It's Grief

The Dance of Self-Discovery Through Trauma and Loss

It's Grief

EDY NATHAN

Copyrighted Material

It's Grief: The Dance of Self-Discovery Through Trauma And Loss

Copyright © 2018 by As I Am Press. All Rights Reserved.

No part of this publication may be reproduced, stored in a retrieval system or transmitted, in any form or by any means—electronic, mechanical, photocopying, recording or otherwise—without prior written permission from the publisher, except for the inclusion of brief quotations in a review.

For information about this title or to order other books and/or electronic media, contact the publisher:

As I Am Press, LLC
edy@edynathan.com

Library of Congress Control Number: 2018906047

ISBNs:
978-0-9971743-0-4 Print
978-0-9971743-1-1 eBook

Printed in the United States of America

Cover and Interior design: 1106 Design

Cover art used with permission of © davecutlerstudio.com.
Author photo: Michael Benabib, michael@michaelbenabib.com

Publisher's Cataloging-In-Publication Data
(Prepared by The Donohue Group, Inc.)

Names: Nathan, Edy (Edy Sue)
Title: It's grief. The dance of self-discovery through trauma and loss / Edy Nathan.
Other Titles: It is grief. The dance of self-discovery through trauma and loss | Dance of self-discovery through trauma and loss
Description: [Port Washington, New York] : As I Am Press, [2018] | Includes bibliographical references and index.
Identifiers: ISBN 9780997174304 (print) | ISBN 9780997174311 (ebook)
Subjects: LCSH: Grief. | Loss (Psychology) | Psychic trauma.
Classification: LCC BF575.G7 N38 2018 (print) | LCC BF575.G7 (ebook) | DDC 155.937--dc23

Praise for *It's Grief*

"This book is a gift and a guiding light for the process of integration and grace after loss. Nathan does a beautiful job of addressing the almost infinite ways we can experience grief, giving us concrete and useful exercises and tools to organize our journey and shape our healing... Nowhere else have I read a more heartfelt discussion of grief or a more valuable and supportive resource than in *It's Grief.*"

— Jessa Zimmerman, sex therapist & author of *Sex Without Stress: A Couple's Guide to Overcoming Disappointment, Avoidance, and Pressure*

"We're all puzzles, Nathan reminds readers, and her clear, winningly sympathetic prose seems designed to help sufferers understand themselves... A sensitive, multipronged approach to comprehending and surviving deep loss."

— *Kirkus Reviews*

"Along with her comprehensive understanding and explanation of grief and the grieving process, [Edy Nathan] provides readers with the ability to discover who they are in their grief.... *It's Grief* is a brilliant, helpful and supportive book. It is a must read for any person who has suffered with grief, trauma or loss in their life, or knows someone who has."

— *Chicklit Café*

"Loss doesn't always mean death; it can include surviving abuse or coping with health issues (yours or someone else's). This open, nonjudgmental approach lets individuals define losses and their significance for themselves. The approach is empowering, showing how individuals can tailor their responses to loss by prioritizing the relationships, meditative practices, and pace that suits their needs. [*It's Grief*] is useful, elegant, and inviting."

— Melissa Wuske, *Foreword Reviews*

In *It's Grief*, psychotherapist Edy Nathan offers an invaluable road map for navigating grief... Like a valuable therapist, she expects readers to do the work: intense self-reflection (guided by many lists of probing questions) and regular journaling... Nathan proves that grief's emotional turmoil can be a growth experience, and that with time and self-care, sufferers can become whole again. Those willing to look deep within will find this a highly worthwhile narrative tool."

— *BlueInk Review*

"Edy Nathan's toolbox is never ending. She has studied and integrated so many different methods to help people that her skills are truly amazing! She is a gifted and seasoned therapist who is sensitive, creative and down to earth. I highly recommend her workbook, *It's Grief*, as well as any other workshop or presentation that you may be lucky enough to attend!"

— Dr. Susan Lipkins, psychologist and author of *Preventing Hazing*

"I appreciate books that are like companions. You want them nearby and available. They have warmth and usefulness but are not shallow. They are friends rather than lifeless objects or heady abstractions. This book can be a companion like that during inevitable moments of grief."

— Thomas Moore, PhD and author of *Care of the Soul* and *Ageless Soul*

TABLE OF CONTENTS

I appreciate books that are like companions. You want them nearby and available. They have warmth and usefulness but are not shallow. They are friends rather than lifeless objects or heady abstractions. This book can be a companion like that during inevitable moments of grief.

~ Thomas Moore, author *of Care of the Soul* and *Ageless Soul*

with grief is an experience that nobody consciously chooses, and our natural instinct is to pull away from the discomfort. However, it's better to confront your grief than to repel and disengage from it. Besides, the effort to disconnect from grief takes a lot of energy. When you move with the flow of grief, seeking to understand its power, purpose, and process can make your journey to the other side a bit easier.

I've written this book to help you sort out what is happening in the heart of your grief. If you can take only one piece of information or lesson found here and use it to help you, then the book will have provided exactly what you need. The self-discovery exercises you'll find in these pages offer coping strategies that can be integrated into your life. I suggest breathing as a useful tool throughout the book. Your breath is something you can count on, it belongs to you and no one has power over it. Even if it seems that you know about breathing, it is often easy to forget just how reliable it is!

Remember to take care of yourself while moving through them. In exercises that have multiple steps, you may be able to engage or follow the first part of an exercise and not be able to do the rest. That's OK! Your inability to focus or to continue may be your brain saying, "I can't do this one right now." You may be surprised to know that when you're ready, you will be able to engage in the self-discovery exercises that are right for you. If an exercise doesn't work for you the first time, or you are unable to complete it (for any reason), please give it another try at a later date.

You can use this book to help you understand how grief impacts your emotions, how your psyche holds on to it, and how to live with it in a healing way. You'll learn to reconnect with who you were prior to the loss, who you are now, and who you are becoming.

When you're in the throes of grief, it may be difficult to imagine a time when grief doesn't permeate all that you feel and do. Although grief can seem like a permanent shroud, the potential for joy and inner peace does exist within you. Though they are presently unattainable, the ability to tap into them and attain these feelings is possible, as they live within you. It is my deepest wish that you can be comfortable in the dance of discovery. The gift of finding your inner Self as you face the daily presence of grief is the benefit of attending to your wounded heart.

I'm not unacquainted with grief. At a very young age, it seemed to me grief was everywhere. There was nothing morbid about it. It was as natural as breathing. Unrest and trauma were imprinted in my young mind as I saw homeless dogs and cats scavenging for food, witnessed loud, aggressive arguments between adults, and watched television news reports about violence and death that were close to home. As a child, it seemed natural for me to grasp the concepts of cruelty, injustice, and loss.

I started my personal dance with grief at the tender age of four, when I realized my inner soul was quite different from that of my family. When turmoil coexists with love, the power of the trauma can often trump any desire to create a loving environment. I learned early on that in order to receive the love I needed, I had to act in ways that quieted the internal forces within me so my family unit could accept me.

Once, my family hired a photographer to take formal photos of the kids. When, in preparation for the photos, I didn't allow my mom to comb my unkempt hair, she had it cut the next day. I had loved my hair. I just didn't like having it combed, but in that crucial moment, her desire to have me look a certain way outweighed my sense of individuality. One of my mother's best qualities was her perfectionism and the desire to have beauty around her, but that desire was sometimes extreme. I never forgot the lesson I learned that day: Be the good girl or have your hair cut off.

It was important for me to have a voice, yet at what price? Kids hunger to be loved by their parents and will acquiesce in order to be "worthy" of that love. The quest to fit in can lead to negating and ignoring conflict or sadness while honoring the desire to find the innocence and delight in the world. It was sometimes hard for me to turn away from the pain and silence the negative. I had an innate ability to feel the pain of others, especially of those who were close to me. Although I couldn't articulate what was going on within my soul or within the soul of my family or social environment, I perceived a lack of safety. Many survivors of trauma and loss have complicated relationships with safety, trust, and truth.

When safety is compromised, the young mind compensates with precocious and curious behaviors. I learned a hard lesson that the kind of love we need is often not the kind of love those around us are capable of giving. As the inner workings of my soul were buried, along with the hope of getting that love or feeling safe and protected, the process of mourning began.

I hungered with a desire to escape from what was already a budding, fearful state of being. This led to sleepless nights, anxiety, nightmares, and roaming in the late hours of the night. My restlessness permeated my daily life. The family lore included tales of little Edy walking out of the house in the middle of the night and "breaking into" (though no one locked their doors) the neighbor's house, and ultimately being found asleep on the couch in their home.

Thankfully, the roaming stopped. My sensitivity to, and awareness of, how prickly things could be within my home never subsided. It was easy to see how I wore my sensitivity on my sleeve, which led to incessant bullying, and ultimately, sexual trauma perpetrated by classmates. I had nowhere to go, no one to trust. Another type of grief emerged, and although no one had died, except perhaps my soul, the internalized trauma turned into self-hatred, self-consciousness, and ultimately, obesity, which was an attempt to nourish the emptiness inside. I could count on grief. It never disappointed me. It was always there leading the way. Keeping people at bay. My relationship with grief continued for many years. I realized I had to change the power of its grip, and no one had the ability, or the knowledge, to do it for me.

Eventually, the theater became an amazing outlet for me that changed the internal messages I was giving myself. I borrowed survival techniques from the many characters I met through the written word. New York City seemed far away from the trauma and losses at home, so I headed there to follow the only dream I had—to be on stage.

There are chemicals in the brain, like serotonin, that control thinking and mood. Once I was in New York, the respite from the negative voices increased my serotonin levels, a "feel good" chemical in the brain, allowing me to self-regulate with greater ease. My brain was changing its relationship to loss and grief. Although my responses to trauma and loss were still extreme, the intensity of the responses was shorter lived and ultimately had less of an impact on me.

The balance I had achieved was disrupted when Paul, my first love, was diagnosed with cancer. I lost him as I was finishing a master's degree at New York University. When he was diagnosed, the life we'd both envisioned suddenly morphed into something completely unexpected. His death changed the trajectory of my life, and the grief and disappointment were potent enough to trigger a resurgence of past grief and trauma. As I engaged with my pain, it was clear that few people were able to help me navigate life while I was in the dark hole. In the darkness, I knew there was the hope of light, even if at the moment I couldn't see it or ignite it. As I embarked on my odyssey, I realized I wanted to help others face their journeys and it became my new goal.

There is nothing more alienating than realizing how alone you are. This sense of being alone in the grief and in the trauma is abstract and often difficult to articulate. There is nothing more empowering and magical than to realize that you will have to create your own path to healing.

Part of that venture involved dropping out of the theater world. Being on the stage would not help me find my Self; rather it would keep me masked in character and in hiding. I found a therapist who witnessed my pain, challenged my silences, and provoked me to stand up to the shadows that lurked within my psyche. He joined me in the journey. I learned to take aspects of the theatre world such as masks, character development, and projective techniques like puppetry, and learned to use them to help others face their own losses and mourning cycles. Thus, my career as a therapist began.

Becoming a therapist was less of a choice and more of a calling. Through the process of professional training and seeing myriad clients identify and break into and through their mourning cycle, it was clear that trauma, loss, and grief needed to be acknowledged and recognized for their compelling and forceful impact. The pervasive power of that impact is unimaginable.

As a therapist in private practice, my clients are my greatest teachers. They often portray their anxiety and depression as emotional prisons from which there is no escape. Many are not only grieving the loss of a loved one, they are also mourning the intense loss of self that can result from experiences such as divorce; sexual, physical, or emotional abuse; job or financial loss; or serious medical issues. And yet, I see them emerge from the confines of grief and marvel as they navigate away from the darkness to grace.

Engaging with grief is challenging. Grief plays games with the mind, often making you wonder how you can feel better without betraying the person or the thing you lost. Grief can be tricky. Many bereaved individuals don't recognize that grief is an umbrella under which a multitude of personal losses reside. For example, if you had been ill for a long time, had been abused, and then years later lost a house, you may find yourself deep in the grip of grief. The loss of the house alone may not have triggered a traumatic response, but if you never dealt with the initial losses, your home being taken away can act as a kind of tipping point for your encounter with grief.

The experience of grief is like your fingerprint, because it is as individual as you are. No traumatic event, illness, or loss of a loved one is exactly the same, so it's logical that no two people will experience the grief related to these events in the same way. The techniques and concepts in this book are adaptable to whatever loss or trauma you have experienced—no matter where you are on the journey.

Move through this book as if you're in a conversation with the part of you that is craving to be released from the grip of grief, and hungers to dance with your own certain grace. Journaling or keeping a notebook for your thoughts can allow you to create a sacred place to respond to the many exercises offered in this book; writing can be a useful tool. Your journal can be the holder of your secrets and your growth. It offers you the ability to refer to the moments of struggle, the revelations, and how and when shifts in your attitude or behavior occurred. Your journal will become a treasure of discovery. Take the time to recover what has been forgotten, what needs to be remembered, and invent the person you want to be as you disengage from the grasp of grief and learn to dance.

Working with grief is a chance to alter where you are, dance in your own way, and find the balance you need in order to live with your losses. In sharing my candid story with you, I want to let you know that it is more than possible to change how you dance within the parameters of grief and trauma. As you move through these pages, think of yourself as an alchemist working to transform the pain of grief and trauma into grace.

CHAPTER 2

Shall We Dance?

"Disappointments in love, even betrayals and losses, serve the soul at the very moment they seem in life to be tragedies. The soul is partly in time and partly in eternity. We might remember the part that resides in eternity when we feel despair over the part that is in life."

~ Thomas Moore, *Care of the Soul: A Guide for Cultivating Depth and Sacredness in Everyday Life*[6]

The dance of turning grief into grace involves learning who you are through the struggle. The experience of loss and mourning influences your sense of Self. At the same time, the things you know to be true about yourself have influence on the way you mourn. This is the essence of the dance. There is a give and take between the familiar Self you've always known and the Self that is experiencing grief.

Meeting the Self at this potent juncture brings meaning to all the work you've done up to this point. The world becomes more real to you because *you* are more real to you. Every shift you make, every new nuance or behavior may be welcomed by a growing consciousness that you are not the same person you were when you started the dance.

Dance can be defined as an art form brought to life through a pattern of movement. I use the term "dance" frequently in this book to refer to the patterns of movement we experience in the active process of mourning. Sometimes the dance takes the form of disjointed movements that make absolutely no sense. A dance that emanates awkwardness is unstable, very much the way you may feel when grief is new. Yet, the dance can become stable and feel less fearful when you allow yourself to move into and recognize the pool of experiences and memories that lie within you.

The dance can lead you into awareness. Or, the dance can allow you to stray from what needs to be addressed as a means of avoiding issues that present themselves. Fear, anger, anxiety, guilt, and regret are examples of the endless emotional choices available to you at any given moment during the process. Remember, you get to meet balance, peace, relief, gratitude, and hopefulness, too. How you move with the various rhythms of your grief will determine where you ultimately land.

Grief is an evolutionary process, and knowing how to dance with it requires the ability to calm and soothe yourself while in the midst of it all. The tools in this book will help you learn when you're balanced or calibrated and when you aren't. It's pretty hard to be in a balanced state when the soul is entwined with active grieving. You'll find that within each exercise, there is a progression of learning-based attempts at stabilization. What this means is your brain will be given different ways to think about what you're feeling. The exercises are progressive in nature. The more you engage with them, the more you actively teach the brain there is a way to alleviate the pain of the grief.

Over time, grief moves and flows from a seemingly simple concept to a concept that is complex and layered. As you learn to develop a keen sense of the ebb and flow of your grief, the meaning of "dancing with your grief" will become clear in its ability to overpower you, flood you, and recede. Flooding is something that occurs when there is too much stimulation and the emerging, often engulfing, emotions cannot be managed. Being overwhelmed, afraid, and physically anxious feeds into a flooding experience. This flooding cycle often transpires when you're in the thick of grief and trauma. When the flooding is interrupted with concrete alternatives, such as breathwork, disrupting negative thought patterns, and physical exercise, it has a chance to shift.

Dancing with your grief is expressed in two major ways: You understand how grief takes the lead, pushing you into a dance that you haven't chosen, while at other times, you lead and take the dance where you want it to go.

When you learn to master your responses to the dormant emotions that become alive and potent through this process, the mourning process will not be able to exploit you. Through the grief process, you will find the opportunity to explore your aptitude for *resilience*. You can then become the choreographer of the dance and an expert in how you engage.

If you think of yourself as the one who leads the dance, you can give your psyche a message that the process is safe and you are in control. You'll come to learn that the dark emotions don't have to feel dangerous. They may become your greatest allies in the quest to understand your discomfort and disconnection from peace and balance. Facing the demons of your loss and trauma will give your soul the message that you aren't backing down in this challenging dance.

The dance with grief is much like the therapeutic process. In my practice, the pace is set by my clients and is a cyclic process of watching and waiting, creating a mutual tempo that establishes the partnership. We listen to the intonation in each other's voices. We watch for what is said and not said in the silences, in body language and through the vitality of expression. Utilizing all five senses—taste, touch, smell, sound, and sight—to assess and modulate the interactions, we ultimately form a relationship that allows us to vigilantly tackle the resistance often present in the dance. The memory of a taste or of a touch can seem so real that it's brought into the therapeutic experience. What is provoked and evoked is done with the notion of acquiring a sense of safety, yet drawing distinctions between safety, ambivalence, and complacency. During the therapeutic process, in thoughtful and artful ways, we enter an agreement that is constantly being renegotiated. Grief can be very tricky in the way it manifests in your soul. It demands consistent dialogue and an added awareness of how slippery it can be.

It takes an observing eye to take note of how you respond to emotional peaks and valleys. You need to assess and determine the degree of conviction you experience when meeting this partner that is grief. *Is it worth engaging? What will the outcome be if I commit to the relationship?* It can be difficult to trust any partner at a first meeting. And this partner has come into your life unbidden. Additionally, prior to your experience of loss and trauma, you may not have known the demands this kind of relationship can make on the soul.

It can be difficult to believe that this strange partner will be able to lead you safely into uncharted territory, and yet grief can put you on a path to grace. It may seem as if you don't have the ability to create the necessary boundaries to shift the dance when it becomes overwhelming, but you can take the lead as you move closer and closer to self-discovery.

You can get to know the union you've formed with your grief by focusing on cues from your body, your environment, and your mind. Did your body suddenly get tense? Is there a scent in your environment that reminds you of your loss? Did a painful memory pop into your mind that takes you down a path you thought you'd overcome?

This understanding of your new alliance comes slowly and methodically. If you can welcome the connection into your life, it can inspire the desire to know more and you can be the master in your dance. You can learn to work with the emotions that live in the burning cauldron of pain. You get to replace that cauldron with a vessel that holds the power to maintain the Self while in an unbalanced state of being.

Learning the steps in your dance with grief is what will bring you to grace.

Are you ready? Shall we dance?

Identify Your Experiences, Your Obstacles and Your Responses to Them

There is a link between the currents of your grief and the unexplored experiences directly related to your loss and trauma. They both live within you. In order to create a sense of mastery, you must understand how intangible the mourning process is. When you believe you know it, more is uncovered and revealed to you, and it seems what you thought you knew about your grief is often just the tip of the iceberg. The emotions and behaviors you identified as aspects of your grief and trauma continue to manifest in your daily life while new information filters in.

There are specific tools designed to help you understand and sort out the complex layers of this process, in order to identify what can aid you in healing. When you embrace what you learn, the tools can be fine-tuned to specifically address your needs.

A first step in recognizing what you're up against is to identify and name an obstacle that gets in the way of your exploration. Some common obstacles include avoidance, anger, ambivalence, anxiety, and resistance.

In the following example, we'll use anxiety as an obstacle so you can see how this tool works:

* Identify obstacles—What experiences and emotions get in the way of identifying your anxiety?

  If your heart races, you feel sweaty and your brain shuts down, this reactivity creates a sensorial experience that is overpowering and uncomfortable. This potent reaction may seem to your brain that it's protecting you, when actually the reaction stops you from facing the intensity of the loss or trauma. This is anxiety. Anxiety is now an identified obstacle.
* What does the obstacle suppress?

  Example of what anxiety suppresses: The ability to tackle the pain. Understand and gauge a range of emotions. On a scale from 1 to 10, what is the level of anxiety you feel, and what level of anxiety is manageable enough to do the work needed to move ahead? Usually a manageable number is between 1 and 4.

* Measure self-understanding.
  What do you understand about the anxiety? To help with this understanding thing about the following questions. When is it activated? Are you in a certain place, with a specific person, or reliving a particular experience?
* Create self-moderation. How would you prefer to react to the anxiety? Can you imagine what a different picture of anxiety in moderation would look like? Focus on that picture. Imagine yourself in it. What's different about the Self in that picture versus when you are engulfed by anxiety?
* Define who or what in your life may cause your anxiety to rise. With whom are you less anxious?

Keep a Journal

A basic tool for working through any of the exercises, like the obstacle-identifying exercise, is a journal or a notebook that documents your grief journey and details the emotional peaks and valleys you're experiencing as part of reclaiming the Self. Writing can shift what you're carrying within you, and gives that material a place to live, while at the same time offering an opportunity to challenge the mind's mourning rhetoric. When an internal discourse exists within you, it either keeps you quiet about how you feel or limits how much you interact with it. When you write it down and make it concrete, you have the opportunity to review, reject, or accept what you're thinking, feeling, expressing, or experiencing.

When in the full throes of grief, you're writing an inner script. The story you tell yourself may have created a habit or custom you're attached to, which fosters a sense of security. I had a client who couldn't reveal what had happened to her. She remembered most of the details, yet felt that if she released her story, she would lose an essential element of who she was. The memory of pain was a kind of partner; it never disappointed her and was always there. It was ritualized to sustain her sense of self as victim. She believed that if her story was interrupted by thinking about her role in a different way, and she found relief with the new thinking, she would have to face the challenge of being the victor rather than remaining in the role of victim. She feared her sense of safety would be thwarted if her ritual was revised.

The script, which can also be called a narrative or internal dialogue, changes as your grief changes, and that change is often a sign of positive movement and growth. Throughout this process you will encounter ups and downs. When the internal dialogue shifts, at times the shift will make it seem as though you are going deeper into the grief, rather than coming out of its grip. Going deeper, and sometimes feeling worse, are part of healing. Acknowledging there is a transformation in how you interact with your active grief can be cause for a dilemma, because you may be thrilled about the change, but terrified to leave what is familiar. Finding a place within you that is balanced means you're no longer sitting in the muck of the grief, and is often accompanied by a sense of relief. This relief can also feel like a betrayal of the Self, disloyalty to the person you lost, or a lack of acknowledgment of the importance of your trauma.

Believing that if you let go and glide with the grief, you'll forget or lose sight of what you've been through is what you put on yourself. The work here isn't to get you to forget; it's about integrating how you live with loss and trauma in adaptable and peaceful ways. When you meet the dance in this way, you'll no longer worry about a lack of faithfulness. Rather, you will have achieved a certain faith in the Self.

Writing allows you to observe yourself via your thoughts and feelings as you express them in your notebook or journal. You can then see, over time, when the script shifts, and how your narrative process is altered. This story—these breadcrumbs, footprints, shadows, or traces—testify to where you've been and where you are now. They can perhaps illuminate a path for the future. As your relationship to the story changes, the currents of grief also change. Think about the following:

* What or whom are you grieving?
* What is your relationship to what you lost?
* How are you affected by the loss?
* What does your grief reveal about your relationships, your philosophical and religious beliefs, your desires, and who you are?
* Are you able to live with the loss?

This is one sacred moment when you get to converse with different parts of you. In this time of reflection, your journal, or notebook, invites you to jot down a few choice words or phrases that best describe your grief. Here are some sample responses:

* *I am grieving my lost childhood after having been abused.*
* *I don't have a relationship with a part of me that I've lost, and what I have lost is my confidence.*
* *I feel deadened and void of feelings. I am desperate and angry.*
* *I don't know who I am. I am terrified. It seems disorganizing.*
* *I cannot live without my loved one who has died, so I have considered suicide.*

Next to each description, note the active way you cope:

* Are you able to change the way you feel? If so, what do you currently do to shift out of the experience?
* What tools do you use to fortify the changes?
* Are you stuck in the emotions of the mood?

What impression does the "stuck" experience make on you? Can you counter and challenge the sense of "stuck" with a different thought or picture? First, see the picture of "stuck," then imagine its opposite. What do you notice when you do this?

* How do you soothe yourself?

  Breathing, meditation, changing scenery, interacting with another (including an animal), writing, and listening to or playing music are a few techniques that can be used to teach the psyche new soothing techniques.

* How do you interrupt the mood to alter it?

  Moods are often affected when negative thoughts emerge. Change the negative thought to a positive thought. See the positive and negative cognitions list on the following pages. Replace a negative cognition ("I don't deserve love") with a positive cognition ("I am worthy of love"). The act of repeatedly taking a negative thought and replacing it with a positive thought can feel challenging even though it seems simple. This exercise will build resilience and is a brain changer.

* Are you able to sit with and immerse yourself in the experience? If so, does that relieve the stress or increase it?

  To sit with the experience means when it is present, you don't avoid it; you meet it with a sense of self-respect and self-possession.

* What does this reveal to you?

  If you discover you can change the feelings, great! Or if it is difficult to interrupt the thoughts, this is good information to be aware of as you become more settled in the dance.

* How would you prefer to respond? Is there anyone with whom you can share these feelings? Is there someone with whom you can share the intimacy of this dance?

Positive Cognitions or Thoughts	Negative Cognitions or Thoughts
I deserve love; I can have love	I am defective
I am a good (loving) person	I don't deserve love
I am fine as I am	I am a bad person
I am worthy; I am worthwhile	I am terrible
I am honorable	I am worthless (inadequate)
I am lovable	I am shameful
I am deserving (fine/OK)	I am not lovable
I deserve good things	I am not good enough
I am (can be) healthy	I deserve only bad things
I am fine (attractive/lovable)	I am permanently damaged
I can be trusted	I am ugly (my body is hateful)
I can (learn to) trust myself	I do not deserve . . .
I can trust my judgment	I am stupid (not smart enough)
I am safe	I am insignificant (unimportant)
I am capable	I am a disappointment
I can (learn to) take care of myself	I deserve to die
It's over; I am safe now	I deserve to be miserable
I can safely feel (show) my emotions	I am different (don't belong)
I am now in control	I did something wrong
I now have choices	I am powerless (helpless)
I am strong	I did something wrong
I can get what I want	I should have known better
I can succeed	I cannot be trusted
I can be myself(make mistakes)	I cannot trust myself
I can have (deserve) . . .	I am not in control
I am significant (important)	I cannot trust anyone
I deserve to live	I cannot protect myself: I am weak
I deserve to be happy	I am in danger
I did the best I could	It's not OK to feel (show) my emotions
I learned (can learn) from it	I cannot stand up for myself

To navigate this challenging and empowering journey counters the fear and stabilizes the sense of Self. There is no "end" to your dance with grief. As author Anne Lamott writes, *You will lose someone you can't live without, and your heart will be badly broken, and the bad news is that you never completely get over the loss of your beloved. But this is also the good news. They live forever in your broken heart that doesn't seal back up. And you come through. It's like having a broken leg that never heals perfectly—that still hurts when the weather gets cold, but you learn to dance with the limp.*

The dance becomes quieter as you become more resilient. The grip of grief is released as you develop a language that converts the pain of the dance into the desire for self-mastery and integration of the loss and trauma stories that live within you.

CHAPTER 3

Me, Myself, and I: Engage With the Dance of Change

"Whenever I considered leaving a bad relationship, I felt paralyzed by two similar fears: the fear of losing my chance at fulfillment by staying, and the fear of losing the comfort of companionship if I walked away and didn't find someone else."

~Lori Deschene, *Overcoming the Fear of Loss: 5 Steps to Get Unstuck* (tinybuddha.com)[7]

Grief is exhausting. Famed dancer Martha Graham[8] once wrote that her body was so tired that it cried while it slept.

I believe the same thing happens to the psyche when it is entangled in the web of mourning. The psyche weeps in both the conscious and unconscious states of grief. The mind in a grief state is like mush. It affects your temperament, your desires, and your perception of reality. Who you were prior to the loss is not who you are now. These differences within you alter behavior toward the Self and toward others.

Although grief has been thrust upon you, you can make a choice as to how to live with it and integrate it into your being. This is an opportunity to meet yourself head on as you face a myriad of challenges. The dance of turning grief into grace allows you to learn who you are through the struggle.

The hand of grief touches every part of your life. Without interruption or respite, the intensity of the mourning cycle affects behavior, relationships, emotions, your sense of self, and your physical and mental health. Internal disharmony created by the magnitude of emotions is disarming and alarming. Although it can disrupt your ability to function naturally, this is a chance for you to appraise the altering reality that unfolds.

Here is Michael's struggle with his grief. Do you relate to what he shares about his experience.

"I was exhausted most of the day. My traumatic memories would pop in throughout the day, and all I wanted was to forget. I felt alone and scared. Alcohol seemed to help, but then at night I was more agitated and could not sleep. I knew I was in a cycle that felt impossible to conquer. This is not the way I used to act. Sleep was always easy for me. I never used to drink."

~ Michael J.

When assessing differences in your behavior, start with what you know about what has been normal for you. It is easy to assess the shifts when they are blatant, and more difficult when they are subtle. Think about how your loss or trauma affects you in the following arenas. Do any of the following behavior shifts apply to you?

Ask yourself,

Where do I fit into these examples?

What was my typical pattern prior to the loss and what is it now?

My clients often feel that their sleep, eating habits, and concentration are most affected during this time.

What Are Your Day-to-Day Behavioral Changes? Time to Dance With the Self

Self-Discovery Exercise

This is an opportunity to raise your awareness so you can understand common behavioral changes in your functioning. These questions can act as a continual assessment of how and when any shifts have occurred. Date the answers, and when you revisit these questions, you will have a record and timeline of your growth or shifts in your behavior.

- Are you sleeping more or less than usual?
- Are you eating more or less than normal?
- Are you able to keep to your everyday schedule or is it chaotic?
- Have you been leaving mail unopened? Are bills unpaid or late? Is everything around you scattered or unorganized, especially if you are normally organized? Conversely, have you become overly organized and obsessive about how you want things done?
- Are you spending too much time on the internet?
- Are you unable to concentrate, or are you hyper-focused?
- Are you reclusive, or do you fear being alone?
- Are you forgetful, or are you obsessive about time?
- Are you engaging in excessive behavior related to shopping, alcohol, sex, and food?

The self-discovery exercise allows you to create a picture of how your behaviors are personally effected by grief. What facets of your behavior are effected, then write them down in your journal. Now, pick the behavior that is most atypical or uncharacteristic for you and work on that first. Tackle each one separately so that you are not overwhelmed.

> *"Everyone can master a grief but he that has it."*
>
> ~William Shakespeare *Much Ado About Nothing*, Act 3, Scene 2

Sleep Problems

Too much or too little sleep affects concentration and the body's ability to restore itself. Your health can be influenced by a disruption of your circadian rhythm (your body's natural internal clock). When this cycle is interrupted, it can cause high blood pressure, depression, a weakened immune system, and of course, insomnia. Trying to get back into your natural sleep rhythm is a first line of defense in helping your body deal with the intensity of emotions brought on by grief. Following are three common sleep problems and techniques that help to significantly change sleep behavior.

If falling asleep is difficult

Find a comfortable position in your bed. Take a deep breath. Hold it and let it go slowly, counting down from five to one. Take in another deep breath, hold it, and when you let it go, imagine a place or a feeling of calm or love or security.

Have you ever seen someone when they are sleeping? Have you noticed how their breath is even, and their chest moves in a rhythmic way? Try to mimic that rhythmic breathing. Let go of any thoughts that arise. When a thought interrupts you, push it away with your next exhaled breath. If you engage in this exercise as part of your nightly ritual, it will become second nature and help you in falling asleep.

If waking up is difficult

Identify the thoughts or pictures that filter through your brain as you struggle to wake up. Keep a notebook by your bed and describe the experience of the struggle. If you would rather not write, then say it out loud, or find a song that fits the desire to stay idle.

Set a specific time to get out of bed, set an alarm, and follow through. Fight the urge to give in to the voice that keeps you down. Having a specific time to wake up is another ritual that is essential for restructuring, restoring the Self, and helpful for the circadian rhythm. Make a plan to speak to a friend thirty minutes after getting up, or go for a walk, or sign up for an exercise class. When you have a specific place to be, it holds you accountable. Accountability is stabilizing. Remember, your brain and your body know when there isn't a plan.

If you get up in the middle of the night

Something woke you; now it's time to soothe yourself so you can get back to nourishing your body through sleep. If you awaken in the night and have trouble falling back to sleep, first try the technique above that is used to induce sleep. If that doesn't work, listen to soft music or a relaxation meditative recording, or talk to yourself in a soothing voice. Rather than reading on an electronic device, read a paper book that won't keep you up (not an electronic reader, as the light can be disruptive to sleep). Have some hot milk or hot lemonade with honey.

Food Problems

It is often hard to feel sated when you are feeling emotionally empty. It is not a physical emptiness that affects your relationship to food. The relationship to food during this time can be fierce. Stress often triggers emotional eating, especially as a reaction to grief or trauma, and is used to control and keep down a rush of feelings. You might find you're either stuffing down the emotions, sometimes with comfort food, or go into starvation mode as a means to have a sense of control. Both impulses can convince you that you are in control, though it is only a temporary illusion. Food, or the lack of it, may help you stay numb or in denial, allowing you to feel a sense of disengagement from the pain. This is especially true when the emotional roller coaster is at its peak. Rage, anger, anxiety, and disorganized emotions can cause you to use food as a control mechanism. To determine if you are stuffing down emotions with food, before you eat, take a few moments to answer the following questions:

- Am I hungry?
- Where am I hungry? My stomach, my head, my heart, my mouth?
- What is each part of my body communicating?

Once the source of your hunger is identified, ask it what (and why) it wants to be fed.

In your stomach: Do you want a piece of fruit, a protein, liquid, or carbs?

In your head: What is going on in your brain? Are you overwhelmed? Disheartened? Having flashbacks? Feeling helpless? What kind of comfort and security does the food offer?

In your heart: Who or what are you missing? What does your heart need from you in this moment?

In your mouth: What do you want to taste? Maybe it's not a flavor, but is more of a desire for savoring beauty or longing for something tender.

In your psyche: Are you conscious of the anger or anxiety that is messing with your balance?

After answering these questions, do you still want to eat? Are you more conscious of where your hunger is lodged? How can you take care of it? Will eating eliminate any of the experiences in your head, your heart, your mouth or your psyche?

If you have chosen to deny yourself food—which is a refusal of your daily nourishment needs—then use the tools you've learned thus far to calm yourself. Depriving the body of food may make it seem as if you have some sense of control during a time when you may feel you have none. Often, it is the *perception* of control that leads to helplessness and ultimately invites deprivation. Knowing this might be happening, will help to identify and incorporate healthy choices of what is in your control.

Here are some options for what you can control:

1. Your response to external stimuli
2. When you smile
3. When you are good to yourself
4. Your breath and how you breathe
5. When and how you exercise
6. When and what you eat

Shift the picture of helplessness as you focus on what you can change—this creates a precise picture that fosters strength. The picture becomes more accurate with greater detail. Start with a theme. If you have been denying yourself food, imagine for this moment, that the new picture allows a sense of control without starvation.

What does this picture look like?
Are you in it or looking at it?
Is it in color or black and white?
Are there other people in it? If so, who is in it?
Are you having fun in the picture?
Are you calm? Are you quiet?

How does your internal voice sound to you and is it honoring what you think, what you believe, and what you feel about the shift?

It doesn't matter what the picture depicts. What matters is that you get to change the picture of perceived control and ultimate helplessness. And even if you can change the picture for a second, that is one second when you interrupted it. The more specific the picture, the easier it is for you to engage your brain and work at realigning the neural pathways that contribute to your core reactions. Keep it up, and your brain will actually change.

Mood Changes and Fluctuations

Nothing is as likely as grief and trauma to make you feel that one minute you're doing pretty well, and the next minute it seems as if a Mack truck has come out of nowhere and hit you. These responses can actually be triggered by sensory communications that occur through smell, sight, sound, touch, and taste. Did you know that the sense of smell evokes a memory faster than any of the other senses? That's why when people sell a house, they make sure to have cookies baking in the oven. They use the smell of freshly baked cookies to lure the buyer in by creating an association with the positive memories of a childhood home. Your senses are working all the time, even when you're not aware of them. When you encounter an aroma associated with the trauma you experienced, the recognized scent can catapult you into a distinct and abrupt change in temperament.

Moods will shift when one of the senses picks up on something familiar, regardless of whether the familiar trigger has a positive or negative influence. If you're feeling good when the same scent worn by your abuser wafts by, or when you are exposed to the medicinal smell of a hospital room, it can affect every part of your being. Your mood shift is directly connected to that scent. The scent triggers a warning to find safety, get help, or hide.

Are you aware of your moods and how they fluctuate? Are there any patterns? To identify any patterns, take note of your moods in your journal. For example, do the mood shifts occur more often in the morning, at work, as you go out for the evening, or when you come home at night? Do they happen more with people you know or with strangers? Do mood shifts come up at the movies, when you are out shopping, or when you are cooking or cleaning?

The cycle of grief is unpredictable. There is nothing quite like it. Extreme and not-so-extreme variations of mood, attitude, and behaviors take place in response to what is often not understood. Whether grieving the loss of a beloved or coping with losing a limb, there will be vast inconsistencies (weekly, daily, and hourly) in how you feel, and you will try to make sense of them. You may find that what once worked as a coping response no longer has the same effect. By attempting to disarm the tension, the mood can shift from acute reactivity, like anxiety, to a need that requires you to retreat, leaving the emotions behind, which is a sort of numbing that protects you.

"Yeah, I'm mad. The whole world has me at their mercy, my life is going down the tubes and there isn't a thing I can do about it. And my husband just sits around watching TV like nothing's wrong. Every time he talks to me I want to bite his head off."

~ Erica[9]

When you go with the flow of what is being experienced instead of trying to understand why things are not the same, there is less of a need for that pendulum swing. It often seems that in the attempt to understand the "why" of any behavioral response, the lack of an answer can create greater frustration.

On the flipside of this, allowing your Self to observe, listen, and ride with the uncertainty, you might meet a sense of balance as you move away from the urgency of knowing "why." When you ride with uncertainty, and are more in the flow, there is a chance that your psyche will reap the benefits bestowed upon you for trusting in the "present": This is the place where you are.

For example, if you participate in an activity that you once shared with a loved one, this may cause a spiraling shift of your mood into agitation or melancholia. Often, the critical expectation of recapturing something that was lost, only to find it can't be rekindled, will create tension. Integrating the notion that it cannot be rekindled, owning it, and having the memory of it without needing to recreate it is being in the moment of who you are in the here and now.

The internal Critic can also participate in mood fluctuations that cause you to feel broken and disconnected. If you made unrealistic promises to yourself prior to the loss or trauma and weren't able to follow through with them, it can cause unrelenting regret. The Critic's voice can harp on the "if only" scenarios, which creep in when you create a belief that you could have controlled the outcome. Anxiety and fear are often in full force when these images appear. They can act as a decoy and blindside you.

Relationship Changes

Relationships may collapse or remain a part of your life. You might be surprised by new relationships that emerge as a result of this journey, and you might find that old ones fade away. Some relationships will shift and change. Have you noticed since engaging in the dance that you respond differently to friends, family, and relationships at work? Here are some things to look for and write about in your journal:

- What distinguishes how you interacted with people previously with how you interact with them now?
- How do you experience alone time? Is it comfortable or agitating?
- Is your self-confidence or self-esteem dependent on others?

* Are you able to remain confident and self-assured in your process regardless of what others think, feel, or say about you or your process?
* Do relationships either deplete or support you?

We will talk more about relationships in Chapter 6, for now let's take a look at this two-circle diagram.

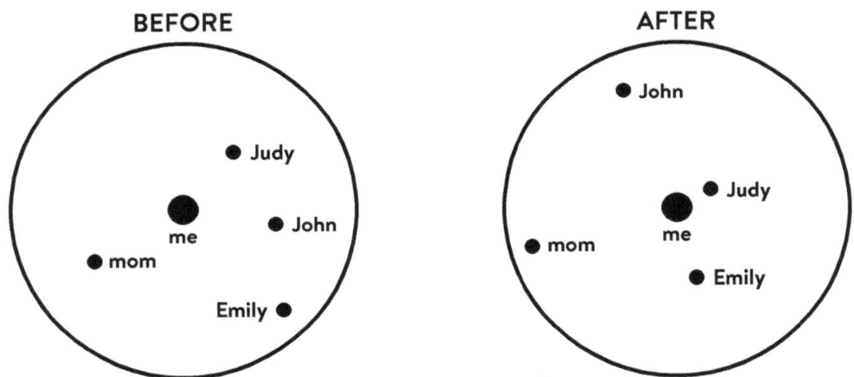

Within the "Before" circle are the relationships you had before your loss or trauma, and the "After" circle represents the relationship you have to those folks "Now." The dot in the middle of each circle symbolizes you. Write down the names of the people who were in your life before and how close you were to them. Each person is represented by his or her own dot within the circles. The dots and their distance from your dot illustrates the degree of closeness you felt toward that person before and now. When you fill in the diagram, it will give you an acute sense of what has changed and what has stayed the same. This is good information. It allows you to notice what changes have taken place, acknowledge them, and assess how those shifts affect you.

When You Are Not Devastated by Your Loss

There are many variables that contribute to a lack of emotional devastation when facing your loss or trauma. Obviously, just because you had a relationship with someone doesn't mean it was a good one. If the person you lost had a severe illness, no matter how much you loved them, you may have shared a desire for the ultimate relief that only death could bring. For some people, their trauma is related to losing a loved one to mental illness. It is often expected that you should be devastated at the loss of a loved one; clearly this is not always the case.

Joan was married to Harry for 25 years. Money was tight, and when Joan was diagnosed with lupus, she had to stop working, which caused rifts and distance in the marriage. The sicker she got, the meaner and more abusive Harry became. When he was in a fatal car accident, Joan was sad, but she also felt a distinct sense of freedom. She was afraid of being on her own, but she had been more afraid of her daily life with Harry. She is now living happily as a widow and her symptoms from lupus have improved. She hesitates to tell her friends and family how peaceful she feels, so she pretends to be deeply grieving when, in fact, she is deeply relieved and finally feels safe.

If not being destroyed by your loss resonates with you, know that you are not alone. You may still experience grief, even if the relationship was bad or not what you had imagined. Sadness often appears as a result of knowing the absence of the grief that might have been felt if the circumstances had been different.

Relief and grief come in many forms. We can find it in scenarios that sometimes go beyond one's understanding. As a sex therapist and grief therapist, I have worked within the gender-fluid and transgender community. Their grief struggle is often hidden in plain sight. Meet Steve in his grief and relief story.

Steve and Charlotte were married for forty-one years. After she died, Steve missed her and mourned her, but also felt relief. His physical body never felt aligned with what he felt inside, and he'd wanted to explore this essential part of himself—a part of him that he'd spent his entire life denying. He'd always thought of himself as more of a woman than a man. He knew that as long as he was married, he would never have the chance to explore his gender identity. It was confusing and terrifying, but once Charlotte was gone, Steve was free to learn more about his emerging Self.

He loved Charlotte, yet his guilt gets aroused and is mixed with his sense of relief. Her death freed him and now he also feels more whole and complete, as he is discovering and living his personal truth.

When Steve's wife was alive, he would discreetly and secretly embody his true Self by finding "safe" outlets that honored the female that lived within his very soul and could not be denied. The internal fire was ignited when he could dress as the gender he identified with, allowing him to feel alive in an otherwise deadened life. When his wife died, the fire that could only be ignited at small, proscribed moments had an opportunity to be birthed, brought to life, and fully honored. Steve faced many dilemmas as he danced with his grief. He was excited to embark on his journey, which could only have occurred upon the death of his wife. Mourning her meant also mourning the life he had yearned for while married to her. Coming into his gender quest, and meeting the Self through this process, also meant leaving behind what was known, for what was yet to be discovered.

Various forces keep the truth away, or support staying stuck rather than living in one's personal honor. Each choice requires courage; even staying in what feels hopeless or uncomfortable speaks to something within the soul that needs to embody those experiences.

Nagging, arguing, and sometimes abuse are integral parts of many relationships. As you can see by the following obituary, the adult survivors of childhood abuse revealed the family secrets of abuse in a public commentary, allowing them to begin the healing process. Fighting, dissension, and/or living in the world as a false Self, as Steve did, can devastate and crush the soul.

"On behalf of her children, whom she so abrasively exposed to her evil and violent life, we celebrate her passing from this earth and hope she lives in the afterlife reliving each gesture of violence, cruelty, and shame that she delivered on her children. Her surviving children will now live the rest of their lives with the peace of knowing their nightmare finally has some form of closure."

~ Obituary of Marianne Theresa Johnson-Reddick, written by her surviving six children, after they suffered years of abuse from her.[10]

You may come to realize that your life and sense of self depended on the soured relationship, or the mental illness, or even the devastation of coping with a loved one's long-term illness. What caused you so much sorrow is surprisingly and suddenly missed. You might even experience a void when the negative interactions are gone. This reaction can seem counterintuitive, yet if the role you had in the relationship is taken away, the imprint it left is like a phantom pain. Ironically, it may have even served to bolster your identity. The more cruel your partner (or parent, or friend, or child, or employer) might have been, the better it may have made you look in comparison to them. What is familiar can be comfortable, even if it is negative.

If you were in the role of caregiver, how you feel in the wake of the loss of that person can be complex. The more you were needed by your lost love, parent, or sibling because you were his/her caregiver, the more difficult it may have been to honor your own desires and needs. The caregiver struggle is filled with contradictions. You want to help and tend to the one in need. However, if the illness is long-term and the friend or family member is no longer mobile, able to communicate verbally, or take part in their own care, the toll it takes on the caregiver is enormous.

It's difficult to separate resentment or bitterness toward the illness, from the feeling of resentment toward the person needing your care. Some people have found themselves wishing for the death of the person in their care because they no longer want to see them suffer, but also because they want to be released from the caregiver role. Wanting to escape that role adds another layer of guilt and confusion. When that person is gone and you no longer have that relationship—when the role has ended for you—who validates you?

If, as a caregiver, you avoid your own self-care, emotional, physical, and soulful disasters are in the making. Becoming aware of how important the role of caregiver is for your own sense of self is crucial. Strategies outlined in this book can help you develop your sense of self outside of that role whether or not the role has ended.

As you process through this muddled and difficult situation, you might become aware that you stayed in the relationship to gain a false sense of self-worth. Following are some scenarios that might apply:

1. You stayed in a bad marriage because you had no other options (or you stayed because of the children).
2. You were a caregiver to a parent, hoping the relationship would improve or that you would be rewarded in their will.
3. You stayed in a friendship because you grew up together and were witnesses to each other's pasts, were loyal partners, and may have held unspeakable truths for each other. Or you may not have been able to set boundaries and say, "Enough!"
4. You stayed in a business partnership because you were needed but did not receive the support that you needed. Or you were stuck with it because of the money, even though you hated the work.
5. You stayed with an abuser because you were afraid to leave.

When a partner, parent, or friend dies, so does the chance to repair the living relationship. Shame and regret can surface when you acknowledge you may have wished for their death, or experienced a lack of remorse following the death. Initially, you might have a sense of freedom. You might feel refreshed and alive in ways you haven't experienced in years, and you may begin to break out of the protective shell the caregiver role gave you. If you find you relate to feeling relief rather than remorse, don't think you're free and clear of the grief process.

Grief may still surface when you form new relationships that echo your prior experiences. If you haven't truly understood your own patterns of engagement, history tends to repeat itself. Even if years have passed since you lost your parent, partner, or abuser, memories of the old patterns can pop up. New relationships may end up with the same results. When you lack an understanding of the urges and desires that prompted you to make the choices you made in the first relationship, repetition of the abuse pattern, lack of boundary setting, or dissension can occur. The theme of your life might persist in a cycle of loss and trauma if you don't do the work to break it. If this is true for you, the grief you didn't feel when you lost the initial troubled relationship will demand to be dealt with.

Health Changes: Take Care of Yourself Physically and Emotionally

"The brain and the immune system continuously signal each other, often along the same pathways, which may explain how state of mind influences health."

~ Esther M. Sternberg and Philip W. Gold[11]

Health changes tend to occur six to eighteen months after a traumatic event or loss. You are more susceptible to getting ill during this period than at any other time. Your body knows that things are not right, and the body often reveals how unattended mourning can cause harm—if you only pay attention to the messages your body is sending you.

Grief left untreated can cause illnesses that may have been dormant, only to be triggered by the traumatic event or loss. Immunity is greatly diminished at this time, and whatever has been in an incubation stage may come out in full force. Rheumatoid arthritis, diabetes, and immunodeficiency disorders are examples of severe health problems that have been known to flare up. This is especially true if you are a survivor of sexual, emotional, or physical abuse. When the Little G's, which are periods in life or situations that have caused you a sense of loss yet don't amount to a Big G, accumulate unattended, illness, anxiety, and a lost sense of self may emerge. The body then reacts as if it had experienced a Big G.

Why does this happen?

The psyche responds in different ways to the cycle of loss or trauma. One common outcome is diminished desire and/or the ability for self-care. You may lack self-awareness, which is an unconscious act of your psyche, or you may have simply stopped caring.

> *"My husband is gone for military training right now. He sent me a text message a week ago saying he wanted a divorce. I am severely depressed now, and have not been able to eat at all. I am practically starving myself. I don't mean to. I just have no drive to eat because I am so severely depressed."*
>
> ~ W

What are the contributors that cause you to stop caring for the Self? In W's case, she is in shock, dismay and reacts to her grief by starving herself. This is often a way to control what seems so out of control. It is important to reach out to friends and family or a professional if you notice extreme shifts in self-care.

There are conscious and unconscious complex aspects to no longer caring for the self. Life can seem unbearable for you, and this sense of "what's the point", as in W's story, relates to the individual relationship you have to what caused the grief in the first place. If you lost a loved one, life without this person can seem purposeless. If you know your perpetrator is still around, you may believe they can hurt you again, leading to a sense of vulnerability. A type of apathy and complacency can emerge.

As we discussed earlier, your relationship to food and sleep may change, and this may make it harder to fight infection. Anger, depression, despair, and regret are some of the stressors that also affect health.

When I met David, he was forty and trapped in unrealized grief. He was able to move through what he called "an immoveable place" only after realizing how badly his health was affected by his loss and trauma. When he was twenty years old, David had been in a car accident and had lost three fingers on his left hand. At that time, he had a full scholarship as a cellist; the accident forced him to give up the instrument. After giving it up, severe headaches turned into mind-numbing migraines.

He didn't want to leave his bed, go back to school, or live. For twenty years following the accident, he experienced body aches and nightmares, but it wasn't until age forty that he sought help. The grief and trauma over the loss of his fingers kept him in a constant state of depression and anxiety. When he started therapy, his focus shifted on specific ways he could heal the piercing emotions that kept him fastened to the past.

Once he was introduced to the notion that he had the power to challenge his negative thoughts and replace them with more positive pictures and cognitions, he gave his brain a break with different mind messages. He worked with his body image, and he talked to the fingers he lost rather than ignoring them. He had to create different images within his psyche. He learned to tap into the part of him he lost when he lost his fingers and, consequently, his cello. When the psyche opens up to new information, a floodgate of new nuances and thoughts get born. These thoughts, these jewels, offered an opening to a world that felt dead, and allowed David to eventually believe that life was worth living.

Stressors within the dance often create physical harm, so it's wise to see your doctor about six months after you enter the dance of grief, loss, or trauma. Get a complete physical. Check your blood pressure, your heart, your lungs, and your blood work. If your eating is poor and sleep eludes you, take extra vitamins, eat less fat, and enjoy more protein, fruits, and vegetables. Exercise is a staple: It stabilizes your mood, balances your hormones, and is extremely therapeutic. No matter how bad you feel, push yourself to get outdoors and *move your body*. Yoga, swimming, and simply walking are appropriate options for people at any level of ability or fitness. When you push through the stagnation and move, the brain responds to the positive shift.

Here are some questions to ask yourself. It would be beneficial to record the responses in your journal.

- What physical stressors are you aware of now that you did not have before?
- What physical complaints do you have now that you did not have before?
- Are you achier or more conscious of not having the energy you used to have?
- Do you have new aches and pains? More frequent colds, allergies, and other issues?

Grief can turn into a state of physical disease in response to emotional *dis-ease*. You have it in your grasp to attend to the hunger of the soul and nourish it by listening to its needs.

Overall Life Changes

Grief can be a brain-change agent because it triggers the unfamiliar, which can lead to your transformation. Life is not stagnant. With insight and intention, you will learn how to modulate your responses. As the picture of grief and trauma comes into focus, you will understand what is tolerable and what is intolerable. Your reaction to the depths of despair can trigger the brain to create new pathways, which can either lead to healing or to greater despair and hopelessness. Challenge the stasis and inertia of your grief. Give your brain the chance to begin learning new ways to function. You can energize your brain by asking the Self to confront the following and writing about it in your journal:

- Are you feeling lost, scared, or afraid? What thoughts contribute to these experiences? How can you challenge them?
- Identify pervasive thoughts. Do they persist in ways that make it difficult to quiet them? What thoughts seem to be inescapable? Ask yourself what purpose they serve. What would happen if they disappeared?
- Do you feel you are lost in a chasm, or an inescapable abyss or a void? Describe this experience.
- How would you like that experience to be different in your mind? Describe the difference.
- Do you experience time as though it were frozen, without any fluidity or movement? When does it freeze? What does it require to thaw?
- Are you stuck because of your thoughts?
- Do your thoughts overpower healthy functioning? If you know what healthy functioning feels like, embody the memory of that functioning. If you don't sense what that feels like, do you have people you know whose behavior and level of functioning

you aspire to? Can you describe the picture when you summon that memory?

- Using all of your senses, see if you can recall a memory that personifies the action of self-care. When you don't have an immediate sense memory of this, remember a scent that you like, a movie that made you laugh, or even a food that you adore. Challenge your statements to the Self:

  Change "*I don't want to exercise*" to "*Exercise can change the way I feel.*"

  Shift "*Nothing stimulates me*" to "*I know that I have laughed in my life. Let me remember one of those moments when I laughed right out loud.*"

- Les Brown, a motivational speaker and one of my favorite teachers, suggests reading books by people who inspire you. He believes that reading thirty pages a day from thought leaders or inspirational teachers inspires change.
- What thoughts do you have about the Big or Little G's? Identify what losses fit the Big G's, and which ones fit the Little G's.
- How do you cope with your thoughts? How do you quiet them or stand up to them?
- In whose voice do you hear thoughts that either admonish you or compliment you? Think about the archetypes. Is it the Mother, the Father, the Teacher, the Critic?

External Conflicts, Influences, and Forces

Forces outside of the Self are part of life, and they can create obstructions that make it difficult to manage your moods. Think about these forces as roadblocks that affect you in concrete ways. An example of an external conflict is a weather condition, like a hurricane, that is outside of your control. What happens at a school board meeting, or even a decision made by a judge, are external. The idea of an "external conflict" is actually born out of literature, representative of the relationship between the protagonist and the antagonist in a story. These roadblocks can exist in relationships between two people, or between a person and an outside force such as society, nature, or even destiny. You are the protagonist in the story of your own life; you are fighting with your experience of loss and trauma, which feels very much like an antagonist.

The external conflicts you face can cause mood fluctuations that leave you unnerved, imbalanced, and fragile, but both positive and negative influences exist within these conflicts. Sometimes the conflicts are necessary to promote and cultivate enlightenment, and this is particularly true for the forces you meet in your grief.

As you grapple with these forces, you face a choice: Break out of known patterns, or remain stuck in them. The outside forces—friends, family, or society—may want you to stay the same, and this may feel like a safe option. The roadblocks get stronger when you give them the power to dictate what is or isn't safe.

Following are some external factors that could affect the fluctuation of your moods. As you read through these examples, identify how you engage with them, what patterns exist in the relationship that keep it constant, what different responses you could have, and what is the desired outcome if you shift your response.

External Factors

SELF-DISCOVERY EXERCISE

As you journal, answer each question and take time to digest the questions before you answer. They don't need to be answered at one sitting. Come back to them again and again. You might find that over time, your responses shift and change as growth increases and the grip of grief lessens.

* Think about which people make it hard for you to hold onto your desire to break through the roadblocks of your grief. How do they keep you stuck? How can you avoid their need to keep you in a pattern that makes them feel content?
* Does your living space provide a place for solace and contemplation? Is it a space that you created, or did another create it? Do you like this space, or does it confine you? This is an outside force that can mute your moods or overly arouse your moods. It is also an easy one to change.
* Do you recognize some people as gaining comfort or power from your distress, your pain, or your moods?
* Energy or emotional vampires[12] sap your energy to keep you down because your pain validates *their* pain. The world revolves around them. Who do you recognize in your life that shows up this way?

It is only through your own intimate process that you get to observe how these outside forces affect your moods. Once you have answered the questions above, try some of these techniques for challenging the patterns and moving through the external conflict:

Quiet the Self by going into a slow-down mode. Slowing and quieting means breathing with meaning, tapping into your mood, and breaking each picture and person into little time-bites. With a new awareness of who agitates you or makes you feel unsure, stay in the role of observer rather than reactor. When you get a clear view of what the antagonists do and how they do it, you gain a sense of empowerment that keeps you calmer. When you stay present in observation mode, use this knowledge to change how you react to the situation, create an itinerary of different reactions, and you can begin to break the patterns of a reactor.

- Take the time you need. If you are sensing pressure from someone to engage in ways that don't feel legitimate or authentic to you, ask for time to respond. Use this tactic to give yourself space to think about what your next move needs to be.
- If your living space causes you agitation, change the energy by adding soothing color, scents, and visual images that compel the environment to change. Surround yourself with colors that make you feel serene by adding pillows or re-painting, even if it is only one wall. Add flowers, a box filled with spices or scents, or a picture of that old dirt bike that reminds you of positive choices or creates a place that appeals to you. Design a corner in that room that expresses a sacred and safe space. You can visit with this self-created space as often as desired or needed.[13]
- Set limits. If being on your own causes you to obsess, then make a plan that nourishes you. Be willing to explore outside your comfort zone. Start in small increments. Do you like to exercise? Then find a class where you can participate, like yoga. If you were comfortable there, return and say hi to one person. You are pushing boundaries incrementally. The goal is to get away from those who keep you down. This changes your pattern and influences the degree to which your moods fluctuate.

Be aware of what you want to achieve when facing external conflicts. By setting strict limits, you disentangle from external forces and influences. It's true, there are roadblocks while in the dance of grief, and in life generally. Be watchful and deliberate in identifying those obstacles and acting on them. That will empower your ability to shift. When you modify your reactions to the external conflicts, you achieve greater balance and fewer fluctuations of mood. Once you acknowledge those areas where functioning is affected, you can begin to devise a plan to thrive rather than simply survive.

Masking the Self

We wear the mask that grins and lies,
It hides our cheeks and shades our eyes,—
This debt we pay to human guile;
With torn and bleeding hearts we smile…

~ Paul Laurence Dunbar (1872–1906) American Poet and Son of Freed Slaves, Excerpt from "We Wear the Mask."[14]

The mask is certainly part of who we are. It has been explored in poetry, books, and many of the arts, such as theater. Dunbar's quote reflects the mask needed to be worn by slaves when facing their masters, the smile that hid their grief and pain, while in his poem, "Masks," Shel Silverstein[15] writes about two lonely people who miss an opportunity for intimacy because of their individual masks. Joseph Campbell also wrote many books that illuminate and contribute to the mask conversation. It serves many uses in the dance. The mask can block you from seeing what may be right in front of you, prevents others from seeing what you don't want them to see, while also showing up with whatever persona works for you in the moment.

The mask is part of who we are. It is universal to all humankind.

Before becoming a therapist, I was rooted in the world of theatre. It was in that world I saw how embodying a character, taking on the role of a completely different persona, or mask, was protective and safe. I liked being hidden, cocooned from the world, and when I was in rehearsal or on stage I was no longer Edy. I could momentarily forget the trauma and the grief that I carried. I felt free. When the show was over, the character gone, it was time to meet myself again. I found the journey of re-entry, after having been shielded from the mild chaos within my brain, both exciting and terrifying. I had to find my social face without an attachment to a character. Sometimes I liked the character better than I liked myself.

Sometimes masks help you hide and sometimes they help you connect with your potency, allowing you to show up more authentically. We all wear masks. There's the mask you wear as part of the core Self in daily life, and the mask that hides the interior, shadowlike aspect of what you don't want others to see—or what you don't want to know about yourself.

You might think of a mask as armor that keeps you, to some extent, unseen. The mask can hide what feels damaged, protect your vulnerabilities, and inhibit any challenge that may come your way. You need to become finely tuned to what your masks actually do for you.

The mask of grief, for example, although different for everyone, is still a mask. Here are examples of expressions that can be delivered from behind a mask of grief:

"I'm okay."

"I'll be just fine."

"I want to die."

"Leave me alone."

Have you heard yourself speaking to people in ways that conceal the truth about your internal pain? What are some of the personae you wear in your grief? What facets of the personae do you normally present to the world? How do they reveal who you are and in what ways do they shroud who you are? What would be exposed if you took off the mask? What do you gain from being unseen and unknown? What or whom are you afraid of?

"I often wear the happy mask because although it is hard to do in some situations it is harder not to."

The mask that is created in response to past traumatic events, prior losses, and of course, in response to current mourning, is the mask of protection. Think of it as a container that keeps you concealed and safe. The goal for healing is to embrace the masks that you need; use them as needed, then put them away or discard them.

The mask protects and stabilizes the psyche, both the unconscious and conscious parts of the Self that are vulnerable and sensitive. When you are exposed to people who seem dangerous and overwhelming, the mask provides a barrier that exists while you are struggling, only receding when you feel okay. The unmasking process involves identifying the masks you wear, including the masks that have been invisible and the masks that are part of your core Self.

Don't judge the way you're handling your emotional turmoil. Don't *should* on yourself! Don't discredit the soul's ability to learn what is needed for healing. The psyche will only move as quickly as it is ready. Trauma and loss are not impediments to insight. Rather, they force you to learn more about who you are. They teach you what masks to assume, and what safety feels like. Masks will diminish when you're ready to do without them. New masks will emerge as part of the letting go of the old ones.

Like denial, a mask can be useful as long as it doesn't get in the way of healing. So often, you need time to figure out what you're doing in this dance, and choosing the "mask of silence" might buy you a little time. This doesn't mean that you don't talk about what's going on with you, yet you're allowed to share the silences as part of the grief. You also may choose not to speak of your grief and remain silent. This mask keeps your psyche as intact as it can be while you're engaging in the struggle.

You'll often change masks, taking off one and assuming another. You'll reuse them and recuse them. Some masks are present by choice; others represent a Shadow. The Shadow is what you don't want to see or be involved with. It isn't conscious. It's sometimes filled with darkness, and until it moves into your awareness, repetitions of feelings and obstacles will occur.

There are positive aspects to the Shadow. They challenge the psyche in good ways. For example, when you find that you're in the same cycle over and over again, chances are that is probably your Shadow at work. Once you see a repetition within your interactions, within your post-trauma responses, like PTSD, you'll understand the brain is giving you crucial information about its pain and internal dilemma. The Shadow shows up in the masks that protect what you're not yet ready to see, and not yet ready for others to know. People who are in your life can also represent the depths of the Shadow. It might show up as an unexplained attraction or repulsion.

Masks are a vital part of the lifelong developmental process. You start creating them at a very young age. The core personality shows up with the agility to move between many roles. To understand the importance of the mask, and how it manifests in your life, it may help to envision the relationship between parent and child.

Think about what it's like for a young child who is not yet ready to leave her mother's side. The child learns that the experience of being with Mommy is safe and secure. She also watches and observes that people aren't always by a mother's side. This awareness begins what I call the "separation dance." The child knows that it's time to begin exploring realms beyond her attachment to her mother. For the child and the mother, this is both exhilarating and terrifying.

As she leaves her parents' protection, the child experiences excitement, plus a type of grief. This is a healthy separation, and although it creates a bit of anxiety, it isn't overwhelming. However, if the separation is fraught with mixed messages from the parent, like "play with your friends but stay close," or the parent is consistently preventing the child from knowing that the parent can handle the separation—giving the child a sense that the parent is not okay when the child forays out into the world—separation anxiety can develop, and will follow the child as she matures.

If the child notices that she gets praise for asserting her independence, that's when the making of the mask begins. She gets the message that it's good to look brave and seem confident, although fear and anxiety lurk under the surface. She learns to soothe herself by fostering a "chin-up" persona that takes her from acting *as if* it's okay, to actually embodying *real* confidence. If the child has not yet internalized the many voices of the parent, her mask will crumble when the parent is out of sight. When the child learns she can survive the absence of the parent, she has found an internal confidence, a belief that she can count on herself. No longer needing the mask, her sense of self becomes integrated. This is the poetry of the developmental process.

Even if you're not a parent, you've probably observed a child who leaves the side of the parent and keeps looking back to make sure the parent is still there. In this tenuous state, the child knows she must make the break from that which is comfortable, and her discomfort in the separation is representative of a grief reaction. This is a *good* grief, a necessary grief, and a grief that aids in growth and maturation. A good grief, for example, is the grief of having a child move out of the house after having lived there for twenty-two years. He's going into uncharted territory, becoming more independent and self-sufficient—and leaving something behind. The leaving can create grief, for the parent and for the young adult, and it's a normal, natural, and useful grief.

What the child learns as part of early leave-taking experiences sets the stage for how he will handle disappointment later in life. As mother and child go through this process, the mother also wears a mask: A mask of encouragement gives the child a sense of support from the parent during the separation process. Although she knows it's an important step, the mother is going through her own grief response as her child grows apart from her. Through the tool of the mask, both mother and child move through the pain of growth—and achieve the next step in the process of development.

It's easy to avoid the subject of masks that people wear, especially pertaining to trauma and loss. Too often, anything that has to do with grief and trauma is considered a taboo topic. Because no one talks about masks of grief, it's difficult to know how to break through them and recognize the need for their impermanence rather than regarding them as an attachment. You want your pain to be unseen, but you also desire relief from that pain. Grief often gets bigger and louder when kept behind a veil. At some point, and that point varies with the individual, the unseen pain can become combustible and must be released. When your pain is unseen, the ability to adopt the different masks is not fluid. Your goal is to know your masks, choose them, and use them at will.

You can move from emotional concealment to freedom of self-expression and achieve a personal metamorphosis when you reveal what you've been hiding behind the mask.

With each new piece of knowledge you gain about your grief, you may re-meet denial, which may be a resting place for you. And that's okay. Take some time to rest, then move on. How do you take that which haunts you and make it less scary so you can do the work necessary to heal? *You take a chance.* You welcome opportunities to remove the veil and embrace your various grief masks.

Don't go it alone. Find places to grieve, people to grieve with, and the internal and external spaces in which to grieve. When you reach out to others, be conscious of the mask you're currently wearing. Take a moment to identify its presence, how it's working for you, and what outcome you would you like if you were less hidden.

Chances are, you won't always experience a sense of relief in the presence of those who want to help you because they will be reacting to the mask—the presented persona—and not to your true Self.

When you're wearing one of your masks, people will see you as you *want* to be seen, which may be different from the way you *need* to be seen. It works to their benefit to respond to your externalized image, believing that the mask is not to be tampered with. Even if they suspect that you're concealing something deeper, they may avoid addressing it, or they'll create a perception of you that enables them to remain veiled themselves.

The positive side to keeping the Self hidden is you might find a certain power behind the mask. This is similar to the reasons why a shaman will sometimes wear a mask: To speak to the power of the spirits, and thus touch the spirit within the Self, he empowers himself while remaining hidden. Not everyone within a tribe is allowed to wear a mask. It's considered an honor. Still, even the unmasked in any tribe have many masks they express. The mask embodies a persona, a social face that is presented to the world. The mask often enables making a connection to that which can't be seen.

Recognizing masks and their potency allows a type of acknowledgment that can be used as a tool for healing. How you engage the masks, disengage from them, or temporarily put them away will influence your energy. Throughout this book, I'll show you how to shift your inner voice through various exercises, questions, and breathwork. Your personal healing will depend on your cultivation of self-talk strategies, to challenge the grip that grief has on your soul.

When you decide to engage with, temper or remove a mask, ask yourself, "What has changed within my psyche to cause the internal shift?" As you learn about the masking process, you'll engage your brain and discover you have more say than you thought.

Think of your brain as one of your greatest tools for healing. When you counter negative thinking, challenge the presence of the masks that serve as protection, one might be the "mask of silence" and be curious about its presence. What other masks could be invited in by you? Masks that are more adaptable, give your psyche resources that coerce change. A mindful relationship with your brain is a major tool for healing.

Until you experience a loss, it's hard to anticipate the specific masks you'll wear to protect yourself. Masks are useful, but unmasking, too, is an essential part of your journey. The masking and unmasking process may lead you to meet parts of your Self that you don't like, didn't know existed, or would rather keep hidden. The shadowy darkness of the Self awakens to the beauty of release—and, ultimately, to a lighter self. Throughout this sacred passage, you may meet others whose gift is their willingness and desire to be authentic with you. Authenticity is a mask as well. The authentic meets the authentic. You drop into it and out of it, and it's part of grief. The journey can feel lonely, but the path is illuminated here and there when you find others who've been on a similar course or who are willing to bear witness to your metamorphosis.

Authentic people tend to attract authentic people: People who have their masks, are fluid and spontaneous with them, and own them. You'll always adopt masks, and have the flexibility to call on them when needed instead of only thinking you use them to evade attention.

Throughout the book, you'll find exercises to help you distinguish masks that work for you and are an inherent part of your core personality, and those tied to loss, trauma, and self-protection. Here are some immediate questions you can ask yourself and write about in your journal:

- Do you have names for the masks you're currently aware of?
- When do you call on the masks? What masks do you embody at work, with friends, with family? (Remember they are often shifting from day to day, person to person.)
- Is your choice of clothing, house, car, or scent part of the masking process for you?

* Which masks are present that you might no longer need? How and why do they exist for you?
* What do you call the masks that create obstacles?
* What masks are part of your core personality?
* Do they interrupt your full engagement with your trauma and grief?

The more you work through the cycles of grief, the more you'll expand, grow, and transition into your new story. Don't be afraid of what appears. Your choices belong to no one but you. Taking off one mask and exposing yourself to other masks makes you confront the dichotomy of wanting to stay safe, while needing to be free. Honor this ambivalence, and be willing to take some risks.

There are many benefits when you unveil yourself and take off the mask. The dance will occur with certain grace when you do.

CHAPTER 4

Listen to Your Grief

"There is no grief like the grief that does not speak."

~ Henry Wadsworth Longfellow

Opportunities for self-awareness and relief await you as you learn to listen to your grief. Think of self-awareness as a kind of listening. It allows for and encourages an assessment of the Self. When you use this kind of listening, it's a way to observe and gauge how the temperament of your grief changes over time. It gives you a chance to collect specific data to remind you where you began, where you presently exist, and where you would like to ultimately land.

When you're not listening, there's a good chance you experience a sense of disconnection from what is going on around you. How do you know when your thoughts are affecting your ability to listen? The answer is: *The messages you tell yourself affect how you listen.* If you tune into positive reinforcement, your brain listens and absorbs this information. If you engage in a refrain of negative commentary, your brain also listens, and the brain assimilates this self-talk.

If your main focus is your pervasive pain, it's hard to be present. You may feel disconnected; you may feel a constant churning in your mind. You simply want it to go away. What if you challenge yourself by asking, "How can I join the pain and change my reaction to it?"

Remember, your interaction with the world and how you work with your grief are impacted by the messages you tell yourself. Make the shift from, "Things will never change. I will never get out of the depths of despair," to, "I know that today is hard for me. I will move with this pain. Maybe learn from it, and breathe into it. I cannot predict what tomorrow will bring. I prefer not to engage in all-or-nothing thinking." That can be the difference between being stuck and engaging in the dance. These two statements result in two different reactions and two different effects.

To inhabit the soul's cry when it is mourning, and hear it, can be difficult. It can feel like an emotionally dense fog obscures access to the Self with little opportunity for natural light to break through. The light is a metaphor for hope. It's hard to navigate and listen to what's going on within the Self when enveloped in this type of haze. It impedes your self-awareness, makes it hard to find balance and proceed with clarity.

Grief is an expert at creeping in like fog, causing your mind to be mystified by the emotionally puzzling ups and downs that accompany it. Breathwork and breathing exercises are tools you can use to re-focus yourself and your senses and move into and out of the fog. Breathe in and you breathe into the fog; breathe out, release, and let the fog go.

Right now, take a breath and let it go. Listen to your breath as you breathe in and out. It makes a sound. Really. Listen for the sound of your breath. Just take that breath with the desire to hear it. How does your breath sound as you inhale? Is the sound of the exhale different from the sound of the inhale? As you breathe, notice what goes on in your body, in your heart, and in your psyche. Tuning into your breath can give you information about the Self.

If, for example, you've been feeling disconnected, it has probably been hard to listen to, and identify, what's going on within your soul. Your body, your mind, and your emotions have become distant, and it's appropriate and natural for the psyche to react in this way when in grief. You move through your day, knowing you have a right to your pain. This type of emotional fog blurs your senses, dulling access to the belief that the pain will lift. The fog is an aspect of the disconnect.

You might come to think that being in a haze is the norm. You reconnect to the self in two specific ways; when challenging the belief that the foggy haze is the norm and by reconnecting to what is a constant, your breath is one constant. To awaken out of the haze, begin to interact with the innate rhythms of breathing. There are other constants that also help to move you out of the stagnation.

You may also be grappling with a desire to stay in the "known darkness" and not listen to what the grief is saying to you. It may be saying, "I'm here, are you listening? Don't ignore me. Dance with me." Instead of yielding to the call, you may want to resist and retreat, because you know that to illuminate the potency of your loss, and trauma might highlight the pain. Most people tend to avoid feeling pain, but at great cost for the mourning soul. It's harder to listen to the Self than it is to avoid what listening would tell you. Once you begin to listen and move with grief, striking progress occurs.

When you exclude yourself from the world, the soul becomes a shut-in. Although it can feel natural to retreat, it's important to establish parameters that will allow you to gently engage. When you establish boundaries, you can give yourself permission to reach out, retreat, and reach out again. This allows you to recognize your limits and realize when it's time to disengage.

This act of listening is like yin and yang. There is a push and a pull; slow, measured movements that create an easy flow. The *Tao Te Ching* teaches, "The soft and the pliable will defeat the hard and the strong." What does a pliable response to the potency of your trauma and loss look like?

Be engaged with your grief as if you're doing *Tai Chi*. A martial art that began in China, this form of exercise provides physical and mental health benefits. From *Tai Chi*, you learn to not directly resist or attack what is coming at you, but rather to engage with the enemy with a pliable motion that causes the enemy to exhaust himself (or herself) and ultimately be propelled back. This creates a balanced dance in the context of battle. Your grief is the battle you're facing, and how you move with it—how pliable you are—can help you or keep you stuck.

Rather than simply avoiding the experience and making grief stronger, engage with it and re-direct the power it has over you. When you don't want to do the work to heal, ask, "How am I getting in the way of the healing?" Do you need to re-group, go to a retreat, find a therapist, or take time to be alone? Or are you avoiding the process with tactics that actually keep you stuck? There are many different types of avoidance.

In his poem, "Simple Twist of Fate" Bob Dylan described one type of avoidance, the avoidance of the soul, when he said, "People tell me it's a sin to know and to feel too much within . . ."

The more you avoid, the easier it is to avoid, allowing the avoidance to intensify. It feeds on itself. A history of sexual abuse, anxiety, loss of loved ones, substance abuse, or a history of being bullied mentally or physically can contribute to your need and desire to avoid what is before you. Past interactions and relationships can inhibit the way you relate to yourself.

When thinking about how avoidance shows up for you, it can often be underscored through excessive behavior that is used as a means for coping. For example, if you're drinking too much, getting high, or are involved in activities that keep you from being with yourself, and this behavior is different from your norm, you might be engaged in avoidance tactics.

> *One of my clients thought of her avoidance as similar to stoicism. Her mother died after a long illness when she was seventeen, and soon after that loss, she learned that her father was gay. She lost two people at that time. Her mother, and the father she thought she knew. She avoided her feelings through stoicism. Yet, her stoicism led to health issues that affected her sleep, her mood, and ultimately, her ability to work. Once she identified her avoidance as stoicism, she could begin to dance with grief.*

Avoidance is often a protector, while at the same time it is cruel toward the Self. It means well, because the withdrawal protects your psyche from feeling the full force of untenable emotions, and perhaps embodying the physical symptoms. However, when you allow yourself to withdraw, even if your intention is to protect the Self, the grip that trauma and loss have on you doesn't release. It goes underground. You're actually being unkind to the Self when you don't challenge what keeps you stuck. When you're in an avoidant pattern, you've stopped listening and reacting.

You can write about the following in your journal.

- Are you avoiding something? How do you know? Name one emotion, thought, or feeling you are avoiding.
- Are you aware of compulsive behaviors? Often a compulsive behavior exists to counter anxiety, yet at the same time, is brought on by anxiety.
- How does avoidance play in your dance? Map it out on a timeline. Look at it from different perspectives.

* Does it help you to shut down and stop listening to your psyche? Remember, the psyche is the conscious and unconscious parts of you.
* Are you having trouble remembering any part of the loss or trauma? Forgetting is the brain's way to give you a break.
* Does your memory seem like swiss cheese when it comes to recalling your experiences? Feeling as if there are holes in an intimate story that are difficult to fill in? Remember: Forgetting is the brain's way to give you a break.

You can change your mindset from avoidance to release. One of the best ways to release the Self from the mindset of avoidance is to challenge it. Begin by creating goals that have intrinsic value to you and write them down in your journal.

What can you do to honor the goals and follow through on them?

If you're drinking too much as part of the avoidance, think of meaningful ways you can limit your alcohol intake. Instead of reaching for a drink, create a go-to list of actionable changes you can make. Maybe you decide to accomplish six tasks before taking a drink. One of the tasks can include reaching out to a friend or family member or exercising for ten minutes.

With any in-depth therapy, the pain is relieved when you stop fighting what's before you and engage with it. When you tangle with the Shadow of mourning, you bring it into the light. Rather than the continuum of pain serving as a form of self-protection, the illumination serves as a reference point for self-protection.

How you listen to yourself is important and actually determines how you'll move in this dance. What are you telling yourself about your reactions to the loss? How do you encourage a shift in your inner voice? How you evaluate your actions as part of the voice that's carried within either stunts growth or enhances it.

Listening and Self-Awareness

Here are some practical guidelines that can support leads to self-awareness. They may seem simple, and commit to them and use them daily, the grip that grief has on you be reduced.

- Be conscious of what you do in your day:

  Make a plan the night before. Map it out. Will you have any downtime in your day? Will you have time to reach out to friends or family? How do you feel about reaching out? Have you made time to eat? Have you made time to exercise? What do you experience or think before you eat, exercise, or go to work? What do you think or experience when you have finished each task?
- Create a self-statement every day.

  The statement can be your mantra for the day: *I will listen to my hunger today. I will acknowledge when something, anything, brings a smile to my face. I will acknowledge my pain today and allow it to be.*
- Be spontaneous. The rituals of each day keep you centered. However, learning to be spontaneous while you rely on the rituals to lend structure to your days enhances the richness in your being and enables you to listen differently. It does not have to be a big move; it is simply about engaging with your comfort zone in different ways.

  Find new rituals and invite experimentation into your world. You can choose to taste a food you have never eaten before or brush your teeth with your non-dominant hand. These activities give you a break from the grief, even if it is for seconds. Take note of the momentary difference. Listen to your grief. Does it shift in those tiny moments?
- Practice patience. Listening requires persistence on your part. Because listening is engaging with the cycle of grief, give yourself "stop moments" in the course of your day.

> Ask your heart, your soul, and your psyche: *What is my experience right now? What can I do to enhance it or change it? What am I feeling? Who or what contributes to this feeling, and how can I engage with this feeling?*

These questions help you get to a more centered and balanced zone within the Self. Being grounded welcomes the ability to assess your state of being with an honest appraisal of how you're handling the experience of loss. It also allows you to immerse yourself in growth. Though some fear may arise about what is discovered about the Self while going through the grief process, your relationship to your grief can be truly transformative when you shed the fear of discovery.

Identify the Voices and Understand the Messages

Your inner voice is like a deep and intimate music that plays within your psyche. It can set the pace and tone of your dance with grief. Sometimes you might not like it, because it doesn't resonate with the way you want to feel, yet it plays in the background, bringing the unconscious into consciousness. If you don't like what your new consciousness presents, you can take steps to change it. The voice of grief co-exists with, and is an aspect of, your ever-present inner voice. When you're grieving, it's precise and specific to your relationship with the trauma or loss. When the voice surges, it's insistent in its presence and constant in your waking moments. Your inner Critic may also be active. The inner Critic is alive in everyone; for some folks it's pretty quiet, while for others it can be firm and demanding. It can be especially unrelenting during the grief process.

Perhaps other voices plague or stalk you. Engaging with those old partners may be a habit that's familiar and hard to let go of, yet it cuts out a possible new partner who could support your transformation.

This new dance invites you to partner with *yourself*. When you're stuck dancing to the same old tune of critical inner voices, you won't find ways to break the patterns. When you change your reaction to the critical voice, the music within is modified, created only by the Self, and you get to engage in a dance that takes you to new heights.

Imagine changing your old directives. The old messages are often the voices or intentions of a parent, partner, or teacher that you have internalized. These are the three most common inner messages or messengers. Who were the people in your life who gave you messages that sounded like a Critic or a Judge? When you hear those messages, ask yourself these questions and write the responses in your journal or notebook:

- Who told you you weren't good enough? In the conversation about grief, it can sound like you are not healing in the right way. In what other ways does "not good enough" translate to this conversation?
- Whose voice is the voice of the Critic? Establishing whose voice you hear can help you discriminate between which voice is yours and which voice actually belongs to another. Sometimes in the reactions around grief, the psyche gets very confused by all the chaos going on in the brain. Separate out the voices; you might find some solace and self-regulation.
- Who was your cheerleader? The same is true here. Is this your voice? The voice of another who was/is supportive? How can you make that voice yours while involved in the dance? The cheerleader counters the voices of the Judge and the Critic.

When old voices infiltrate your psyche, I call this the "invasion of the memories." Some memories can certainly bring you solace, for example, when you remember a happy time, while others can mess with you and feel more like an intrusion. Sometimes the same memory can yield a different effect depending on the day, the moment, or the specific trigger that brought you to the memory. You'll notice that these memories can make a lot of noise in the recesses of your mind and soul. Vivid pictures, sense memories (such as aromas), and replayed conversations from years past all contribute to how you hold on to your trauma, loss, and grief.

Memories of the traumatic event or of the lost loved one can become emotionally oppressive. Usually, the repetitive traumatic memories result from the soul's need to work out unfinished business. You put yourself under scrutiny for what you didn't do, what could have been different, or how you could have changed the outcome. How you sit with the grief depends on your willingness to challenge these memories. If you find yourself preoccupied and replaying the same feelings, desires, or thoughts, this is often considered to be obsessive thinking. Conversations you wished you'd had with your lost loved one, or ruminations about how you could have better defended yourself, keep you living in the past. The past is what you know, and it seems safe. Painful, yet safe.

These memories are like warriors, and when they invade, you can reflexively respond with actions that you know, consciously or not, have helped keep the overwhelming and intense memories at bay. Here is Robin's story. See how she reflexively responds while her unconscious and conscious states are aroused.

> *I got so used to running that I didn't notice when I was doing it. Nothing I did was ever enough to get rid of the fear that held me; no success or bar that I reached could keep the memories of my mother's bloody face after being attacked by her girlfriend from my memory. I kept myself "busy"—this led to much success, however its greater purpose was to keep from remembering each trauma, and ultimately it created more grief within the family. Anxiety attacks, high blood pressure, and physical ailments increased substantially over time. I felt unable to stop and be with myself. If I did, what would I have*

to look at? In every relationship, I kept creating the same scenario of trauma. This included my marriage to a sexual deviant. Until I stopped running and faced the monsters of my past, I did not understand how avoidance was the fuel that kept the monster alive.

What do you notice about Robin's story? Her response to her trauma was to avoid and emotionally run. How do your responses key into things that have happened in the past? Do they address what is happening in the present? Do you respond to chaos created by these old memories with old ammunition that has little effect in the current situation? Are you running, or avoiding what is in front of you?

This time of grief is for separating what belongs in the present from what belongs to the past. Do it now! What belongs in the past? What belongs in the present? Ask yourself these questions and allow your curiosity to get involved in the answers. When the past starts to move in, what is it trying to communicate? What do you need to understand about yourself when past images or voices show up? Can you quiet them simply by acknowledging their presence? Can you say, "STOP IT!" and re-orient to the present? Keep what works and throw out the rest.

How will you know when the choices are working? You'll notice when the impulses and obsessive thinking quiet down. You'll feel less stuck and overruled by the thoughts and actions that kept you in the grasp of loss and trauma. Awareness of the present becomes more abundant, ultimately creating the emotional space for healing. The grieving soul needs different care and attention from the non-grieving soul, which is often quieter and balanced.

Obsessing about old memories and outdated self-talk keeps you in the past. When you move your responses into the present, without predicting what lies ahead, you're invited to remain in the present. This shifts the obsessive thinking out of the past and welcomes you to the here and now. Then you can tackle the vestiges of loss and trauma.

Bil Keane, the cartoonist and author, once wrote that, "Yesterday's the past, tomorrow's the future, but today is a GIFT. That's why it is called the present."[16] It's certainly a challenge to stay in the here and now. It's much easier to return to the past or imagine a future story. How you've responded to adversity, including your internal critics or external events, may not have prepared you or given you the necessary tools to cope with your present loss or trauma. Imagine allowing yourself to get out of the complacency that sabotages growth as you welcome a new repertoire of responses that help you meet your grief head on. Start this conversation by identifying what hasn't worked--knowing what has failed you is as important as knowing what works. This is the beginning of breaking out of the grip of grief.

- Identify what you have been telling yourself.
- Change the language.
- Speak it out loud.

The memory invaders are noisy and can be relentless when you don't listen. Knocking, knocking, knocking!

You can create a reprieve from an active state of mourning. Sometimes, without knowing, you'll receive a kind of hiatus. For example, when you laugh at something funny or sleep through the night for the first time in a long time, or when you're less disorganized than usual, you can feel the grip of grief is letting up. This brief intermission might seem alien to you, because you've been so hyper-focused on the loss or trauma. When grief isn't present in every waking moment, fear of forgetting the source of your grief and the imprint made by your Big G can cause the anxiety around it, along with the intensity, to revisit your psyche. Remember, it's not about forgetting. It's about learning to live with this part of your story with ease and grace.

Even when the source of the grief is from physical or sexual abuse, that part of your history is what contributes to your sense of self. You may want to let go of it, yet also hold on to it as an integral part of you: "Never forget," your psyche says, "or else you'll repeat it." Allowing for the reprieves one at a time lets the brain know it can let go and adapt to changing the way the voice of grief takes up residence in your psyche. Welcome the easing of the grip of grief, and enter the healing dance.

The Crowded Room

I often say to new clients when they walk into the office that they may think we are the only ones in the room, when there's actually quite a crowd. Shadows of parents, siblings, grandparents, and friends also walk through the door, sit down, and take up space. Whether you're conscious of it or not, all these people have made an imprint on you and to some degree, each of them is carried within your psyche, and they each have a voice or perspective that you're listening to.

They're part of an array of influences that both celebrate and annihilate you. In the crowd, you can encounter "the Judge," "the Critic," or "the cheerleader." Their voices can be loud and abrasive, or loving and warm. They can be admonishing and cautioning, or they can be supportive and encouraging. They appear uninvited, but because they're so familiar, asking them to leave creates some anxiety, and it'll take courage to make the request. Being willing to let them go so you can linger in the darkness and hear the silence is part of the dance. When you learn that darkness and silence are not threatening experiences, the imbalances encountered on the journey of grief can be digested and normalized. The Crowded Room exercise may help clarify which friends and phantoms exist in your crowded room and what purposes they serve.

Please note you do not have to complete the entire exercise. You can do part of each exercise. If you get overwhelmed, stop, breathe, and re-engage when ready.

The Crowded Room

SELF-DISCOVERY EXERCISE

Think about all the people who are in your crowded room. It could be Mom, Dad, aunts and uncles, friends, and/or teachers. Write down their names and think about what "voice" of theirs you carry internally. Think about how their presence helps, hinders, or hurts you. Now go through every name and put a voice to it that best represents how you hear it. Is it a kind, loving, supportive voice, or does it warn you? Does the voice judge you? Does the voice undermine you, or speak for you and make it seem as if you are being emotionally annihilated? (*"Don't socialize tonight. Stay in, feel bad, just say no to the invitation."*) Does the voice encourage you like a cheerleader? (*"You can feel better by challenging yourself. Push a bit harder and you might be surprised by the outcome."*)

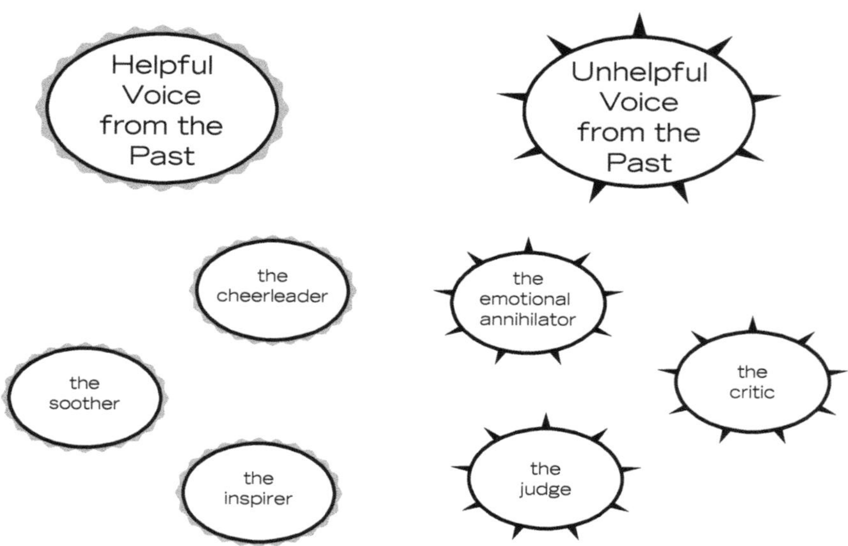

Name of Person	Mom		
What did they say?	"Get over it!"		
How did you respond then and now?	Then: retreated Now: *Get over it* is repeated in my head and I can't shut it down.		
How do you hear it?	Something is wrong with me.		
Age you first heard the voice? How old is the voice in your head?	8 years old		
What kind of voice is it?	Judge		
Mental image that goes with the voice?	Getting bullied and teased by kids at school.		

- Identify which of these voices have been helpful in the past. Can you imagine that they could be helpful in the recovery process? Which have been less helpful in your life and may not support your healing now?
- Discern how *long* the voices have been with you. What is the age of the voice? Is it younger or older than you are now?
- If you were in a conversation with one of the negative voices, how would you hear it, and what would you say to it?
- What would you say to a voice that is kind and supportive?
- How can you encourage the positive voices so they can continue to encourage you?
- How do you give less potency to the negative voices?
- Did you find a voice that feels like "The Judge" or "the emotional annihilator"? What about "the cheerleader"? or "the soother"? If so, who do you think of when these voices are highlighted? Almost everyone I have met has as least one of these.

Sometimes you listen to them; sometimes you silence them. How you respond to them is an essential element to loosening the grip of grief. Knowing how to sort and manage the voices can lead to essential insight. This self-discovery exercise lends itself to understanding the voices. You want to create a skill set that helps you diminish the internal pandemonium caused by the voices. The result is empowerment. Mastery of the ups and downs helps with the healthy integration of grief into your life.

Please know that a negative voice is just as much a teacher as is a positive voice. Here's a variation of the above exercise that can help you work with the negative voices. It requires some colored pens or pencils.

* Give the negative voice a name that best describes what the voice does to you when it is present. For example: *Soul Crusher.*
* Write the name of the voice, using whatever color pen, pencil, or marker best represents the array of emotions present. Using colors may help you see the variations of your emotions as they relate to the character of each voice.
* *Soul Crusher: feel mute (in yellow), ill-equipped to face my loss (dark blue), stuck (red), afraid (brown).*
* What phrase or chant would you use while releasing the negativity? Write it down. *Soul Crusher, you don't have power over me. I will persevere. You can't make me feel bad, I am a survivor!*
* You have options for what to do with this piece of paper. You can tear it up into tiny pieces, burn it, or put it into an envelope so you can revisit its contents at a later date. You might be surprised how the impact of time and your own healing can shift your reactions. *I choose to bury this paper and hope that time will disintegrate it.*
* Negative voices often inhibit growth and joy, so while you are either tearing up or burning the paper (or just putting it away for now), you can replace that lost growth and joy by saying something like:

I will replace the voice of the Critic with a "You go-girl" voice that encourages my growth. The voice will be cheerleader-like in its intentions (these are my words . . . feel free to use your own).

Or, you might say something like, *I will introduce the voice of the Critic to the cheerleader, because I may need both of these voices to create an essential balance in my understanding of me.*

Call in the Positive Influencers

What can you do to enhance the voices that are positive? When you acknowledge and recognize the Critic, you actually diminish its power. You weaken its ability to influence you, while you also learn how it pushes you to go beyond your limits. Conversely, by acknowledging the positive voices, you *increase* their power and authority. Here are some of the ways you can counter the negative voices and develop the positive voices.

- Encourage a more positive voice to emerge once you have recognized the currency the negative voice holds. If you can't imagine a positive voice, begin to identify constructive and encouraging comments you might hear from others or might have read in a book. On the internet, if you Google sites like Pinterest or Goodreads, they offer positive, proactive, and helpful quotations. You can access these sites through your phone, computer, or connected device. Use them, try them out, and assess if they work for you.
- Write about the voices and their need to exist. Each voice is important. This is a tool that helps sort out why the negative voice is present, whether you need it, why you need it, and what purpose it serves. If you determine it is no longer needed, then formulate what you would prefer to be thinking, and determine how the new internal voice is a better choice.

* Replace the Critic's thoughts with new thoughts. Make a list of the old negative voices and enhance the list with new voices. You can counter the voices with something like, *I don't want to engage in the painful rhetoric you are offering me, even though we have been companions for a long time. I have the power to change my reactions to you.*
* Create a new plan that consists of the voices you want in your life, or formulate a revised story that honors who you are right now. Who do you want in your story, how do you want to feel in your story, and what needs to be different in this new chronicle?
* Have the courage to face what needs to perish as you engage in changing the impact of the known and negative voices. Now is a good opportunity to give a name to each new voice that you adopt.

You have a choice when you hear judgment: Internalize it or refute it. Counter with the power of your own voice.

Grief Speak: The Universal Archetypes

The term "archetype" was used by the well-known psychiatrist Dr. Carl Jung[17] to describe universal symbols or patterns, like prototypes for ideas often used to interpret dreams, the world of the psyche, and ultimately, the Self. Jung thought of humankind as having a "collective unconscious." He realized that all people are related to one another, as if by a string that connects universal experience and ultimately makes up our unconscious states of being and our consciousness. We hold a universal recognition of symbols and relationships regardless of ethnicity, religious background, or education.

A call to the archetypes can help conjure traits that you need, yet may not be evident in you. When the archetypes reveal behavioral options, their influence can be rewarding and *free you* from being in a holding pattern. This information can move you into a sense of release.

The archetypes can actually help you imagine how you can position the Self in the healing dance.

The Hero and the Mother are good examples of universal archetypes. If I ask you to describe a Hero or a Mother, you would be able to conjure up that image. Based on the culture from which you came, each image, the Mother or the Hero, may be different, yet ultimately these archetypes do not need translation.

Think about what a Hero does or how the role of the Mother functions. The response to these two archetypes operates on both a universal level and a personal level. They exist in the depths of the unconscious mind, and they also exist in consciousness. Your consciousness is what you know; it's your reality. Jung also identified archetypal *events*, such as birth, death, marriage, and initiation. **It is this universality that allows the conversation about loss and trauma to be understood by all: By every man, woman, and child.** Although no one experiences pain in the same way, grief and trauma are universal experiences.

In addition to the Mother and the Hero, Jung's archetypal figures include the Father, the Wise Old Man, the Trickster, and many others. We will touch on some of these in the following pages. Jung identified four major archetypes—the Self, the Shadow, the Anima and Animus, and the Persona. The focus during your dance of grief will be on the Self, the Shadow, the Mother, and the Hero, which are discussed in Joseph Campbell's *The Hero with a Thousand Faces* (1949); however, please consider any other archetypes that speak to you. It's curious that the Hero seems to be consistently present in the trauma and loss story. Perhaps because the Hero speaks to the impulses in your brain. Although the Hero is not one of the four major archetypes, it is an important archetype to meet, converse with, and integrate.

You can own what's going on within you through keen observation and action. You can join a self-created pity party, or you can stand up and fight for your life. If you don't have an internal impression of what "fighting for your life" feels like or looks like, engaging with the symbolic and metaphorical powers of the archetypes can demonstrate and show the immense ways they're helpful and valuable.

The archetype conversation is a personal one. It doesn't matter which you choose, and the choice can certainly be fluid. Some people will choose "the Warrior" archetype for his unending strength, while others will choose the "Wild Woman," because she represents honoring desire and finding truth. They both tap into surviving, while at the same time tapping into savage aspects of the Self. Both archetypes have characteristics of anger and rage.

Your psyche also plays a major role in how you interact with the archetypes. The psyche is a window into your conscious mind and a knowing observer of what is yet to be uncovered in the mysteries of your unconscious. Jung called the psyche a "self-regulating system" that he likened to the body regulating itself. The body strives to initiate balance among its systems, and the psyche endeavors to find a balance between equal but opposing benefits. The psyche wants to know the conscious and tangle with the unconscious—things yet to be known. The psyche hungers for growth and ultimate understanding. Jung also believed that archetypes were limitless. This means there are many, many archetypes, many more than what he delineated. For this discussion, we'll look at archetypes that can inform the ways you grieve and interpret your trauma and loss; we'll consider which archetypes you need more of and which you need less of.

The archetypes enable you to gain new insights into the internal and external voices you hold, while also accompanying your interpretations about the varied roles you access in this process; these archetypes can actually help you progress through this dance. As you read, think about which archetypes are present in your loss, grief, and trauma. How do they mingle with the many different aspects of the Self? Their potency can introduce you to how they represent the internal voices, as well as invite you to bring them to life through specific behavioral choices.

As you look at the descriptions of the archetypes, think about which you would invite into your life to inspire growth, change, and internal power.

The Self

In your loss and trauma, you are intimately dancing with the archetype of the Self. You are aware of the conscious Self. The unconscious self, remains hidden until its mysteries are revealed, the abundance it carries can be both scary and protective. When the unknown is exposed, the psyche can begin tackling the obstacles that keep you stuck.

The meaning of who you are as a being marks the difference between you and another. The Self is represented in so many ways. It's revealed in the psyche, the body, and the voice; it's revealed through relationships, introspection, and revelations.

The Shadow

"I guess we're all two people. One daylight,
and the one we keep in shadow."

~ Bruce Wayne/Batman, *Batman Forever.*

The archetype of the Shadow refers to the part of your unconscious mind that consists of what you don't want to see or engage with. Every archetype has a Shadow side. This is an important factor when meeting the archetypes. The Hero, for example, has a Shadow side that shows up when a Hero uses his or her power to enhance his ego through indifference, arrogance, and superiority.

The Shadow's essence is filled within your instinctual nature, your weaknesses, and your wishes. It's an element within you that doesn't want to be seen or known, but for growth to occur, it cannot be ignored. We all have these shadows, and we all have a choice whether to engage with them or not. Simply because you choose not to engage with them doesn't mean they disappear.

Your Shadow is much like a diamond in the rough. It's raw, and embedded with history. It's yet to be cut into brilliance. The shadowy parts of grief may appear within your dreams, for example, as snakes, demons, dragons, or dark figures. *What* you don't want to look at, *what* you would prefer to ignore, and *who* you don't want to tangle with are all aspects of your Shadow. Yet within the Shadow, within whatever you don't want to look at, there is information that's useful in the dance. There are symbolic and metaphorical aspects of the Shadow, as well as people in your life who represent or bring out the depths of the Shadow.

The Anima/Animus

The Anima/Animus archetype represents a very specific aspect of the unconscious Self. The Anima is found in men, is like his soul figure, and is expressed as the inner feminine within his personality. The Animus is found in women and is expressed as the inner masculine within her personality. It's part of the universal experience; an inward and subconscious experience. As part of the unconscious mind, the Anima/Animus not only affects how you relate to the opposite sex, they impact how you engage in emotions.

In grief, the Animus will show up in the woman with fixed notions that can keep you stuck. The Anima is like the Tarzan who needs his Jane—without her he is lost, while with her he wants to be the all-powerful male. As a male, ignoring the internal feminine may result in ignoring or revolting against emotion.

The Mother

Understanding the potency of this archetype is one essential key to unraveling the response to your loss and trauma. The relationship to the Mother archetype influences your ability to engage and disengage. It prompts your need for others to see your pain as a means to validate it, and it forms lasting impressions that can help you or hurt you. Sometimes it helps to think about your own mother as you write the answers to the following questions:

- Do you see her in your mind? If not your biological mother, is there a Mother figurehead that you relate to?
- Do you experience the Mother as forgiving, remote, loving, or protective? Do you experience her connected to some specific emotion?
- Do you hear her messages as consuming and shrewd, or nourishing and kind? So often, a consuming message plays: An internal repetition that cannot be shaken.
- Identify your responses to your loss and trauma. Are they the same as your mother's response to you, or are they different? How are they different? Do you seek out the "Mother" in others? Are these mothers male or female? Are they caretakers? Are they harsh?

While in the cycle of your bereavement, the wish for the archetypal, "Good Mother" may be present. If you have internalized a *consuming Mother*, you might hear her voice echo in the conscious and unconscious aspects of your psyche, saying, "Get over your grief, so I can have you back. Your grief creates distance between us, and I don't want you to leave me. Your grief is less important than our relationship." This response shatters the hope for the Good Mother to be present when facing the tenacity of these feelings.

In contrast, a *nourishing Mother* encourages you to engage in the work of the psyche, to go into the depths of your grief process without needing to adapt your healing for her comfort. She wants you to be the strongest version of yourself. She is not intimidated by who you are. She represents the archetypal Good Mother.

You can choose between these very different Mother archetypes to create conscious messages that work for you. It would seem the consuming Mother would be worth disregarding, as that internalized archetype is not on your side. Certain people may have taken on that role for you, even though they aren't your actual mother. It's common to form relationships with people who are symbolic representations of the mother, father, or parental influencer. Who are those people in your life? Do you seek them out in the midst of your mourning? Take a moment to think about these questions and answer them. If you write them in your journal, you can revisit your answers to see if they change as part of the process of healing.

The Mother Shadow: The hungry and devouring Mother is an all-consuming figure. She can be seen and illuminated in both the feminine aspect of the Self and the masculine aspect of the Self. If you find you experience an insatiable thirst or hunger, it can mean you carry components of fear, loneliness, and dependency with you. How do the forces of this Shadow rule and create boundaries that seem to address safety, yet merely conspire to control and keep you down? The need to control everything is part of the Mother Shadow, and can affect how you handle the dance of grief and how you disengage from its grip.

There are many different archetypes that might make an appearance during your journey. What follows is a list of some of the other archetypes you may encounter along the way. As you think about loss and healing, do you relate to any of the descriptions? Again, this is an opportunity to use your notebook as a way to record your intimate thoughts.

THE MAGICIAN

Gifting you with the mysteries of change, chameleon-like in its presentation and alchemical by nature, the Magician is a change agent who begs for the transformation of the Self. What happens within the Magician's powerful presence is a creation of that which is held to be sacred, privileged, and potent. Transformation and mystery are associated with this archetype. And you *will* transform, because after dancing with grief, it's not possible to go back to who you were. At the beginning of your journey you may not recognize the Magician. It's through your desire to be healed that the lens of grief offers many gifts. Gifts that could only be accessed after having joined and survived this journey.

The Magician's Shadow: This archetype erupts into the psyche to tease you into the belief that you will magically "get over" your grief by wishing it away. It's a form of denial. Self-esteem, competence, and your own internal light are darkened when this Shadow is present. Illusions are at their pinnacle, making the pain of loss and trauma seem different from what it really is. In situations where there is a perpetrator at hand, the Magician within them can appear innocent as they hide their cruelty. This is not unlike some of the priests who abused children as they hid behind the cloth. The dark side of the Magician doesn't allow you to clearly see what is before you. You cannot grasp the hope beyond your pain. It's hard to see a way out. What you want to believe is healing may really be an illusion. *Ignore the loss* or *ignore the trauma* may be messages you hear or believe will aid in healing and in finding a sense of balance. It's not so. It's the Shadow of the Magician that creates blinders.

Do you recognize the Magician in your life? Your friends and family often want to be the Magician while you're in this dance. Why wouldn't someone who cares for you want you to "get back to your old self"? What they don't realize is how necessary it is for you to engage fully with integrating your grief into your life. This is part of regaining balance and reclaiming the Self. They cannot protect you from the pain, the process, or the resulting transformation.

The Magicians in your life might think that if they don't talk about your trauma or loss, or if they act as if everything is good with you, your healing will accelerate. This is an example of their magical thinking.

Who in your life right now is a magical thinker? How does that magical thinking affect you?

THE TRICKSTER

The Trickster invites you to break taboos, face life with a lighter spirit, and take on the Self with less seriousness and more frivolity. In one moment, the Trickster tempts you to ignore what's present, almost snub the grief and loss you feel, and act like everything is fine. And in another moment, it will remind you how sad you feel. The activity of this polarizing agent is seductive in nature, and keeps you off guard. The Trickster shows up to surprise and shock you, and yet, arouses you, reminds you, like a renewed alert, to pay attention to how grief can engulf you. Awareness of the Trickster's wiles enables you to care for yourself and prepare for your potential triggers. Because triggers come at a moment's notice, just like the ups and downs of a mood, the Trickster prepares you for the inconstancy of grief.

When you honor the pace of your needs, you'll meet the virtue of understanding that the ground you stand on is shaky one minute and stable the next. When you meet your internal Trickster, a breaker of illusions, you may sense that intentions or personality traits of others around you will be uncovered, giving you ample information that can help you protect yourself, separate from them, and understand them. This allows greater tolerance on your part, or enables you to see how their agenda could impact how you heal. The Trickster will bait you and teach you at the same time. That is what trauma and loss do as well!

The Trickster's Shadow: The Trickster, in its darkness or Shadow, is hard to cope with when it conjures its cunning practical jokes within your unconscious. When it emerges, it can show up in living color. The internal practical joke is emphasized when you believe headway has been made in the dance, and then an unanticipated memory filters through, triggers you, and evokes within you a sense of doubt about your progress. Startled by this new sensory information, you are presented with something you didn't want to look at in high definition. You cannot ignore it. In this dance, you move with certain grace while realizing the inevitability of occasional rocky moments, hours, or even days, that can often come out of nowhere. It's in these surprise moments that you may become uncertain, surrounded by emotional powerlessness and filled with equal but opposing personality traits: Smart and defiant versus powerless and faithless.

One essential element to the Shadow aspect of the Trickster is the belief that you must challenge how you heal, challenge who can help you along the way, and question how much you can trust anyone to help you on this journey. Believing there is a "truthful" or "manipulative" way to heal is magical thinking. It's part of the Trickster rhetoric. It's great to think that you're going to be the one person who can transcend feelings around loss and trauma.

The Trickster, as Shadow, puts you into chaos, creating havoc and making you ill at ease with the complexity of your grief. The Trickster wants you to laugh in the face of your grief, and will make you feel as if you're done with the dance, when it may have just begun.

THE JUDGE

In a court of law, the roles of the Judge are to find truth, to create balance between what is right and what is just, and to accurately convey the laws of the land. Harmony of these roles is often disrupted by the need to decide who is innocent and who is guilty. As a mediator, the Judge archetype appears when you're trying to make sense of what you're facing. The dichotomy of good and evil, death and life, grief and release are dilemmas faced when this archetype is present. The Judge wants to keep you safe. You might find that its voice filters through your day regularly without an acute perception of its presence. The Judge offers you the chance to negotiate within yourself and find your most pragmatic self, while working through issues like loss, grief, and trauma; ultimately, the Judge wants what is right.

The Judge's Shadow: Although you might be unaware of its powerful presence, the Judge can be a major player in your unconscious. This voice is the Critic when it's in the space of Shadow, assessing the way you act, how or when you speak, what you wear, and how you show up. It can be a governing force to be reckoned with when it's in its Shadow. You might hear the Judge as loud, overbearing, and difficult to assuage, depending on how long it's been around you. It can be a dark force, especially when you confront it and defy the rules it has set for you. Its influence varies and depends on how you have been able to quiet it when it's in full force.

When you succumb to the echoes of this voice, it can shut you down. The shut-down, which feels like you're sloshing through emotional molasses, effects motivation to change. When you hear the internal voice, "You aren't healing in the right way. Be pragmatic and get over it! Your loss is in the past, and it's time to get back to life," this is the Judge at work. It's this message and other messages like this that cause undue stress on the best pace for your healing and integration. Friends and family who want you to "snap out of it" because of their own inability to cope with grief will often support this voice. If they lack compassion, they often have a secret, manipulative agenda. When you think vengefully, or selfishly push your own agenda, the Shadow aspect of the Judge may be at work.

We'll take a closer look at the Judge in the next chapter.

THE HERO OR JOURNEYMAN

The Hero is an archetype who can be an ardent supporter and cheerleader, finding ways for you to meet your grief and loss directly. Known for strength, ingenuity, and the desire to be courageous at all costs, at the core of the Hero's existence is the need to show how valuable it is not only to the Self, but to others as well. The Hero offers stability.

In the Hero, you will meet the part of you that is capable of fighting what's before you with a dragon slayer's mentality. The Hero has been depicted with both masculine and feminine energies in movies and comic books. If you're tackling part of your trauma that is particularly difficult, imagine calling upon or conspiring with the likes of a Wonder Woman or Spiderman to help you navigate through a difficult time. It might seem funny, yet this is a journey that awakens you to an internal understanding of the Self. This is a gift offered to you as you enter the dance and meet all the aspects of the psyche.

The Hero or Journeyman's Shadow: The Hero detests weakness. You will know that the dark aspect of the Hero has shown up when you feel more powerful in relation to the weakness of others. You feel better when someone else looks worse than you.

Obstacles faced by the Shadow of the Hero have to do with the need to be engaged in a fight, so with nothing to fight, the Hero may feel lost. This can cause emotional hardship within the Self. Questions may arise such as, "*Who am I without an active state of grief? Who am I when the role of survivor is only part of me? How can I use the roles I've played and make a difference in another person's life?*" These questions engage you in the present, bring out what has been hidden within your psyche, and participate with the power of the Hero's Shadow.

The Lover

The Lover desires to create intimacy with another. Tender and committed, it strives to build a sense of camaraderie. The Lover is connected to your sensations, hunger, and desire. The desire to find balance in your psyche, the hunger to be nourished as you move through the grip of grief, and the commitment to thrive are primary needs of the Lover in grief. The Lover is alive, aroused easily, passionate, and filled with compassion for the struggles of others.

The Lover's Shadow: The Lover often fears being alone, unloved, or rejected, and therefore makes the dance of loss and trauma harder to live with and comprehend. The Lover often gives too much of itself and jeopardizes losing the essence of the Self. Helplessness, chaos, and undefined emotional structure, which is often present in the face of grief, causes the Lover to feel disconnected, without a sense of internal resources to shift the journey that may require other means to nurturing the Self.

THE WARRIOR

The Warrior's energy defends, creates strategies, and is decisive, which is certainly needed when facing loss. Known for loyalty, endurance, and courage, this archetype contains a wisdom stored within the soul. This stored emotional energy is often released as anger. When anger is released in relation to your grief or trauma, this may be the Warrior at work. This emotional energy also accesses the wisdom of the collective unconscious and informs healing.

When you're ready to defend yourself or need a guardian, this archetype combines elements of security and refuge, and is a true trooper who cares about the integrity of the fight, although this can sometimes look like unexpected violence or rage. The Warrior, like the Hero, might have feminine and masculine attributes, or combine them as part of understanding this archetype's extreme core. The psyche is a potent aspect of this core and can help you touch the desire to succeed and conquer—and the knowledge that success is defined by you and only you.

The Warrior's Shadow: Some of the Warrior's greatest fears are the show of weakness and to be abused, neglected, or ignored. When you feel these emotions, know that your Shadow Warrior is present. It's hard to fight a valiant fight when you lose a connection to humanity and your psyche. Unconsciously, this loss enhances the losses you already feel, and can lead to cruelty, heartlessness, and untendered eruptions. Cut off from humor and self-defense, your thoughts become a lone pathway to more of the same. Interrupt them, and remember that when you honor the Warrior's tale, you will tap into courage, power, and the decisiveness needed to shift into the momentum to heal.

I present the following archetypes in less depth. Should you want to learn more about them and their Shadow counterparts, you'll find abundant information on the web if you look up "Archetypes," "Shadow," and "Carl Jung." Think about how the core, the Shadow, and the fundamental desires of each of the archetypes resonates with you.

The Explorer

The Core: The Explorer strongly dislikes feeling trapped by anyone or anything. This archetype begs you to know more about what defines your loss, grief, or trauma.

Shadow: The Explorer fears boredom, which pushes it to experience new and illuminating situations.

Fundamental desire: To create and secure a life that is fulfilling and real. When you have integrated the losses into your being, it means they can be quiet without a need to keep them at a heightened awareness.

The Rebel

The Core: The Rebel is at its best when breaking rules, or as part of a revolution or group that wants change at all costs. The goal is to change what's not working by creating disturbances and shocking the audience. It's a selfish way to stay powerful and, ironically effective. The Rebel in your grief disrupts the stagnation of this dance.

Shadow: Often on the fringe of life, a lone ranger who fears apathy and being immobilized, lacks self-care, and easily puts others in danger.

Fundamental Desire: The Rebel will work to confront negative societal beliefs by changing the thought processes of others. When others project a healing timeline for you, it will be the Rebel within or that you call upon to reject their projection and honors what you need.

Wild Woman

The Core: Erotic and powerful, she can hold the intent of a Mother yet with unmatched intensity. She is the feminine Warrior, and can make the trek into the unknown elements of loss that exist within your soul.

Shadow: The Wild Woman Shadow has a shrewdness that pushes away those who stand in her way and those whom she holds dear. She is a clever manipulator who navigates the world in careless ways. The Wild Woman in loss will think she's right, even when she's in unknown territory.

Fundamental Desire: To be the Feminine Divine, in its purest form, allows for vulnerability, inner strength, and the fortitude to challenge wrongs and make them right. It's through vulnerability, challenging what's before you, and the inner strength to meet the darkness that discovery of the Self emerges. The masculine and feminine aspects to this archetype are part of this journey.

You will discover a power within you by confronting, challenging, and understanding the influence that these archetypes have, and in doing so, the potency of your grief can begin to shift. The archetypes will teach you to discern which aspects can help you with the dance, and which aspects thwart your efforts to heal. Whether the Mother, the Judge, or the Warrior are present, when you listen to the presence of the archetypes, you're observing and hearing the Self, unveiling the path of your journey, and creating your course. As you change, the people around you will react and respond to that change.

The dance with grief is often like a roller coaster ride. Your companions on the ride can be any of these archetypes, either metaphorically or in the embodiment of someone you know who is assuming the role of that archetype in your life. Encountering ups and downs, turns and twists on the ride, will, in time, help you land on your feet.

CHAPTER 5

THE DANCE OF AWARENESS—HEAL AT YOUR OWN PACE

"Time is the coin of your life. It is the only coin you have, and only you can determine how it will be spent. Be careful lest you let other people spend it for you."

~ CARL SANDBURG[18]

No one can tell you how to heal or give you a map or timetable for processing your loss. One of the archetypes that shows up and may try to tell you what to do is the Judge. The Judge can be part of an internal dialog that's critical to how you face the dance of grief, or it can be embodied by those around you who, although well-meaning, try to dictate the steps they believe you need to take. Being aware of the Judge and how it manifests in your life can help you set your own pace and timing.

The Judge brings order and truth to this process, while its Shadow and its voice, wherever it comes from (internal or external), is destructive and can interfere with uncovering the right steps for your healing.

By acknowledging the Judge, you gain the gift of a potentially more positive healing outcome. Though you may want to, it's tough to annihilate the Judge. This archetype is quieted when you no longer give it power. Know it's there, recognize it, and allow it to walk with you, yet not determine how you walk. When you stop reacting to the Judge, and walk your own way, you'll determine your own sense of authority and feel that you're in discovery of your voice—a voice that stands on its own. It's a voice, a perspective, and a belief that is securely constructed by you. The challenge is that when you balance your reaction to the Judge, your dance must then be based on *your* needs and not on the needs or intentions of others. Here is the judge in action as it felt by another.

> *"I lost my mother at nine and my father at twelve. I remember feeling the expectation of a grief expiration date for myself. I remember being fifteen, five years after my mother died and three years after my father died. If I had a tough day missing my parents, people looked shocked, or avoided the subject, or avoided me. Sometimes I would hear insensitive comments, like, 'Aren't you over that?'"*
>
> ~ Lynne B. Hughes [19]

Facing the Judge

To transfer power from the Judge to yourself, you develop "a voice with a choice". That way, instead of listening to the Judge, you call on your new voice, which will offer a different and potentially more healing response to your situation. Facing the Judge with your new voice can be exhilarating, especially when you see how your attitude, your behavior, and your psyche begin to shift. You will know you have achieved this metamorphosis when you:

* Stop listening to only what the Judge says.
* Consider what the Judge says and consider what you believe, then respond.
* Develop an internal voice that counters the criticisms of the Judge.
* Talk back to the Judge.
* Identify who the Judge sounds like. Is it the adult you may have feared or the teacher who admonished you?

Here are two sample conversations. The first is between the Judge and your old voice: A conversation that's similar to those you've probably been having a lot of lately. The second conversation is an example of the strength and authority you can master when you speak with the voice of choice.

Conversation 1

Judge: Get over it. You are not healing fast enough!

Self: You're right. I am stuck. It is safe here, and it's hard to shift away from what I know.

Judge: That's right. So just put on a better face, and if you feel bad, don't let anyone know. They can't help, and they are tired of your grief.

Self: (Defeated, sullen, quiet, scared, silent. Apathy has set in.) You're right.

Conversation 2

Judge: Get over it. You are not healing fast enough!

Self: I'm moving in my own time. I am learning new aspects of myself. Who are you anyway?

Judge: I am the one who pushes you to keep going. Without me, you would be stuck. You need to get over this now!

Self: And *you* need to quiet down. I am a survivor! I will face my grief, my trauma, and my losses in my own time! I know I have a lot of fear. You are not helping me. I need to learn that my fear will not hurt me, and could teach me something. If I face my fear rather than avoid it, it will not get bigger; it will diminish. I don't know all the steps to this dance. I must learn to crawl before I can stand upright. When you push me, I feel angrier than I already am. The next time I hear your voice, I will shut you down. You are not allowed into my domain. The next time you try to interrupt my dance, you can just dance on by.

Which conversation would you rather have?

Heal in Your Own Time: There Is No Clock

As time goes on and you grow, the tenor of your grief changes. No one has the right to say you need to change how you mourn, or it should take a particular amount of time to get through the dance. Don't let anyone "should" on you. They're not in your skin, they don't have your history, and they don't know what you have experienced.

If friends or family tell you to *get better, get on with your life, stop being bothered by this,* or *hurry up,* you can respond with:

> "I know that you are concerned. I will do this in my own time. Here are some ways you can help me: Ask me if I want to talk about what is going on, and I'll answer honestly. Sometimes doing simple self-care activities, like going to the grocery store, are difficult for me. Give me a call when you're going, and maybe I can join you."
>
> *Or*
>
> "I know you want to see me as my old self again, but that self has changed. Whoever I become through this process, I will probably be wiser, more self-assured, and different in ways that I cannot yet imagine. Some parts of me may not be recognized by either you or me. I need to go through this in my time, and not yours."

When you teach others how to help you, it satisfies many parts of this nurturing dance. You get to explore the interior of your soul, you learn more about what you need, and you understand how to receive help from others.

Grief work identifies the internal voices, and also helps find the voice that belongs to you. Your dance is a private process that only you are privy to and doesn't have to be shared with others. However, too much privacy can make the journey more solemn and difficult, because it's often hard to get out of the mire of grief. If you prefer to heal alone and keep your dance of grief to yourself, do so with care and keen observation. If you don't know someone in your immediate circles who can give you the needed support, seek out a group or therapist to help sort out the confusing dynamics.

It takes a strong sense of self to communicate your needs and reveal your vulnerability to others. The ability to articulate what you know about who you are right now can be difficult, yet finding your voice is one of many gifts this process brings to you. You're learning to create boundaries. Your assessments of how others can support and assist you will become more distinct and clear with time. At first, you may not know exactly what you need, and that's okay, because you do know what *doesn't* help. That's a great start!

The Four Seasons of Grief

As a survivor of trauma, the loss of a beloved, a debilitating illness, or any circumstances or losses that you consider to be a Big G, be aware that certain days or months of the year can provoke depression, anxiety, or some resonance of emotional reactivity. Take note of time periods such as the holiday season or other important dates (birthdays, anniversaries, and so on) that have been historically important to you and are connected to your loss. You'll need to plan for these challenging times. This is an essential process, especially during the first year following your personal trauma or loss.

Bring awareness to these dates and make a plan that keeps you from being caught unawares, and ultimately, blindsided by a new wave of grief. If you don't plan ahead, time can surprise you. The element of surprise can reignite the drama of the trauma. When you note these dates on a calendar, you are forewarned, and can prepare accordingly. You have a greater chance of feeling more empowered in relation to your grief. As time goes on, dates can also signify where you are now and how life has changed for you. These dates may become a time of remembrance, of honoring the person you lost, or celebrating an integration of loss or having worked through a life transition. The calendar marker exercise described below enables you to prepare for what might emerge during that time.

Calendar Markers

Self-Discovery Exercise

- Sit down with a calendar and mark your zones of vulnerability and days of success (holiday seasons, dates for an annual vacation) as well as specific days that hold meaning (birthdays, death days, emotional release days, and anniversaries).
- Ask your children, friends, or other family members if they have any dates to add to your calendar. This will allow ample time to plan for the sensitive upcoming date. Enter the dates into whatever application you use for a calendar—phone, datebook, computer or printed calendar—and create notifications for those dates at least one week before the marked date.
- Planning for these charged times and noting the times when you have shifted will give you a sense of empowerment. Remember,

planning ahead to combat the cognitive and emotional danger zones creates a greater chance of achieving a balanced state of being. The danger zones can manifest months before a charged time. If your emotional norm is different as a date approaches, for example, you are aware of anger that emerges in situations that are usually benign for you, or your sleep is more disturbed, or your time spent thinking about the trauma or loss has increased, then you may have entered an emotional danger zone. The goal is to lessen the intensity through deliberate and mindful planning. These are reminders that *you* are the one in charge.

* Acknowledge what you believe you might experience on each date, and write the feeling down. Are you sad, angry, helpless, depressed, or anxious? Create a grid that outlines what you can do during that time to soothe your soul.

Date	What You Are Acknowledging	Emotions	Soothing Coping Mechanism—Actions Taken, Plans Made
June 22	When my dad died	Anger Fear	Take a walk in the park, see a movie and talk to my family.
Feb. 10	My rapist was released from prison	Terror Helplessness	Go to walk-in support group at the church, stay with friends for a few days.

When the world feels out of control, it's important to create space where you're in charge of your life. During the dance of grief, when you lose sight of the potential crisis moments, it's a set-up for emotional upheaval. When these moments arise and you haven't planned for them, the element of surprise and your reaction to the surprise might interfere with your progress. When you choose to be more awake and aware, the result is you get to be accountable for self-care. Welcome to self-discovery and awareness.

"This is the third anniversary of my brother's death and for the past two years I have noticed I get sick right around that time. Is this something that just happens to be coincidental or is this something that subconsciously my body does?"

~ Cara [20]

By creating a plan, like Cara, you gain a sense of self-empowerment, and a formula that supports you. Throughout the year, you'll feel content at certain times, and experience agitation at other times. Mark the times that have been filled with the good stuff as well. You're going for balance. For many people, December is often a month when memories become painfully alive. For others, it's only another holiday season. When you plan for the trigger days in the months ahead, you create an intention around the event and define how you'll respond to it rather than having it take you by surprise. However you choose to cope—to be alone, go to the movies with friends and family, take a walk, read a book—the day is in your hands.

In addition to significant days in the calendar, weather can impact your mood. Hot, cold, sunny, or rainy days can influence your emotions. More significant than the weather itself is the season that coincides with your loss. The story of what happened at this time, whether it was one year ago or ten years ago, can replay in the mind, body, and soul. The body always remembers, even when the mind wants to make the memory disappear.

Do not underestimate the importance of the seasons.

Having a plan in place for all the tough and complicated firsts following a loss (first birthday, first Thanksgiving, and so on) is important. How you cope may be something you do for many years; it's not time-limited. You might think you're finally "over" your grief, and yet at some time during the year—usually the same time every year—you become uneasy, anxious, or sad for seemingly no reason. Triggers can come out of nowhere and leave you feeling as if your recovery has stalled or there is a setback. This is OK. It doesn't mean you haven't been successful in your healing journey. It just means grief is revisiting. And that's perfectly normal.

The body remembers things the mind may forget. When you're prepared for the dates, your body is less likely to remind you of the significant milestone with an illness or injury. With less preparation, clients will often find they get sick around the anniversary or important date. The illness occurs in direct response to what they haven't recognized. Sometimes, if the date isn't pre-acknowledged, the illness can show up as a delayed response to what was ignored.

"I will readily admit that my own rape was the single-most defining challenge in my adult life . . . So each year, on a certain weekend in April, I make sure to walk around a park on my own, wherever in the world I happen to be.

I walk to commemorate another walk I took one afternoon in Colin Glen Forest Park in West Belfast, when I would be faced with something that would change my life irrevocably. But I also walk to realize how far I've come since."

~ Winnie M. Li, Huffington Post Contributor[21]

Respect yourself by noting when you may need extra support. Stop and listen to the Self. Be in discovery for what you need. This is one of the healthiest responses you have in your healing arsenal. In the beginning, healing takes place with baby steps. Little by little, the determination to shift from what *was* to what *is* will become more insistent as you begin to emerge out of the darkness.

CHAPTER 6

Who Are You and How Do You Cope?

"Life belongs to the living, and he who lives must be prepared for changes."

~ Johann Wolfgang von Goethe[22]

If you've survived abuse, become a widow or widower, experienced the death of a child, or had a long-term illness, the crisis frames and informs your very being. Transformation of the Self is a primary experience that takes place in this process. Your metamorphosis occurs as the dance progresses, and moving through these changes is cathartic. When you learn who you are, how you react to situations, and how to master practices you can use for comfort, you'll be better equipped to manage the profound, emotional pressure cooker of your grief. Out of that pressure cooker will come features of the Self that you may not have been aware of, and you'll come to understand them in impactful ways.

In the following pages, you'll conduct self-assessments that will help you to recognize and discriminate among different aspects of your personality.

The three sections of assessments are:

Introvert, Extrovert, Ambivert
Fixed, Mutable, Cardinal
Under-distanced, Over-distanced, Calibrated/Balanced

By knowing who you are, knowing what triggers you, and acquiring awareness about your coping styles and skills you can procure specific ways to help yourself (and understand how you may be getting in your own way). You'll learn to navigate through this personal process. Remember that who you were prior to the loss is different from who you are *now*. How you've reacted in the past can be similar to how you react in the present, yet as you learn about the Self, there might be new reactions to what you're facing.

Learning to assess your personality not only facilitates insight, it also encourages you to become the champion of your healing. Knowing the Self in this meaningful and intimate way enables you to learn how to go the distance—so you can soar.

Getting to Know You

Three distinct areas of assessment will help you determine how you typically respond in stressful situations. They will help you discover how to best find the help you need from yourself or others:

1. Are you an **Introvert, Extrovert, or Ambivert?**[23] The first assessment section introduces you to the specific tendencies for each of these coping styles. You may already think of yourself as either an introvert or extrovert, but review the characteristics and see which category, including ambivert, seems most like you.
2. The second assessment introduces **three personality types** of ***Fixed, Mutable,*** or ***Cardinal.*** Each category is broken down into positive

and negative characteristics. Understanding your personality in this way is vital to healthy long-term healing; so is getting the help you need. You'll read three scenarios and answer questions at the end of this section to help you accurately define and evaluate your go-to coping and personality style, especially when stressed.

3. The last assessment considers reactions to emotional stimuli, which include situations or people who provoke you. Responses are represented on a scale that measures whether you're in an ***over-distanced, under-distanced,*** **or** ***calibrated/balanced*** state of being. This might sound overly clinical, but the concept is simple—the "distancing" concept is based on determining the relative distance between you and a particular emotion. It also measures the degree to which your reactions to external or internal conflicts cause you to either overreact or remain in a state of inertia. By understanding distancing, you'll be able to label your reactions to stimuli and be introduced to tools that can help you change those responses as needed.

Introvert – Extrovert – Ambivert

Fixed – Mutable – Cardinal

Under-distanced
Over-Distanced
Aesthetic / Calibrated / Balanced

Believe it or not, your physical brain plays an enormous role in how you heal. You have natural internal chemicals called *neurotransmitters* that communicate between your body and your brain. Neurotransmitters control your mood and your thinking. They also determine how you recharge.

Some people recharge by being alone and reading or engaging in other solitary activities, while others recharge by being around friends and family.

Your moods and your thoughts are linked to behavior. How you refresh the Self or engage in a reset, which we all need to do, depends on whether you are an introvert, extrovert, or ambivert.[24] It's good to become familiar with the ways that, for *you,* are the best methods to recharge and regain your energy and balance. Knowing this helps you clearly define how you interact with the world, what you need to do to make the cycle of grief easier, and how best to communicate your needs to others.

In the simplest terms, you can think about introversion or extroversion as the way you gain energy, or the way you get back to your internal safe place. It's the soulful mechanism that brings you a sense of peace, which for the extrovert may be reaching outward, and for the introvert, turning inward. The ambivert is somewhat of a balance that moves between the scope of the extrovert and the introvert.

To honor how you cope is important, as it informs what goes into your personal toolbox to facilitate healing. The coping mechanisms you'll gravitate toward will depend on many factors, including mood, situation, access to people, the environment you're in, and your brain!

This next section will explore the tendencies that exist within the introvert, the extrovert, and the ambivert. Please understand as you read this that you might not exhibit all the characteristics of a particular type, and in some situations, you may think or behave like another type entirely. Most people will lean more toward one type than another but have characteristics of multiple types.

Introvert Tendencies

Have you heard yourself saying, "I get my energy from being alone, in a calm environment, and I prefer to recharge and soothe myself *by* myself?"

Introverts not only like to recharge on their own, they relish solitude, because they get stimulated easily and can quickly become overwhelmed.

For this reason, spending time one-on-one or in small groups is preferred. As an introvert, you think before you speak, and don't usually take big risks because you dislike conflict. You probably have a gift for concentration, and focusing on a goal can make the journey of mourning more powerful and deep because you won't let it go until you've reached resolution or a sense of peace. The grip of grief tends to be a lone journey for you. It's what you need.

Introverts require a lot of time to think and reflect. This is how you take care of yourself. You're more comfortable as an active observer rather than an interactive participant. But just because you're an introvert doesn't mean you're only friends with introverts, so your extrovert friends may not understand your desire to hibernate. This may add to your discomfort, although if you're secure in your place as an introvert, how your friends react may have little or no impact.

Jenny is an introvert who waited years to seek therapy. She's a woman of few words who prefers to be alone rather than with others. People often think she's angry or anti-social because she's quiet, an observer, and would rather listen to others' stories than speak herself. She's used to spending time alone. She likes to recharge at home, reading a book or watching sixteen episodes of her favorite series.

Jenny couldn't imagine reaching out to get help. As an introvert, her tendency was to believe that if she spent more time alone, her symptoms of rage and anger and anxiety would dissipate over time. Unfortunately, this didn't happen. Her impulse control got worse. Unable to help herself, and sitting alone in her apartment, amid the broken glass that was the remnants of her rage, Jenny made a call to her family doctor for help.

Her introversion created an obstacle to getting to a professional sooner. By the time she reached out for therapy, she was in a full PTSD crisis. She came in to see me because during the previous five years, her father and two sisters had died, and her surviving mother was consistently cruel, using verbal assaults to bully and emotionally annihilate her. The grief over having lost her two siblings and her father while also coping with PTSD from years of turmoil with her mother caused her brain to react traumatically to stimuli beyond the reasons for which she sought help.

If you are an introvert, and relate to Jenny's story, seek out one person who you feel safe with. Safety is often hard to feel or trust and to assess, especially when grieving. To help your psyche access the energy needed for emotional support, look to one of the archetypes described in Chapter 4, pages 77–88. The Warrior is often great to call upon when needing a stronger inner voice and actions, especially when reaching out to a therapist or doctor is called for.

Extrovert Tendencies

Are you more in tune with your emotions when people are around rather than when you're alone? Are you aware that now, in the clutches of grief's grasp, your normal desire to be in the company of others is magnified?

As an extrovert, you gain energy from others. When you spend too much time alone, your energy is depleted. Being in the company of others facilitates calm and supports your sense of well-being. You may wear your emotions on your sleeve, seek out social interactions in the worst of times, and react to external stimuli with quick responses rather than with forethought. Because you tend to be more of a risk taker, you may be comfortable with coping methods that might be outside of your comfort zone. And that's a good thing! What might get in your way of healing is failing to stick with something if it doesn't offer immediate relief.

Familiarity with these aspects of the Self can inform your ultimate healing. If you feel diminished and overwhelmed when you're unable to find others who will listen, this may be an opportunity to learn some techniques for calming yourself. Solely relying on others has its drawbacks because they won't always be available. Learning to self-soothe may be one of the greatest gifts you can give yourself as you move through this process.

Ambivert Tendencies

Legendary psychoanalyst Carl Jung said, "*There is no such thing as a pure introvert or extrovert. Such a person would be in the lunatic asylum.*"

Ambiverts fall somewhere in the middle of the continuum between extrovert and introvert. An ambivert can exhibit the tendencies found at either end of the spectrum and can find relief from stress when with people or alone. Those involved with an ambivert might find their seemingly contradictory behavior confusing. The ambivert might sometimes be eager to spend time with a large group of people, but might seek solitude and quiet at other times. An ambivert might want to be near a crowd, yet be alone at the same time.

The spectrum is huge, and moving on a continuum between two very different soothing methods is powerful. The power is derived from the ability to adjust coping mechanisms based on current need. It can be a situational response, yet the response to the same situation may not be the same each time. Drawing on both types of coping, extroversion and introversion, allows your psyche to call upon what is needed for you to find balance based on the immediate need.

It may seem your responses aren't in your control. You *can* regulate your emotional reactions and influence your reactivity. Grief and trauma often keep you from remembering what you need to help yourself, and what you're capable of.

Now that you know where you fall within the category of introvert, extrovert, or ambivert, make a list of go-to strategies that you can use when your emotions overwhelm you.

The following are some examples of go-to strategies.

Introvert:

Write in a notebook or journal, take a bath, meditate, watch a movie, read a book, listen to music, create a playlist, dance in your living space, cook, draw, color, cry, clean your closet, or exercise.

Extrovert:

Chat on the phone, go out with friends, invite people to share a meal, go to a movie and dinner, find a yoga, boxing, or spin class, cry while others are around, make a list of fun activities and whom you'd like to do them with, change your environment, or join a webinar online that interests you.

Ambivert:

You can pick and choose from the above lists based on your present feelings.

Fixed, Mutable, or Cardinal Personality Type?

The more you know about your personality, the more effectively you'll be able to identify your personal coping skills. Information about where you fit into the three personality types helps inform how you process information and how you live in the world.

Identifying the complexity of your personality can help you recognize what causes the dance to lose its rhythm and flow. Knowing yourself in this way helps you understand how your personality type contributes to how you react internally to any external situation. You have learned to cope based on many different variables, which include how your family of origin handled stress, what you mimicked, and the mechanisms for survival and happiness that you've created in your own life.

The characteristics within each of the fixed, mutable, or cardinal personality types are heightened or diminished based on what you witnessed and what coping methods your family of origin used. Adaptive patterns get created based on the environment in which you were raised. If your parents were both mutable, your temperament may not have been able to tolerate their indecisive and unclear natures. A reaction to their natures and the environment that was created by them might have caused you to become more fixed in your character and core personality style. Although it may not have seemed as if you made a firm, discernable "decision" to become a particular type, your psyche, or rather the unconscious part of the psyche, created a sense of internal safety for you by seeing the world as black and white.

Gathering pertinent information about these traits informs you about the way you function in the world. Picture yourself socially, at work, with family, or alone. What do you know about how you interact within these contexts? When looking at the following descriptions of *fixed, mutable,* and *cardinal*, what words best fit who you are in those realms? Look at the following chart to assess your traits that best align with both the positive and negative qualities.

Fixed

Positive: Tenacious, Stable, Contemplative

Negative: Arrogant, Critical, Skeptical

Mutable

Positive: Adaptable, Curious, Street-Wise

Negative: Fickle, Cowardly, Absent-minded,

Cardinal

Positive: Visionary, Confident, Risk Taker

Negative: Egotistical, Bombastic, Manipulative

Here are three scenarios to help you understand these three types of personality styles. See where you fit in.

Scenario 1. Let's say you are invited to join a support group. Here are three different reactions to joining this support group.

Fixed: It is be difficult for you to believe that a support group could actually help, stubbornly holding on to a belief that nothing outside of your safe sphere will alleviate your pain. Alternatively, you know you have it in you to be resourceful. If a group is not for you, talking to a trusted friend could be just as helpful.

Mutable: You go to several support groups, believing that more is better. Since you are flexible and curious, you decide to go to two support groups, assess the one that is best for you, and stick with that one.

Cardinal: You attend a support group, yet would look for ways to undermine the therapist, believing that you know the best way to run the group. As motivated as you are, the grief process is one that you want to take head on. Instead of a support group, you might get more out of a classroom situation, where discussions about loss or trauma create more interest for you, thus allowing you to show up with what you know and get support at the same time.

Of the 3 choices, which reactions best fit your style? This information is helpful in finding the right type of support for you.

Scenario 2. Three people are traveling along a road. One is cardinal, one is fixed, and one is mutable. They come upon a boulder that blocks the road, and this is how they respond:

Fixed will spend five years drilling a hole through the center of the rock. They will stay their course.

Mutable will simply go around the outside of the boulder and carry on, or change direction altogether and find another road.

Cardinal is likely to see this as an interesting challenge, and will scale the boulder with climbing equipment, going straight over the top.

When thinking about your loss or trauma, how do you assess the way you would tackle the metaphorical boulder? How would you react, and which reaction described best reflects your personality style?

Scenario 3: You are feeling angry at a person who has made comments about the time it is taking you to heal, stating that your progress is too slow and you need to be over it.

Being more of a *Fixed* personality style, you will create a plan to either disengage with this person or to challenge the person with specific data that proves their lack of understanding. You tend to dislike people who are not trustworthy and genuine. You will have a difficult time if someone has shown up unpredictably angry, which leads you into a more stubborn, unrelenting, reaction toward them.

You are an energy changer as a *Mutable* personality style. What this means is that your anger will shift. One moment you want to have a face-to-face conversation with this person, and in the next moment or day, you have changed and shifted, to the point you no longer need to talk. The ups and downs of emotions cause you some distress, yet you prefer to go with the flow.

As a *Cardinal* personality, you will talk with others about initiating a conversation, and share the anger that you feel. Chances are you might not follow through, ultimately avoiding any engagement about the anger with the person who angered you. Though you will continue to complain about the anguish and anger.

How do you see yourself responding in each scenario? This is not an exact science, however, identifying what drives your responses assists in generating an internal knowledge of which tools will work for you and which ones won't have as much impact on healing.

The Fixed Personality Type

When you're more of a fixed personality type, you create a steady life that is often predictable, based on internal self-reliance and confidence. Decisions are well thought out. You take the time to think about how best to proceed, and you can sit with your pain until a pragmatic resolution appears. If you're facing an impending loss, such as a life-altering situation—for example, a health issue or a divorce—you manage the emotions the same way you manage your life. Sometimes that modus operandi works, and sometimes it doesn't.

The stubborn quality that enables you to stay your course regardless of the obstacles can also hinder you. Skeptical in nature, the ability to trust others as confidants does not resonate with you. Coping styles that have worked in the past, like keeping people at a distance, may continue to be effective, yet in the currents of your grief an opportunity exists for new methods to be learned and put into practice.

The fixed personality style might choose excessive use of food, sex, alcohol, or drugs to break out of their rigidity. These soothing, yet unhealthy choices seem to break you out of the rhythms of being fixed. The pattern of rebelling against your usual constraints by over-indulging is as comforting as much as it is internally combustible. Engaging in excessive alternatives relieves the sense of being ensnared; at the same time, you are in a safe and knowing cocoon.

If you find yourself rebelling against your status quo, it might be time to imagine yourself out of your fixed box. In your journal, write down what constitutes your "fixed box." What alternatives do you have to what you identified in the box? Can you attempt to engage in one action that you identified as an alternative action?

For example, if you've used drugs or alcohol in the past to calm the Self and want to alter this behavior choice, try engaging in physical exercise, like walking or running. Think about integrating creativity into your world to replace inaction or addictive choices. You might try to work with your hands. Clay, wood, and plaster are materials that resonate with a fixed personality style and engaging with them can lead to a sense of calm. The idea of combining grief with self-discovery as a partnership is a potential challenge to your comfort zone. Challenge behavior you've used repeatedly, especially when that behavior has yielded the same response and kept you emotionally in the loss and trauma.

Honor the characteristics of the fixed personality type by committing to focusing on something new and challenging. Remember, no one can take your typical fixed reactions away from you. They are yours; they are generally how you operate in the world. If you know this, then everything you do results from your choice. In any shift you make, you remain in control.

When you confront the stasis of the old choices, and do so with the power of focus that is part of you, you can maintain your style as you develop ways to use it to break into your grief. You will still be you when you cultivate and increase your choices. As you expand, coping becomes easier and more fluid.

The Mutable Personality Type

For a mutable personality type, coping with loss and trauma may seem to be an easier process because you're communicative, adaptable, and talkative. You're willing to share your innermost secrets without discretion, so joining a grief support group or discussing deep feelings with friends isn't alien to you. When a mutable personality type dances with grief, it may appear easy—to others.

Don't fool yourself just because it's easy for you to self-disclose. The disclosures may not reveal the gravity of your story. You may have fooled those around you, and perhaps even yourself, and the irony is that sharing yourself in this way may not actually reach the true depths of the emotional vortex that pulls you down into its darkness. This character type includes an avoidant aspect that knows how to keep intensity at bay through constant mutations. You may not ever allow the Self to go deep, or run deep.

It takes courage to learn how to handle mourning. By wanting to please people, you want others to think that you're following the necessary protocols to heal, even when you aren't. Acknowledging that life is no longer as it was before your loss leaves you bereft and often scared. It's likely that anxiety is an emotion you know well.

The dance requires you to access the parts of yourself that are adaptable, teasing out and unearthing the parts of you that dwell in the loss, while learning to tolerate and engage in the discomfort of it all. Internal arguments arise because of your scattered nature, making it difficult for you to stay focused on the dance. A support group is not foreign to you, yet committing to it *is*.

Snakelike, you can slither in and out of the dance, sometimes moving slowly, then quickly, making it difficult to shed the skin of grief. Being mutable, you vacillate between sharing what you feel, doing your healing dance, feeling good, and then shutting down and feeling stuck. Generating a new skin requires that you engage differently. You need to use all the best parts of you, and flow between extremes, which enables you to borrow a little from the fixed and a little from the cardinal traits as a way to create a new skin. Mutable behaviors will be your go-to, yet you can be spontaneous and adaptable. Use these aspects of psyche to work through the dance.

The Cardinal Personality Type

As a cardinal personality type, you are often seen as the support system for everyone else. You like being needed, and you like having all the answers. The word cardinal actually means "a hinge" on which something turns. If others rely on you when they are in crisis (or if you make people believe they can rely on you), it may be difficult to cope with your own mourning. The mask of the cardinal personality type rarely comes down, and if you experience emotions such as fear, shame, or anxiety, they may show up as arrogant or conceited behaviors. These characteristics can arise when you blame someone else as a way to divert attention away from yourself, or when you feel terrible (emotionally or physically), and you take great pains to look "too" good.

The good news is you're self-motivating, and that's powerful. Often unstoppable once committed to a project, rather than being stubborn, your self-motivation expresses an internal knowing that guides your decision-making. Confrontation will often lead to disputes, so anyone who wants to help is pushed aside, potentially feeling impotent in their desire to help. This puts you in a bind when strategizing to comfort yourself. Although you'll be involved in activities that include others, such as a support group, you may challenge the leader's ability.

Be aware that you can be manipulative and calculating. These are prominent aspects of the cardinal personality, and this can get in the way of how you engage and heal. The psyche's normal responses can become magnified when grieving, and even if they've been well-moderated in the past, they can be harder to tame now. Be mindful of how the worst in you is expressed. It alienates those who can and want to help.

Fixed, Mutable, or Cardinal?

Self-Discovery Exercise

In your journal, answer the following questions with the category that most resonated with you. Count the responses. If you have more answers in one category, then take a further look at that category. You might find your personality has a little bit of all three traits, or you might find there is one trait that is more prominent than the others. Again, the answers to these questions can help you determine what kind of healing interactions will be helpful to you and which alternatives may not work as well.

- How I handle arguments is:
- When I'm in my loss or trauma, I use the following behaviors:
- In my time alone, I experience myself as:
- How do others see me?
- Does my personal perspective match the perspective of others? How are they different or similar?
- How do I regulate emotion?
- Do I reach out to people for comfort or comfort myself or both?

When determining if you're more of a fixed, mutable, or cardinal personality, remember that the information you've gathered doesn't mean you fit only into that personality style. You might find you have a little of each of these personalities. This conversation is to facilitate getting the right kind of help based on how you currently live and cope in the world. Your relationship to these aspects can change as you change. It would be helpful for you to revisit the characteristics outlined above, to see what modifications have occurred over time.

> *"The rhythm of the waves as they moved in and out below us felt analogous to the waves of grief I had experienced since Kristen's death. At times, the waves of grief pounded with a force that threatened to pull me under forever. At other times, I was free.*
>
> *Sitting on that rock, I was aware of these internal waves, but they didn't engulf me. I was as distanced from the grief as I was from the waves surging below. It was symbolic of all we had been through in the year prior. Kristen was gone forever and nothing would bring her back."*
>
> ~ Carol Kearns, *Sugar Cookies and a Nightmare*[25]

Distance in the Dance of Grief: Under-distanced, Over-distanced, Calibrated/Balanced

The concept of distancing enables you to define where you are on the spectrum of emotional response and the degree of emotional distance you experience while in the throes of active mourning.

One goal in this section is to understand what emotional balance is and how you can achieve a sense of balance—or *calibration*—while living with grief and trauma. The term "calibration" is like balance and is used to describe an emotional state that does not have broad swings—it rests somewhere in the middle of two extremes. When your psyche is *calibrated,* it is neither *over-distanced* nor *under-distanced*; your conscious emotions are balanced and measured, rather than chaotic and extreme.

Over-Distanced, Under-Distanced, and Calibrated/ Balanced

In 1981, sociologist Dr. Thomas J. Scheff identified three basic states of emotional reactivity: *over-distanced*, *under-distanced*, and *aesthetic distance*,[26] (also referred to by me as a *calibrated and balanced* state)

* In an over-distanced state, feel removed from emotions, spiritless, apathetic, impassive, numb, or unfeeling. It is difficult to make decisions. You may feel paranoid, distrusting, or bored by external stimuli. Sleep may elude you; it also can be a way to escape the pain. Too much sleep might affect your ability to function. Judgment, clarity, and decisiveness seem to elude you in this state. To cope with the inertia, you may choose drugs, alcohol, or cigarettes to overcome the internal numbness.
* In an under-distanced state, your emotions verge on hysteria. You might display behavior that is over-reactive and potentially abusive. You may interact with angry outbursts, uncontrolled behavior, or become abruptly loud and vocal. You might use sleep as a means of escape, although it may be hard to quiet your brain long enough to get the rest you need. Untamed hostility, lack of clarity, and obsessive narratives may cause you to abuse alcohol or drugs, or act out in sexual ways that are different from your norm.
* When you reach aesthetic distance, which can also be referred to as a balanced or a calibrated state, you have reached a place where your reactions are optimal for you. You can ask for what you need and calm the Self because you've found a way to flow with the intensity of emotions. In this balanced state, you are

> highly motivated to maintain it because it feels good. And, when you are alert to the messages within your mind and body, you tap into a chance to realistically assess and respond to external stimuli with appropriate emotional reactions. This is the place on the continuum that offers you a sense of empowerment, resiliency, and knowing. Ultimately, this calibrated position allows for consistent reactions, while introducing you to the needed core that empowers healing. This is your strongest position. In it, you have less need to seek out drugs or alcohol to calm the Self.

The term "distance" refers to how you respond to your emotions, and these responses are not static. Let's use anger to demonstrate this concept. For example, one day your anger is triggered and you become enraged; your body is shaking, your voice goes up an octave, and you're extremely agitated. This is an under-distanced—completely sucked in and emotionally dysregulated (a dysregulated state is one where emotions fluctuate and are not in balance or controlled). On another day, when once again your anger is triggered, instead of being under-distanced, you react in an over-distanced way by being quiet, withdrawn, numb, and even depressed. You may be physically inhibiting the anger by grinding your teeth or through some other unconscious gesture.

How you dance with these emotions depends on your environment, your prior coping skills, and the internal depths you're willing to explore. The dance of grief will constantly move you in and out of under-distanced and over-distanced states, just like the tide.

Locating where you lie on the spectrum of over-distanced to under-distanced gives you a chance to manage emotional upheaval with greater ease. Ultimately, by understanding the many levels of responses, over time you—and others—can detect and observe these behaviors. Ask your friends and family to share what they observe in your behavior patterns. This is often a self-reflective moment, inviting personal insight and discovery. Think about your emotional responses: Are they over-distanced, under-distanced, or in a balanced/calibrated/aesthetic distance?

In the beginning, when you first engage with grief, you'll probably be less in touch with your emotional, physical, and sensory awareness. Often feeling stuck, the emotions, whatever they are, may seem impossible to shift from an extreme point on the continuum to a less extreme, more balanced position. As the emotional experience becomes familiar and you pay closer attention, you'll find that movement occurs more fluidly, because you're accurately assessing where the emotions live on the continuum. Aesthetic distance might be achieved as you break the cycle of staying at either extreme. The goal is to teach your psyche and your brain the experience of being calibrated, attuned, and regulated.

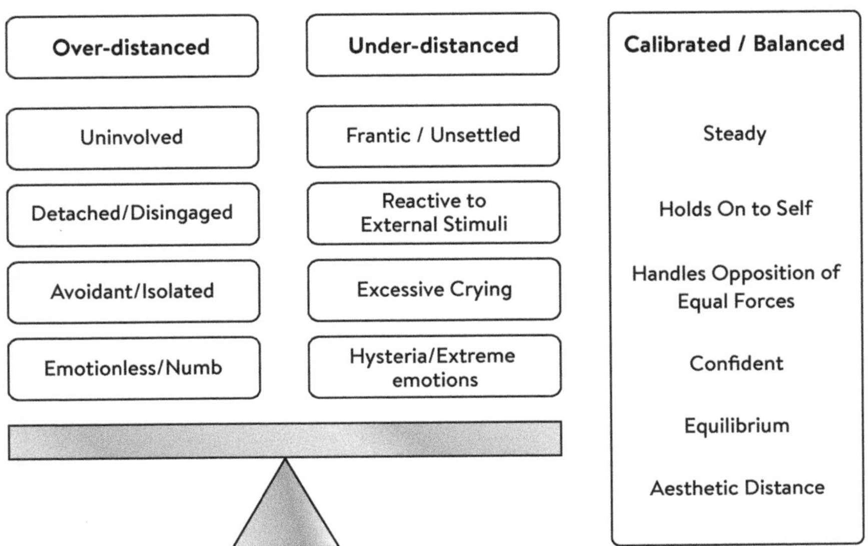

To encourage a shift, choose behavioral options that counter your current state. When your emotions are under-distanced, it usually means that you're focused on what if scenarios, which direct your attention to the future. One way to interrupt the under-distanced state is to shift your focus to the present moment.

Perspective Shifting: Engage in the Present Moment

Self-Discovery Exercise

The goal of the perspective shifting exercise is to refocus, and these simple methods for re-directing your attention can often yield the greatest results. Remember that you can intervene when emotions are in the under-distanced position.

* Summon the present by looking around and really seeing your environment.
* Focus on specific objects that are in the room, in your wallet, or even on another person.
* Count to 100 or sing a simple song, like "Row, Row, Row Your Boat."

Shift the intensity of the under-distanced experience by replacing it with calmer options, which is like acting as your own cowboy, lassoing your out-of-control emotions, addressing them, and noticing them, but giving them a different platform in which to exist. It is as if they are moved outside of you to a place where they don't have power over you, allowing a different message to be sent to your brain. When you do this, those neural connections in your brain have a better chance of finding balance.

For example, when you walk, your brain is communicating to your legs and your arms and telling them to move. Your neurotransmitters call on your body to follow through on this task. Move one leg in front of the other, and put a foot down on the ground while you pick up the other foot. For most people, once you've learned to walk, little conscious thought goes into the process of walking. When the ground is covered with ice or is slick with rain, the dormant mind engages, sending messages to be safe, take slower steps, and be more thoughtful about how you navigate the obstacle. Your mind and body seek balance in a situation that feels less safe. When you are challenged by the environment and respond with disconnected or jagged movement, it may influence your coordination as well as affect your emotional balance. When you regain a sense of balance, the conscious effort to walk is no longer an issue. It reverts to its typical automatic state.

When you have learned the skill of how to assess when the under-distanced or over-distanced states affect you, it is in your power to shift your interactions with them. The ultimate goal is to achieve the ability to be "both an observer and a participant"[27] in how you interact with the dance. This perspective enables you to challenge your relationship to mourning, your relationship with others, and your relationship with the Self. As grief comes and goes, surfacing and disappearing and surfacing again, the potent triggers will also modify accordingly.

Let's use the ocean tide as a metaphor for how you gauge and assess emotions. At times, the ocean's water is calm, while at other times, it roars with waves and a strong undertow. No matter what the sea's level of activity, the tide, which is a constant, always moves in and out, in and out. Calibrating your emotions is like finding the point where the water looks like it is neither going out nor coming in. You can also imagine being on a see-saw where you are poised in a balanced place with no severe ups or downs.

Over-Distanced

When the tide moves out to the depths of the sea, the beach is left bare. The human emotional equivalent of this is feeling barren, numb, and disconnected. When over-distanced, you're hidden behind a false, fixed demeanor that veils your internal battle. Although this stiff upper lip may look like strength, it's not. It is *over-distanced.*

> *"Sometimes I think I am so good at this acting stuff, that I convince even myself nothing's wrong . . . I can literally act myself into thinking there is nothing wrong with me."*
>
> ~ Tamiko[28]

If you're over-distanced you may feel disinterested, lethargic, apathetic, listless, and as if you're going through your day in a fog. Are you unaware of sensory elements in your life? You might notice a coldness that infiltrates your body. Your mind is quietly detached. The tears you smight have had are not accessible, and if they were, you wouldn't want them.

In your numbness, you tend to avoid contact with others. You may have created a story that justifies your isolation. If this resonates with you, and you build a story to explain the choice of isolation, what is that story? What contributes to the need to avoid others?

In this over-distanced state, when people want to interact with you, you don't hear them, connect with them, or care to know what they're saying. When you're over-distanced, you believe this place of dullness and hopelessness will never change. It seems that you've abandoned some part of the Self and constructed a Self that is alone, isolated, and resides in a cold cave where you sit within the poignant emotional darkness within your soul. You perceive no light at the end of the tunnel. Internal agony will not relent. You feel stuck and permanently tethered.

Not surprisingly, within the over-distanced position, your mental state is often hidden from others. You go about your day saying, "I'm fine," or "Everything's okay." You are not okay. You may project a sense of balance to yourself and to others. It's one of your masks. Some people might be fine with you being over-distanced, because it takes them off the hook. They don't have to take care for you or face their own pain as they watch you cycle through your grief.

In the following exercise, the goal is for your brain to learn how to change course and get out of the over-distanced state. Understandably, you landed in this place because you don't feel safe. It's a necessary go-to. Your protected internal harbor relies on keeping emotions tied up and hidden. What makes change more difficult is the fact that so much of this is not conscious. Becoming aware of what your psyche is doing in the over-distanced state is part of this exercise. Staying in the over-distanced position may work for a short time, but in the long haul of healing, it can lead to physical and psychic pain that diminishes many levels of functioning. So, give this a try.

HINT: When engaged in any exercises, take them one step at a time. If you get overwhelmed, stop, and start again when you're ready. Respect what your body and mind are saying to you.

The Emotional Map

SELF-DISCOVERY EXERCISE

You will create a map of your emotions. Look at the diagram on the following page as an example. The goal of this exercise is to expose you to hidden emotions, become reacquainted with them, and offer the key to unlock that which you no longer need to keep hidden inside.

Get a piece of paper or do this in your journal:

Put a circle in the middle of the page. Each time you're asked to add information, draw another circle, put the asked-for information into that circle, and draw a line connecting that circle to the first circle. Continue to do this throughout the exercise.

Identify an emotion that is hidden. Write it down in the main circle.

* How old is the emotion?
* When do you remember first feeling or experiencing it?
* What circumstances caused the feelings?
* What do you remember about hiding it from others?
* Why did you start to hide it?
* What other emotions surface when you think about sharing what you feel?

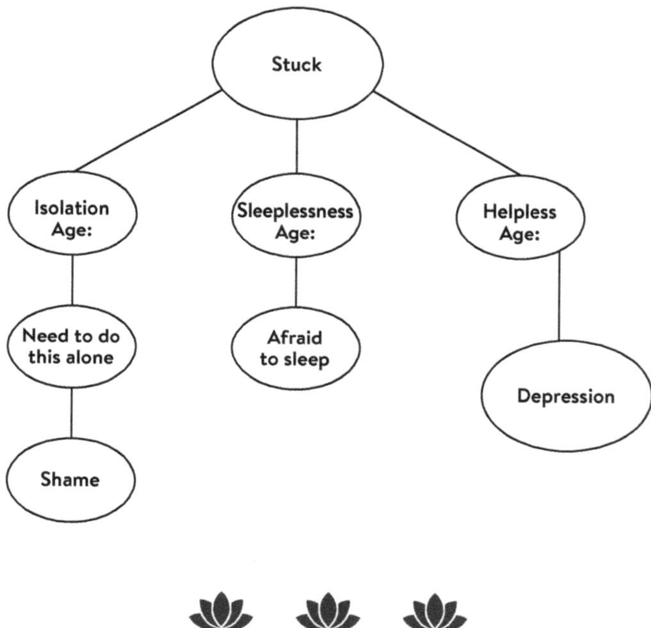

PEOPLE, PLACES, AND FEELINGS

Name a place/person/feeling that allows you to experience a sense of safety.

* Go back to the first circle. Ask yourself: If I could let one person know this about me, who would it be and why would I want to

share it with them? If you don't have anyone who feels safe to you, then *you* be the person to trust.

* Picture doing this in your mind. While that picture is formulating, allow yourself to tap into a sense of calm and safety. (If you have no specific person in mind, then use yourself. That is a great place to start.)
* What elements add to that sense of safety? For example, you believe that person has integrity and would be the holder of your secrets. Think about what the best outcome could be and what the worst outcome could be.
* Define what a feeling of safety is for you. Cultivate that sense within yourself by remembering a moment in time when you knew you were safe. It can be very small: Listening to a piece of music, a conversation with a friend or even a stranger; a meal you cooked for yourself; a time when you laughed at something with abandon. If none of these suggestions work for you, go to your breath. Talk to your breath—hold it, let it go, pant, and stop. Allow your breath to be a safe place within you.
* What would be different if you allowed one person in?

Revisit what you wrote in the first circle. If you were to have a conversation with the emotion in the circle, what would you want to say to it? What is it saying to you? Imagine how you would feel if you were willing to allow the emotion to be witnessed rather than hiding it. How would that shift you from the over-distanced position to the more calibrated position?

This is an exercise that can be done every day. The goal is to be in the discovery of the Self and how different emotions reside within you. You are desensitizing the Self, getting in touch with elements of confidence and reassurance while challenging the impulse to keep everything the same.

Under-Distanced

When the tide moves in, covering the sand and changing the complexion of the beach, the flooding overwhelms the shoreline much in the same way your emotions overwhelm the Self. While under-distanced, your triggered emotions are exposed, creating a feeling of being naked, unprotected and engulfed.

Under-distanced emotional states can, at times, be perceived as a type of hysteria. Your senses are so alive that you feel ready to implode as they course through you. Your tears come from a deep well of pain. Without the necessary self-soothing, you almost *become* the hysteria. When you're under-distanced, you express your emotions with a level of drama that might elicit negative reactions from others or prompt them to stay away. In an under-distanced state, constant tears, tantrums, and an inability to console the Self impact core functioning.

Anger, regret, rage, and anxiety pierce you with an unrelenting potency, causing an outward over-reactivity. In this state, it feels as if you're drowning in the enormity of the emotional tide. At the same time, it can seem as if you're disappearing and losing the sense of who you are, which is certainly scary and consuming. If this sounds familiar to you, think about the following:

* *Do you sense that your thoughts and emotions are racing? Do you experience them with acute magnification, as if you are being attacked by them?* This is *personal flooding*. It is a cascade of emotions that are out of control and magnified. Once you are besieged by emotions, it can feel as if you're primed to stay in this state with no hope of finding relief.
* *Are you frantically moving from one person to another seeking advice and help?* Have you created a story of doom and gloom, believing that no one will understand? Are you disappointed in the people around you, perhaps responding with an outpouring of rage, anxiety, or fear?
* *Does your body feel agitated?* Your flooding emotions can seem to be externalized through body language. I notice the following clues

when I am observing a client in an under-distanced state: Poor eye contact (or wild eyes), hunched shoulders, pacing, and jitters.

* *Are you unaware of what you're saying?* Do you feel you have to repeat thoughts or phrases in order to be understood? This is due to your lack of concentration. You may not even remember what you just said. Also, if you have not shared your pain with anyone, when someone is ready to listen, you might discover you unleash a frantic rant.

If you have assessed that you respond in an under-distanced way, try the following exercises to break the cycle.

Name and Tame Your Thoughts

SELF-DISCOVERY EXERCISE

In this exercise, you're asking your brain to be plastic and pliable. Through repetition, you can change the way your brain holds onto the trauma of loss. The neural connections actually change when you repeat and stick with new behavioral responses. This exercise is an opportunity for you to delve deeper. Take out your journal to record and date your answers. If you go back to the exercises, you can compare and have a timeline for any changes you've experienced.

1. Identify what you are thinking in the under-distanced state.
2. Slow the thoughts down by taking one thought at a time. Name and number each thought.
3. Don't move from a thought until you feel the thought has slowed down. You might notice your breathing slows as your reactions to the thought shifts. Notice any other shifts in your body, mind, or breath. Write down any differences you notice.

4. Practice slowing down each thought before you move to the next part of the exercise. Notice what emotion is associated with each thought; this process can contribute to an internal quieting down. Identify how you would rather feel when having this thought.
5. Go back to the thoughts you identified. Is there an image connected to each one? What is the image? If an image does not automatically come to you, that's fine. Do the identified thoughts arouse any of your five senses? Take note of those senses. If an image has come up for you, is it in color or black and white? Is it an image from the past, or present, or something you have thought about for the future?
6. What is your reaction to the combined thought and image? What would you like your reaction to be? Is it different from what you thought your reaction would be? What modulated reactions could be more helpful for you?
7. Between each combined thought and image, take in a slow, deep, deep breath. What are you learning about yourself when in an over-distanced state? As you move through this exercise, take the needed time-outs so your brain has a chance to process the information. Ask yourself if it's good to continue or if you need a break. Listen to the response. Breathe.
8. Breathe. Breathe. Breathe. Your breath can ground you and is always available.

Emotions obstruct your access to the grounded or calibrated state when you're under-distanced. Still, wherever you are is where you need to be. You might be physically and psychically uncomfortable in this state. Join it and honor it. Learn to catch your breath and regulate it. This helps to positively influence the physical toll of emotional under-distance. If you're crying hysterically, regulate your emotions by using the breathing exercise below. When you talk to yourself, bring in one of the archetypal voices to help you break the cycle. I have a client who is calmed when he taps into the Warrior. When he's in an under-distanced state, he accesses the voice of the Warrior. This helps him tap into a more balanced state.

When addressing the Self in the under-distanced state, ask yourself how the hysteria helps you. Does it relieve your pain or make the feeling of loss dissipate? Keep in mind that the under-distanced state is a reaction to your loss or trauma, and it may not ultimately help you feel better. It's a feeder that keeps the emotional frenzy alive, which you need to honor, yet it contributes to the distance between you and balance.

Biofeedback and Breath

Self-Discovery Exercise

This biofeedback exercise has terrific results. It's a technique that helps you take something that seems involuntary, like your hysteria, and gain control of it by interrupting its hold on you. It also requires the use of your breath.

1. Identify the thought that contributes to your under-distanced state.
   Identified thought: Anxiety.
2. Take note of what is experienced in this state of mind. Where is it in your body, thoughts, and beliefs? Write the responses in your journal or speak them out loud.
   Spoken: I am anxious. My heart is racing. My palms are sweaty. This is never going to stop.
3. Take in a breath, and as you take in the breath, say, "I am."

4. As you breathe out, say to yourself, "Calm." As you let out the breath, you are releasing one thought, one piece of tension, or one piece of emotion.
5. Do this breathwork ten times.
6. What, if anything, has shifted? To assess what you are experiencing after the breath, stop for a moment, take an inventory to assess if your brain has quieted, if your body feels less tense, and if you notice a change in your sense of being. Is your heart still racing? Are your palms still sweaty? Did the pervasive thought *This is never going to stop* quiet down?
7. If you notice any shifting, that's great. If not, remember this is a process and your psyche is doing whatever it needs to do to keep you in perceived safety.

Although this may seem like a simple exercise, when done repeatedly and over time, it works with the chemistry of your brain to override the impulse to stay immersed and enmeshed with the under-distanced emotions. It calms anxiety, regulates your breathing, and can even change your heart rate. This is a process that invites you to check in with all the parts of you to take note if they have settled down.

Calibrated/Balanced

To envision balance, once again, let's think about the movement of the tide. Imagine that the tide is neither going out nor coming in. Instead, it's in perfect balance. This slack tide represents an appropriate and equal distance between under-distanced and over-distanced responses. In this position, you are neither veiled nor dramatic in your responses. This invites depth to your understanding and awareness. Experiencing the full range of emotions and not getting caught up in them or trying to control them allows you to move fluidly in and out of the dance.

Have you ever seen a play or a movie that moved you to tears or laughter? In that moment, you were transported into an experience and connection that you expressed. Whether you cried or laughed, you had an emotional release, and then *poof*, you left the theater and went about your day. That is what balanced emotional distance looks like. Once you get a sense of what the balance looks like for you, your brain will begin to register the change and realign itself.

In this calibrated state, emotional balance includes moments of agitation and moments of calm. You know intrinsically that you can get through your day little by little, taking small steps toward healing and stability.

The emotions are there, yet you have enough distance to have a harmonious relationship with them. It's important to know the continuum on which your emotions exist. To move through them is not only beneficial, it's critical to learning the movement of your grief. When over-distanced, your emotions aren't available to you, and when in an under-distanced state, your emotions overtake you. In the balanced and calibrated state, you can meet your emotions with greater clarity, allowing the dance to be full and the grip of grief to be less powerful. This is a gift.

Whether you're angry, anxious, or experiencing an array of emotions, when in a state of balance, you're able to notice them, sit with them, respond to them, and move with them. The presence of emotions doesn't stop you from living; they're merely part of who you are.

"After placing my daughter up for adoption in August 1969, I chose to hide under a shell of protection for the next twenty-five years and not discuss her. Burying that part of my life deep inside, I allowed myself time to think about her only when I was safe at home alone where others could not see my pain. Sharing with others the hurts, struggles, and joys of my life has been healing for me."

~ Sharon Fieker, author of *I Choose This Day: Mournings and Miracles of Adoption*[29]

You'll recognize you can find balance when you can ask for help when needed, soothe yourself, and find the appropriate time and place to cope with strong emotions when they surface. Create a picture on paper or an image in your mind of how you'd like to experience yourself in a state of balance. What does it look like?

Noticing where you are on the over-distance and under-distance spectrum is the essence of understanding how to gauge emotional responses.

I have a client who has a talent for detecting when she's beginning to go into an over-distanced state. She perceives when her reaction doesn't fit the situation. She thinks about a rainbow of emotional reactions, and if she could choose a response other than over-distanced, which emotion would she select? She imagines what the outcome would be if she allowed herself to have that reaction. When she catches her over-distanced state before it settles in, she can recalibrate and reposition her Self. She also knows that her over-distanced state may be a protection device. In that case, she has a series of questions she asks:

- What do I need to protect myself from?
    - Feeling overwhelmed and scared.
- How can I make sense of feeling unsafe?
    - Acknowledge it's an old feeling and has nothing to do with who I am today
- What am I really reacting to?
    - I am unsure of myself in this moment
- Of my five senses, what senses have been activated?
    - Smell and Kinesthetic
- What can I do differently to tap into balance?
    - Focus on what I know about my bravery and resilience. Remember that my breath helps to focus on the present, and that is powerful and calibrating. Remember that my fear is an ally and when I join it, it lessens.

The responses to her questions work to get her back into a state of balance. She is calibrating herself. She is staying present. She is alive.

Balance is the goal, yet you'll have ups and downs as part of the cycle of grief. Think about under-distanced, over-distanced, and balanced/calibrated states as part of a deep understanding that can offer relief and empowerment as you integrate self-discovery with the dance of grief.

Once you have a sense of where you fit into the above descriptions, you'll be able to develop a set of skills that can be added to your toolbox for moving in and out of the dance. As you get to know these intimate aspects of the Self, an internal lightbulb can go off within your psyche. When you realize you're a cardinal personality and more of an extrovert and your emotional scale tends to be under-distanced, these pieces of knowledge enable you to mitigate the imbalances through perceptive and informed awareness.

Awareness of the Self is a tool. If you're cardinal in style, an extrovert, and under-distanced, helpful strategies might include learning to quiet the reflexive impulses through breath work and keeping busy, yet finding some time to document feelings and experiences or even identify the archetypes that resonate with you. When you know who you are, it's easier to grasp what you need in order to heal. Gaining knowledge of the Self is a gift that the losses in your life are giving to you.

Shift Happens
Neuroplasticity Allows Your Brain to Heal and Reorganize

"Grief does not change you . . . It reveals you."

~ John Green, *The Fault in Our Stars*[30]

There's nothing like grief to goad you into meeting a raw, true, and honest *you*. As you work through your grief, be prepared to engage in the process of revealing the Self to the Self. You may encounter some personal dilemmas when challenging the Self. What you've felt, seen, heard, and been aroused by has made indelible marks on you and your behavior that cannot be ignored. Additionally, they've had an impact on your brain. Understanding there is a reciprocal relationship between behavior and the brain increases the prospect of engaging in the dance with a greater sense of hope and courage.

The shifts that happened, either suddenly or over time, were made in your brain as a response to the situation that triggered your grief, and ultimately your sense of loss and response to trauma. These experiences signal your brain to be in protection mode. Flight, fight, or freeze are very real reactions that are abundant when trauma strikes and part of the common language when discussing traumatic reactions. Dr. Peter Levine, in his October 15, 2014, YouTube video, "Nature's Lessons in Healing Trauma: An Introduction to Somatic Experiencing® (SE™)"[31] discusses the ability of animals to discharge after a fight, flight, freeze response. They can, essentially, "shake it off." He states that humans don't discharge from this engagement quickly and can get stuck in the reaction. Once the brain is "hijacked," the fight, flight, or freeze response that is meant to be temporary isn't temporary at all. It remains within the secrets held by the body. This often leaves the body responding to nonexistent threats that are perceived to be present. Understand the symptoms of the fight, flight, or freeze experience so you can recognize if you're stuck in these states.

Fight

Your jaw is tight, there are excessive feelings of anger and rage; it's as though an internal tornado is going off within your body and brain. Your body is in a hyperactive state, wanting to hit, hurt, and even howl. You can vacillate between an over-distanced state and an under-distanced state.

Flight

Wanting to flee quickly, breathing jaggedly in a way that leaves you feeling breathless, feeling unsafe, believing that you're your own prison, your body is twitchy, edgy, and the whole of your psyche feels on edge. This is an under-distanced state.

Freeze

You are cold, solid, and immoveable. It seems you might break or crack. You chase your breath, as if you cannot get enough air; it feels as if you're moving through molasses, terrified and yet not able to do anything about what is being experienced. You feel stuck, unable to make a move. This is an over-distanced state.

You can break the fight, flight or freeze response because your brain has the capacity to make long-term, sustainable change through a variety of techniques. First your body needs to be calmed. Calming self-touch, like stroking your own arm while taking in a slow breath, or focusing on a pattern on the floor or closing your eyes while imagining a waterfall, are all ways to help the brain refocus the body into a state of calm. Of course, you can choose any protective means you believe fosters safety. The previous triggers that gave you the fight, flight or freeze responses can be given new context and connections that actually wipe out the old responses.

Have you heard how your brain is plastic? Not really plastic, yet what's been recently discovered is how the brain changes over our life-spans. New connections get formed and you can be the source for the new connectivity.

Your mighty brain, because of its plasticity, can divest itself of the default trigger responses. By sending different messages, a new balance is achieved. This happens when you change your cognitions (thoughts), engage in exercise, and meditation and adapting the desire to adjust to the new magic within.

Tempting as it may be to stay harnessed to the old responses and remain in the same cycle of it all, you have an opportunity to change how your body, mind, and emotions respond to stimuli that affected you in the past and continue to affect you in the present. The science of neuroplasticity offers more than just hope for change. The brain, the Self, and all those neural connections are active participants in how you live in, and get out of, the hold of emotions and memories, like those that your loss and trauma have forged.

Your soul is going through a metamorphosis. This journey is encouraging you to re-form the Self by creating new information and adapting to it. Your brain and body know you cannot go back to the reality of how you once operated.

Understanding *neuroplasticity* or *neural plasticity* can be important as you find ways to grow: Your pain may be your greatest teacher. While it sounds complicated and scientific, it simply means your brain can reorganize itself by forming new connections. It can change its wiring and its structure according to your actions, your beliefs, and your experiences. This is great news for you because it means *real* change can occur. Yet, for the re-wiring to occur, the brain needs you! It needs a willing and devoted partner in the dance. Knowing change is in your hands is powerful.

So what is *neuroplasticity* or *neural plasticity*?

Both terms refer to the same concept. Neuroplasticity is merely the umbrella term for the brain's malleability, not unlike clay. You've heard the adage you "can't teach an old dog new tricks." Well, until recently, that's how scientists believed the brain functioned. Not so long ago, they thought the pathways in the brain were fixed, and once a neural connection was made, it stayed that way. (So much so that if a brain were damaged due to stroke or injury, it was thought there was little hope of meaningful recovery). Thinking the brain is hardwired negates the chance that it's flexible enough to sustain reorganization.

The good news is the brain isn't static. The physical structure of it actually changes throughout one's life. *The brain forms new connections* that allow it to override what is already in place. As you learn the new responses, and repeat the new responses, the responses become modified, actually replacing old thoughts or behavioral patterns that may have been formed in reaction to an environmental event such as those that occur when encountering a trauma or loss.

You can discover what patterns you're holding onto by asking yourself the following questions. Take a moment to write your answers in your journal.

- Do you hear yourself saying, "I don't know who I am anymore"?
- Do you feel the Self you thought you knew is not there?
- Do your thoughts feel scattered in one moment and clear the next?
- Are you experiencing rapid-firing thoughts, emotions, and mental images throughout the day?

You encounter internal warfare and the crisis of confidence as you enter the uncharted territory of grief. Each person's loss is intense for them. Anyone facing loss or trauma feels their experience cannot be compared to or equated to other losses. This is the ultimate truth. It's horrific to lose a loved one. The grief of a person who survives a mass shooting is monumental and causes internal chaos and crisis. The struggle of grief is individual, and each moment in grief is hard, potent, and sometimes unbearable. These are the Big Gs.

I had a client who was the sole survivor of an ATV accident eight years before he came in for therapy. He lost his two best friends in the accident. He struggled with PTSD, nightmares, and physical imbalance. He developed a weakened immune system. He self-medicated with alcohol and opiates until he reached bottom. He never grieved the loss of his friends, had survivors guilt, and it impacted every part of his life. He became a recluse, struggled with intimacy, and was challenged in business. His trauma sponsored feelings of shame and embarrassment. He had to mourn his friends, get in touch with what he had been telling his brain about his loss, and tackle his sense of being disabled by the loss. The confrontation of the Self enabled the grief he was holding in his body, soul, and psyche to shift, allowing him to find the ultimate freedom: a reduction in survivor guilt, business success, and a solid relationship with himself and his partner.

A Big G—such as the loss of a loved one, the loss of a limb, bullying, a life threatening accident, sexual or verbal abuse—disorients your thinking, your behavior, and ultimately your internal compass and can cause changes to your brain. This disorganized thinking is a hallmark of being in the grip of grief.

When a client comes in with a history of sexual abuse, their stories are often confused, their timelines seem inaccurate to them, memory recall of the past is often disabled, and emotional balance is out of reach. They have often reported blacking out or feeling dissociated during the time of abuse. In that moment, that very second, the neural connections are altered. Those neural connections change in the brain when the abuse occurs as well as when the stressors from the abuse are prolonged.

Reminders of the loss or abuse that remain in your environment can exacerbate the reaction and keep you linked to the trauma. This makes it difficult to break the connections made in your brain, since it believes those connections create protection. You can re-wire your emotional and behavioral responses by challenging the lifelong patterns of behavior. This is part of the grief cycle.

In *Necessary Losses,* Judith Viorst wrote, "We each are artists of the self, creating a collage, a new and original work of art out of scraps and fragments of identifications."[32]

We now know that behavior patterns are developed over time and can actually affect the way the brain is formed. In terms of your responses to loss and trauma, the way you hold on to pain, depression, or anxiety can actually affect the physiology of your brain. In other words, the structure of your brain can be altered through your experiences and the behavioral patterns that follow. If you change those patterns and create a new collage, you can change your brain.

We're all puzzles, and each distinct aspect of the self is like a piece to that puzzle. Imagine that in the past you had a clear picture of your personal puzzle; you knew how each piece fit perfectly into the next. Your borders were firm, and they held distinct aspects of you in perfect alignment. Now, imagine that something smashes into your puzzle, shattering it to bits. Pieces are flying everywhere, and the border is gone. The pieces that are destroyed will never fit quite as perfectly as they once did. Even if only one piece is destroyed, the rest of the puzzle is incomplete. Instead of staying in the destruction of the puzzle, you create a new border, and new insides, using some of the old pieces of the puzzle while designing new pieces that can be incorporated into the puzzle. You're merging the old with the new.

Your brain is a work in progress. For that matter, you are a work in progress. Shifting the perspective and breaking through old habits and damaging beliefs requires self-awareness. Trusting your brain's ability to change means you must be willing to fully engage in converting to a new way of thinking and behaving. Adopting a new approach doesn't mean you'll forget where you've been. It simply means those past experiences don't get to control you and don't dictate how you behave in the present (or the future).

If your trauma is from the past and exists in memory, it is likely your behaviors adjusted to the trauma and created safe connections keeping you stuck in the past. What was created in those synapses and connections can actually be undone by teaching the brain to think and respond differently. When you release the old ways of thinking and engage with new elements of thought, the complexity of the brain connects and fires in new ways that are safe and transformative. Knowing your brain is quite plastic and can reset and adjust itself gives hope for what Dr. Peter Levine refers to as "flow, vitality, and wholeness."

The neurons in your brain are *dancing*. They are jarring and resistant, hopeful and constant, and they break down and restructure as you shift and learn to live gracefully with the grief and the trauma.

"Is it even possible for one event to completely change who you are, and the entire foundation of your being? I didn't think so before, but now I don't know."

~ X. [33]

Choosing to heal can be one of the hardest choices a person ever faces. Your brain won't change until you're willing to counter the overt negative thoughts and bodily responses that control your attitude, mood, and behavior. Some of these thoughts might include:

* If I change, am I willing to release my expectations of the people who cannot accept my transformation?
* I know I am not the person I used to be, and I can't pretend to be the old me.
* Am I afraid they won't understand the new me? Should I even care if they do?
* I don't like who I have become. Sometimes I feel too harsh or angry.
* Should I hide my growth to maintain my current relationships?
* If I do that, am I being dishonest to them and mostly to myself? I can't be in that mask any longer.
* Who the hell am I anyway?

Self-confrontation is a fundamental component of the grieving process. What you thought you knew about your psyche and soul is challenged by self-questioning and confusion. This is to be expected. No one ever really wants to change; we have a strong desire to keep things in a kind of stasis. When struck by monumental shifts, the big questions are . . .

* What do I understand about why this is this happening to me?
* What do I need to understand in myself?
* What causes self-confrontation to be so difficult? What will help me heal?

Drawing on your grief tool kit can help create new neurons in your brain. There are simple activities that can help you heal and pave the way for future health and growth. For example, physical exercise is known to help alleviate some symptoms of depression.[34] Exercise also drives the creation of new neurons. These neurons can actually break the cycle of depression. Exercise activates the production of serotonin and dopamine, essential chemicals called "endorphins" that are commonly associated with feeling good and support happy moods.

Finding the motivation to move through the pain is essential. Create a self-care program that you can commit to following daily. Practice, practice, practice! Every day, challenge yourself in ways that may be uncomfortable, knowing you will ultimately reap rewards that support a balanced state of being. When you've chosen a different approach to coping with grief's emotional narrative, and you've had success, take note of it. Don't shrug it off. Noticing and becoming astutely aware of what works is *essential,* because your brain is listening! Change takes time. The more you initiate new coping skills and use them consistently, the stage is set to help yourself out of the swirling vortex of grief. Your soul can access the prospect of succeeding and the gift of healing.

It's human nature to believe we're in control. The hope that control is completely within our grasp is like fool's gold; it's wrapped up in a fantasy that creates undue stress. When it comes to external conflicts, you cannot control what comes at you. Luckily, you *can* regulate your responses to external events and conflicts. It might seem a lot easier to keep your head buried in the sand than to face what's before you. If you lift up your head and squarely face your external and internal battles, you can make change happen. When gripped by life-altering, soul-devastating experiences such as profound loss or trauma, you can still achieve balance, and ultimately, the deepening of the psyche's potency and restoration.

CHAPTER 7

The Dance of the Support System: Friends and Family

"The truest help we can render an afflicted man is not to take his burden from him, but to call our his best energy, that he may be able to bear the burden."

~ Philip Brooks
American Episcopal Clergyman/Author 1835-1893

Creating a support system is as much of a knowledge-based decision as it is instinctive. Friends and family can give you room to grieve, a shoulder to cry on, or become a sounding board for your sacred thoughts. However, they cannot do your work for you, and they do not replace the work you need to do on your own.

Family and friends can help, however what they're able to offer isn't always enough. If this is the case, it might be advisable to seek out the help of a therapist or other professional whose sole purpose is to be objective, giving your pain a place to safely exist while challenging the stasis. A professional will act as a guide with insights and support, giving you the opportunity to learn to live with your grief in more peaceful ways. It takes courage to reach out and share the profound intensity of your grief.

Think of friends, family, and professionals as a collective network that can offer emotional, practical, or physical support. This network can help you create a kind of shelter or holding area for emotions, information, and pivotal growth plans.

"Tons of new people and changes are coming into my life as the result of my job loss and my new job. All of which has skyrocketed my anxiety level. The only loss was the one person I used to work with (not the boss) who is keeping her distance. I believe it is out of self-preservation, as I am no longer there as a buffer and [the boss] will take all of his frustrations out on her now."

~ Carol H.

The relationships in a support system serve many roles. Long-standing friends and family relationships may remain constant during times of tragedy and sorrow, but just because they're family or friends doesn't mean they know how to provide the type of support you require. Depending on the individual or the situation, they can endanger your progress or enhance it.

As you move through the depths of mourning, your needs will fluctuate. Your support systems may change in response to your shifting moods and needs. In some cases, friends will grow with you; while others in your life previously might distance themselves from you. This is all part of the dance, and it allows you to pursue and develop fresh connections with new partners. You may meet new friends through support groups and other networks. Experiencing similar losses can unite people. Those who've shared the same type of loss or trauma tend to gravitate toward one another, and that synchronicity can form positive new bonds.

Cultivating the right people in your network is vital to the task of healing. Choose people who have the ability to honor the pace of how you mourn. They are the people who don't drain you, who are able to listen without making it about themselves, and understand your personality style.

People who have shared a similar loss can feel like reminders of your loss or trauma. If this is the case, you may need some distance from those folks as you heal. The need for distance is a decision you can make with each person in your circle. As you heal, the need for distance from people who provoke you also shifts.

The gift of learning about your personal style (introvert, extrovert, or ambivert; fixed, mutable, or cardinal; and under-distanced, over-distanced, or balanced/calibrated) results in clarity about what you need and who can offer the most support. Clarity will be enhanced as you continue to learn about your needs, wants, and personal style. When you know more about yourself and who you are, the people you choose to be around will align with you.

> *"My marriage ended due to my breast cancer, at least, I thought that is what ended it. Looking back, I realize there was always just one of us trying . . . if not for this it would have ended anyway. Cancer may have sped the death of the marriage up as it opened my eyes to, 'Is this all I get? Is this what I deserve?'"*
>
> ~ C.

Friends

When you survive a severe trauma, abuse, or the loss of a loved one, or have a history of chronic illness, the people around you shift and change like new dance partners. Relationships can get stronger, fracture in some way, or remain as they were.

Nothing changes you more quickly than the struggles associated within the dance of grief and loss. When you freely express anger, regret, depression, and anxiety, this can create "stay away" messages that put you in a virtual danger zone that can be difficult for outsiders to handle. They may be unable to fathom the intricacies of your personal process and because it seems strange to them, they need to retreat and honor their own need for safety. The friends who have witnessed your pain may have difficulty being with the new, post-loss you. Your danger zones may also trigger their own yet-to-be-resolved loss issues. Of course, that is *their* problem to resolve, although you are affected by it because it creates conflict or possibly distance in your relationship. They may not be available to help you if they are in the midst of resolving any of their own loss issues.

"I don't blame my old friends—they tried their best to keep in touch with us, but they are very comfortably off, and we live day to day—we have nothing in common any longer."

~ Jane K.

Consider how your dance triggers their fears. When someone is in the throes of a Big G, like illness, remembered trauma, divorce, loss of a loved one, or any situation that has caused them to feel the gravity of grief, others can react to them as if they carry a contagious disease. Friends and family may feel if they get too close, they'll catch it. Of course, all they'll catch is having to feel their own fear and meet their own triggers.

This reactivity is sometimes seen in cases of divorce, illness such as cancer, and with folks who are immersed in their loss and trauma. There is a universality to this response, though not everyone reacts with a triggered flight, fight, freeze response. Is it the Big G they're responding to or the emotions that are expressed as part of being embroiled in the Big G? Separating the two reactions is something to think about, and it's okay to not yet have the answer. Clearly, their emotions are aroused while witnessing your darkness, and this can lead them to abandon you. Staying away from you keeps them from facing their own internal terrors.

Friends often don't know how to respond appropriately when you are actively mourning. If your spouse died and your circle of friends was comprised of other couples, their discomfort with your glaring singleness may lead them to disengage, creating yet another loss for you. If you have been out of work due to serious illness, and as a result had to sell your upscale home, some friends may desert you when you're no longer part of their exclusive neighborhood. As painful as these losses-on-top-of-losses are, you'll see your friends for who they are. When you observe which of your friends can tolerate their own discomfort in order to be supportive of you, you achieve valuable insight into that person and gain someone whom you can add to your support system.

New friendships are primed to enter a rich gateway that nourishes in ways that could not be imagined. At the same time, deepening of old friendships will occur as you move through your grief dance. Like the cleansing aspect of the tide, you'll wash away the sludge to reveal a clean foundation on which you can dance from grief into grace.

FAMILY

You choose your friends. You don't choose your family. You might hope the family will be a foundation of unconditional support. Oddly enough, however, no two people have the same growing-up experience, even if they were brought up in the same home and had the same parents. How often have you heard siblings describe childhood memories as if they lived in different homes? Knowing this occurs, you might ask yourself how a family can be a source of support in times when facing personal and emotional distress. Dropping any expectation of how each family (and family member) will respond relieves the anticipation of how they will help. Each reaction by any individual is likely to be different.

Everyone holds a diverse meaning of what family is to them. You define family based on who you consider to be part of that group: Parents, aunts, uncles, cousins, and even people who aren't blood related can be part of this crew. They represent an aspect of your support system.

This is a good time to take out your journal and think about each person in your family and how you believe they would respond to your needs, or if they would show support.

- Will they be there when you reach out? How do you know?
- Can you count on them to be part of your support system?
- Will they respect your unique way of engaging with the dance?
- Can they tolerate your distance when you need to step away?

Reactions to your family of origin are determined by many variables. The family dynamics are often mirrored in how you cope. Family life can be filled with joy or anxiety, anger, deep connection, or a lack of it. What you experienced within the family, how emotions were expressed, and how family members reacted to you influence the way loss and trauma touches your psyche.

To assess how your family of origin affects the mourning process, take a moment to remember what it felt like to be in your family dynamic, especially during conflict or in times of trouble. Take yourself through a timeline that represents a span of ages. It doesn't matter what ages you remember. This is another journaling opportunity. Think about the following:

- Did your family create safe boundaries? What were those boundaries? How were they implemented? Were you able to speak up, disagree, or engage in an activity outside of what the family wanted you to do, without repercussions?

Or

* Did your family regulate your actions and your voice through dominance, power, and an insistence on following the family rules, inhibiting personal development and a core sense of self that was not tied to the totality of the family?

If you were encouraged to explore, take reasonable risks, and stand strong within your own beliefs, it's likely you cultivated a positive sense of Self, leaving you secure and able to be autonomous and independent. With these qualities, not only can you withstand the pain of grief and the ability of your psyche learned to sustain itself,[35] tolerating the necessary steps it takes to unmask parts of the self where grief is imprinted.

However, if your family could not tolerate diffences, felt a sense of contentment when everybody held the same point of view, and acted as one unit, anxiety would likely arise if you stepped outside of those limits. If they taught you that the only way to be stable is to stay attached and obedient[36] (and you followed their lead until you could claw your way out), it's probable the familial glue probably affected your sense of self-esteem, making it harder to develop effective tools for managing life and now, your grief.

If members of your family or clan have historically gathered to give support, offering non-judgmental and unconditional love while anyone in the family unit was in a crisis, you can probably count on them. They know how to help you through bereavement's internal and external chaos, but they don't need to *join you* in the chaos. Instead, they simply acknowledge your pain, offer help, and support your growth.

Family members may thrive on what is called "group think."[37] One of the pioneers of family therapy, renowned psychiatrist Murray Bowen,[38] developed a substantive theory that focused on the combination of togetherness and individuality in a family. He wanted to help people understand how their functioning was affected by too much togetherness, which he called fusion, or too much individuality, which causes distance and estrangement from others.

While moving through the many phases of grief and trauma, it's helpful to have a complete picture of who you are and what you can emotionally endure, while also gaining an understanding of your limitations and strengths. The reason Bowen's concept of balance is important is twofold:

1. When you have a greater sense of balance, you're not concerned about what others think.
2. Your emotions are held intact without moving into the extremes of over-distanced or under-distanced responses.

Bowen focused on what one needs in order to live in a state of emotional balance, which he called "differentiation." This means balancing not only emotional reactions to external and internal conflicts, but also to balance the desire to be attached to another while honoring the importance of a separate Self.

His term "group think" refers to an undifferentiated and merged position that can be held by a family. Within this kind of family, the belief is sustained with adages like "What's good for one is good for all." Family rules, ways of behaving, such as "no one cries in public" or "we don't speak ill of the dead" (or speak of them at all) or acting like everything is fine, are examples of the group think process. They are created to keep the peace, to keep control, and to keep everyone attached. If members within the family structure do not abide by a certain conformity, the result may feel like a literal or symbolic displacement from the family. In the family where group think is present, you might find that family members who have had losses similar to yours feel especially attracted to you, seeing you as a comrade in crisis, and want to merge with your pain. When a family is more differentiated, meaning they actually tolerate differences in each person's individual perspectives and actions and don't become reactive to the differences, someone with a similar loss will be able to offer support, rather than feeding off of your pain to enhance their own pain or using your pain as an opportunity to talk about their pain and eclipse your suffering.

Or their response to your pain and loss might go in the opposite direction: "Stay away. I don't want to be reminded."

> *When Thomas sought therapy he was grieving the death of his twenty-five-year-old son, Ryan, to cancer. Thomas was in a state of shock because he thought his own parents would offer him support and care during this hard time. Instead, his parents suddenly left for a trip to Europe, and explained they couldn't be with him because his loss reminded them of the death of the infant son they had lost many years before. They couldn't tolerate losing a grandchild after having survived the loss of their newborn. Sadly, Thomas not only lost his son, he also lost his parents. They couldn't emotionally tolerate a similar grief.*

They took leave and acted as if they were avoiding the pain. However, is anyone ever able to get that distant or removed from this kind of trauma and feel relief? Maybe a sociopath could. Based on their reaction to the death of their grandchild, probably they avoided all situations that made them remember the loss of their own child. Thomas realized the parents he trusted and relied on couldn't be present for him in his time of loss and grief. If they had been able to separate their loss from Thomas's loss, and had been able to integrate a graceful solace from the loss of their infant son, they may have been able to be the supportive parents Thomas craved. They were bonded in the loss of their infant son, yet also stuck.

A good-enough[39] *differentiated family*[40] does not rely on group think to help their loved one. They do not expect you to respond as they would and are able to honor and respect differences.

As you can see, not everyone within a family is the same nor will they behave similarly under the same set of circumstances. If you came from a family that saw itself as one unified body where everyone was expected to think and behave in the same way, it may be very hard for you to create distance from them. Move away from seeing the family as a unified force and as individuals that make up the family, and you're on the right track to autonomy. Meeting your own sovereignty aligns you with self-sufficiency, and, ultimately, healing. Face the Self and you learn to face grief. An entire world opens up for you when you do!

> *"I survived Hurricane Katrina, but it transformed me. I am a different person. I feel more loved than I did a week ago, and I very much appreciate all of the friends and family and even strangers who both helped me directly and who contacted me to say they were concerned and thinking about me and my family."*
>
> ~ Michael Homan[41]

As you change your behavior in relation to the familial status quo, they might feel there is a threat to the composition and unity of this collective. They also may become concerned when they notice you're not going along with the overt and covert agreements of the family unit. They may consciously and unconsciously want to maintain the status quo of the family and expect you to stay exactly where you are, rather than support you challenging yourself. Part of your growth requires breaking from this pattern, and ultimately allowing you to see the Self as primed to become more psychologically and aesthetically balanced. This is an ultimate benefit of successful healing. You might find your internal sense of calm and balance positively shift when you oppose what has been the norm.

If your family has historically offered little or no support, they're unlikely to act differently in response to your current situation. Set aside the expectation that the people you've known all your life will be part of your dance. Some simply don't know what to say or do for you in the midst of your emotional storm. They're unable to reach out because they feel helpless or are overwhelmed by your pain, they're reliving a previous loss, or they're suffering from the same loss you're going through, which may contribute to their discomfort in your presence. Their leave-taking can feel like abandonment, but in all likelihood, their reactions have nothing to do with you. They—like you—are in the process of learning to come to terms with who they are as they cope.

Donna found the support of her family while she struggled with a marital crisis. Her husband was cheating as well as watching a lot of porn. She had two young boys, and was afraid they would find the porn. She had no money to leave and felt as if she were in an inescapable prison. She wore the archetypal mask of the Trickster, who looked like the archetype of the Hero, to show a certain persona to the world that all was well, yet behind it lay abundant layers of shame and fear. She believed it was a way to protect herself and her children. She held fast onto the mask, until one day she had a major psychological breakdown.

She sought therapy when she could no longer hold the mask. She wasn't sleeping, eating, or caring for her children. That mask was tearing her apart. She shared her story with her mom. Donna's mother had been the more parental of the two parents when Donna was a teenager. Reaching out to her helped Donna realize that her mother could bear more stress than Donna thought possible. This allowed for healing to trickle through on many levels.

She'd never been close to her mom. A new relationship emerged as they learned how to work as a team. Donna grieved the loss of her marriage and got to rebuild her core sense of identity while meeting her mother woman-to-woman. She is learning to tackle the shame of her past and the masks that betray what lies in her psyche, and she is discovering the gift of a renewed relationship with her mother.

In meeting Thomas and Donna, does your grief experience parallel any aspect of their narrative?

Some families have the appropriate distance to manage emotions when witnessing the suffering of a loved one. Others don't. Even families that are higher on the differentiation scale and rely less on the need to identify as part of a pack may not give the exact support you need. Unless you do the work to know what you need, you won't be able to let them in on ways to help. At the end of the day, your movement toward grace and self-discovery always begins with *you*.

CHAPTER 8

THE ELEVEN PHASES OF GRIEF

"You can't prevent birds of sorrow flying over your head—but you can prevent them from building nests in your hair."

~ CHINESE PROVERB

You define the steps of your personal dance of grief: Nobody else does. Listen to your soul; it will reveal the areas that need attention and you will move accordingly. The way you mourn won't necessarily follow a script or unfold in any prescribed order. The phases described in this chapter invite you into an exploration of the experiences that can accompany grief and the grieving process. You can decide to engage with any phase or phases that speak to your pain, your thoughts, or your emotions, and what you're experiencing in the moment. Eventually, you'll reach a personal resolution as you achieve greater balance, which means you have integrated the loss into your life. The memories of your trauma and loss won't be erased from your mind. They will be carried within your soul with mastery and grace.

We know of no timeline to work through any or all the phases, nor one correct protocol. It happens in your own time, and, like your fingerprint, the dance of grief is individual and unique to you.

You might have heard that grief follows five specific stages. Some experts still subscribe to this way of thinking, but it's good to know the field has moved away from this perspective, because there is no formulaic or strategic way to mourn and reconstruct the Self. Trauma and grief will dance with you in ways that are unimaginable, profound, and sometimes, when you awaken the Self, joyful. Your growth, your enlightenment, and your healing depend on many variables. Grief is not a linear process.

You can move in and out of the eleven phases discussed here; layer them if two or more seem equally important; skip some of them; stay with one that resonates with you—all without being confined to a particular order or viewing them like a checklist that, once completed, will mean you have conquered your grief. As you know, the dance is neither stagnant nor predictable, therefore no clear-cut boundaries or rules need to apply as you encounter each phase.

As you look at the list of the eleven phases of grief, even before reading about them, gauge the reaction that each phase inspires in you. *Then, in your journal or notebook, list the phases and give each phase a number ranking from one to ten, with one for the least intense and ten for the most intense.* It's helpful to rank the intensity of the phases to create a memory place mark of where you began this journey. My clients have taught me that it's quite easy to forget where you've been as you grow and shift.

Numbering the phases (even before you have gone through them) allows you to see where you started and perhaps where you go once you've read through each phase; a ten can shift to a two, and a three can change into a nine. This is a way to establish the facts about what is affecting you, what needs more time or less time, and perhaps what is quiet and is no longer part of the grip of grief.

Push yourself to go into unknown territory as you explore these phases. If you have a strong reaction to a particular phase, you may find yourself trying to avoid it entirely. Pay attention to what you're resisting. Push into it and onward, understanding this phase is an opportunity to become more intimate with your psyche as it unfolds and discovers the lessons of loss.

The Emotional Armor phase is the first phase and includes numbness, denial, hysteria, and shock. This is a phase you will likely visit and revisit many times. It can serve as a re-grouping and resting phase. It's the phase that prepares you for the next meeting of the Self in your grief. It offers you respite from the hard work, and lets your brain disengage a bit before moving forward. It's very much part of how your brain creates a safe haven for you while you move through the phases.

Depending on what caused your grief, trauma, and loss reactions, you might find that some phases strongly call you to engage with them. Some phases will be more notable at the beginning of this process. Moving through the phases will be influenced by your desire to engage in the exercises offered within them.

Once you've read through the initial list, go to the sections that speak to you. Whatever topic you're drawn to will be the right one. Even when the journey seems to be hopeless at times or lacking in direction, trust that it opens a way out of the cocoon that grief and trauma have created, so you can discover your ability to fly. Knowledge of the Self, inner growth, and integration are realms to be uncovered and discovered in this dance.

The phases give you an opportunity to meet the Self in transformation. They can be cathartic. When you find relief from active grief, you will birth a reconstructed, restored, and balanced Self.

The Eleven Phases

1. Emotional Armor: Numbness, Hysteria, Denial and Protest, Shock
2. Role Confusion
3. The Three D's: Distraction, Depression and Detachment
4. Fear and Anxiety
5. Anger, Rage, and Despair
6. Regret, Guilt, and Shame
7. Sadness
8. Forgiveness: Letting Go with Insight, Purpose, and Understanding
9. Re-Patterning, Calibration, and Integration
10. Resolution
11. Grace

PHASE 1

EMOTIONAL ARMOR: NUMBNESS, HYSTERIA, DENIAL AND PROTEST, SHOCK

Numb
In a distant fog
What I knew no longer exists,
Fire burns inside yet I'm blank
The sun sets, the sun rises
The distant fog surrounds me
I cannot see or feel or act
Numb
I am the fog
All has stopped
There is no one but me.

~ Anonymous

Numbness, shock, hysteria, protest and/or denial all serve as types of protective armor. These reactions are automatic; you don't *choose* to feel numb in response to the depths of your shock. These are healthy defense mechanisms that protect you from being overwhelmed. During this phase, you hunger to find protection that offers security and safety. In its infancy, the power of your loss and trauma erupts. The bottom has dropped out of your internal infrastructure, and you need to be shielded from the outpouring of emotion.

Your brain strives to resist the powerful emotions that are aroused when faced with loss. Your psyche can feel as if it's being attacked. To fend off the attack, you either retreat by cocooning yourself and barricading your emotions, or you expose yourself, meet the emotions with your own force, and ultimately, reveal them.

Whether you bare the mask that is your soul or firmly keep in place the masks that create a barricade, both approaches have the goal of helping you cope with the intensity of your experience. Grief calls loudly for your attention, asking you to make it better, and your unconscious responds—sometimes loudly and hysterically and at other times; from within a place of hiding.

"I feel numb. I feel like my whole world has just been taken away from me, crushed after a two-minute ultrasound. The thought of "terminating" is horrifying to me . . . he/she still has a heartbeat . . . and is still MY baby."

~ Brandi[42]

Within each phase, your emotions will range along a spectrum, and this is especially true in this first phase.

If you're numb during one part of the day, and hysterical during another, know you're not going crazy. You're experiencing the unpredictability of active mourning. Numbness and hysteria, although on opposite ends of the spectrum, provide you with the distance that enables you to face the tasks at hand, such as planning a funeral or making medical decisions. When you shut down in numbness, you're over-distanced, and when you're in hysteria, you're under-distanced.

Denial can surface whether you're numb or hysterical. It can seem easier to stay in this phase than to step into the multilevel emotional dimensions of the Big G dance. Yet as hard as you try to avoid an emotion, for example, anger, it often emerges when your mind would rather stay numb. These emotions can be triggered by reminders that come in strange packages. An object, a color, or a familiar scent can trigger an emotional response and remind us that grief and trauma cannot be forgotten or ignored.

Joanna came to see me for help with her grief after her fiancé was killed by a drunk driver as they were on their way to a party. Joanna's injuries caused her right leg to be amputated. Joanna's multiple losses were almost too much for her to bear, and she wanted to stay numb. But her injuries and intense medical needs demanded that she stay connected as she followed up with an array of therapies to help her manage and learn to live without her lost limb.

"When I got home after being in the hospital, every time I saw a red car that looked like John's, I turned and followed it," Joanna described. "Even though I knew my leg was not part of my body any longer, I continued to believe that it was there because of the phantom pain I experienced. It was the same with John. I kept looking for him, and he wasn't there. I knew John was dead, and I did not want to believe it. He was alive in my heart, even though I knew intellectually that he wasn't."

In this phase, the soul wants the pain of the present to stop. The psyche, in its desire to protect you, will go to great lengths to make it seem as if the pain has ceased. The psyche is bound to a feeling, and also to a sense of aloneness and alienation. In this unfolding journey, you face the monumental task of soothing your Self while submerged in the power of loss. Thankfully, the brain takes on its protective armor as a way to mitigate what does not want to be felt or seen.

It's good to have emotional armor in the infancy of the grief cycle. The truth about learning to dance with your loss is that it's a painful dance. The truth really hurts. As difficult and agonizing as it is, this journey contains many truths that serve as conduits to awareness and personal transformation.

The emotional armor phase includes several subcategories. Observe how they manifest in your own psyche and behavior.

Numbness

You're almost in a stupor, indecisive, and unable to make important decisions. Apathy holds you hostage. Marked by a stillness, you have limited, if any, desire to actively participate in the world. Emotions are in hiding and often inaccessible. You're in a foggy present, watching everything go on around you as if in a fog. Although you're not denying the truth about your loss or trauma, you create a protective, defensive armor, until you're ready to begin the dance. This is an over-distanced state of being.

> *When newlywed Andrea discovered her husband's suicide, the world became surreal. Her heart seemed to stop beating, and she couldn't grasp information to make sense of what was going on. She describes the shock as being like watching a horrific car accident in slow motion and not being able to do anything about it. After that, the numbness became a welcome reprieve to her pain, anger, rage, and depression.*

This is also a place to gather strength. When you're numb, it's a protective and safe resting place. The brain is taking a time-out. When every part of you is flooded, the mind, the body, and the conscious need to shut down. Numbness allows this to happen. It can act as a safe place until you're ready to emerge from being detached.

Hysteria

At the opposite end of the spectrum from numbness, emotional overload, causes a kind of frenzy and madness known as "hysteria." Bouts of crying, moaning, babbling, behaving unreasonably, and sometimes contempt for being in the potency of grief can flare up. In a strange way, these reactive manifestations help block what you're not ready to acknowledge or feel. Hysteria represents being in an under-distanced state.

The dance within hysteria is often irrational and unpredictable. However, experiencing hysteria may lead to a breakthrough. Your body and mind are actually experiencing a release that occurs when your internal conflicts are externalized in what looks like spasms of distress.

The brain stays hysterical until it's ready to move out from under this protective layer. Your psyche must believe it has a foundation of support before it can refocus and undertake the task of unraveling the layers of the Self on the journey.

Denial and Protest

Denial is probably not a new concept to you. Frequently used, even by those who aren't immersed in grief, it's a defense mechanism that helps to avoid pain, truth, and seeing what you must face. Ultimately, it's an attempt to make what is, *disappear.* It leads to a turning inward, refusing to engage, or not seeking help when needed. Denial and protest are over-distanced.

Protesting the facts keeps denial alive. The act of protesting reality is often the mind's way of avoiding the truth. Anger may feed into the protest, working in tandem to keep the arousal and energy fed and the denial intact.

Denial isn't all bad. It's actually a necessary part of life.

Healthy Denial

Denial has a bad rap in popular culture. There is such a thing as *healthy* denial when it comes to death and loss. If you thought about death, trauma, or loss every day it would probably lead to insanity. Denial in this sense is an element of human survival. It allows you a respite from dwelling on our own death. You probably don't think about that very much and that's a good thing. The brain actually organizes itself to be cloaked as your mind keeps the reality of death at a distance, allowing you to feel a sense of well-being.

This protective denial is different from the kind of denial that keeps you frozen and unavailable to engage in the dance or the denial that prevents you from identifying and recognizing the sources of your grief. As you face the struggle and pain in the currents of healing, your shield of healthy denial is tested and provoked. This integral part of you that has served as a protector loses some of its ability to maintain a sense of balance and control. The stability you feel when you're in denial is rocked when you face unmistakable facts about the loss or trauma. Denial has its uses:

- It provides a safe place to rest until you're ready to engage and interact with what you don't want to see.
- It keeps you from confronting the demons, so when you're ready to face them and engage with them, you can promote growth rather than distress.
- It gives you time to regain a sense of balance to help you cope with the ongoing fluctuations within your psyche as you contemplate partnering with your grief.
- It enables you to avoid what is before you.

Any loss alters aspects of the Self. Healthy denial, without even knowing it, allows you to accumulate lifelong coping skills that teach endurance and survival. It can often be difficult to access those skills when facing the loss of a part of yourself. Moving out of denial isn't easy because you become caught in a vicious cycle of craving balance, which you don't have when in denial, and wanting to face what's on the other side of the denial, which is turmoil and truth. Neither place is particularly comfortable.

You may desperately want and need to share what's happening, yet the words aren't accessible to you, so your denial becomes an unconscious go-to. Carried within that sanctuary is the illusion that you must handle this journey all on your own. The consuming turmoil is compounded by this imagined sense of being alone in your pain, as well as being alone in finding your way through the pain.

If you feel there is no one who understands the depths of your pain, online discussion groups can offer care and guidance. You will find the names for some of them at the back of the book, in the Support and Support Groups section. It also may be time to reach out and engage with a therapist or counselor. It takes far more courage to reach out for professional help than to sink deeper into a diminishing sense of balance and hope.

It's imperative to find the balance between healthy denial and the denial that is an obstacle to healing. When you do so, you can meet the grace in your grief.

You might want to stay occupied by anything other than looking at what's before you, particularly when it's painful. However, unresolved grief will continue to haunt and taunt you when you delay the necessary engagement with the Self. Rather than choosing to allow your grief to linger, it's best to step into the pain. A gift awaits you when you do. You learn that discomfort and even agony cannot destroy you.

Shock

Shock occurs in the body and in the brain. The effects of shock can sometimes be more devastating than the original injury. Physically, shock is a protection when one is in an accident and the body shuts down. Keeping the body warm and staying engaged in conversation are two keys to surviving the physical shock response.

Emotionally, when you're experiencing or re-experiencing a personal or psychological loss, disbelief contributes to the waves of shock. The re-experiencing can take you back to the initial trauma or loss, allowing the first imprint of the trauma to come alive in real time. You are more than dazed, and it affects the soul. How you've handled loss and trauma in the past impacts how you handle loss in the present.

Your memory of how you handled past situations informs your capacity to tap into the ability to ask for what you need, and enables you to move through extreme psychological, emotional, and physical reactions.

"As I walked home later that day I felt as if the universe had slowed down; I was more aware of my surroundings than ever before. 'Am I dead?' I asked myself. 'Am I walking around not knowing I've died?' I couldn't help but purposely bump into pedestrians just to reassure myself."

~ Michelle Cruz Rosado, survivor of the attack on World Trade Center Tower II.[43]

Shock often mingles with numbness, denial, and hysteria. Shock affects all your functioning, as though you were in the middle of a bad dream. Its tentacles are far-reaching, affecting your breathing, your sense of calm, and your ability to think clearly or focus. It can even cause physical sensations of instability and unsteadiness. Unable to comprehend what you've witnessed, heard, or remembered, you may find that you need to ask the same questions again and again, because it's difficult to concentrate, focus, or retain information.

Shock is your psyche's response to an array of situations, including:

- If you were unprepared or surprised by the suddenness of an event.
- If you felt powerless to defend yourself or remove yourself from a situation.
- If the experience occurred when you were a child.
- If you experience interpersonal violence.

Shock can impact you differently if you generally approach the world as an introvert, extrovert, or ambivert. If you are an introvert, shock will send you into your cocoon. Remember, you isolate to recharge. If you suddenly and uncharacteristically avoid your normal group of friends, family, or social situations, it might be wise to reach out for help. You don't want to stay in shock longer than necessary.

As an extrovert, you risk believing that you can only reach emotional calm if you're around others. When dealing with shock, you might manipulate others, so you don't have to be alone. Anxiety may be quite high, and the shock can adversely impact the coping skills you need to still the Self. An ambivert may react as either the extrovert or the introvert does.

When the shock subsides, you will often experience something like an emotional clearing or release, also known as a catharsis. Catharsis enables you to blossom, because you're reacting to the loss and traumatic information differently. Empowering by nature, catharsis offers an ever-changing and freeing perspective. You suddenly realize grief isn't taking you over. You understand how it functions and what its boundaries are. A deeper understanding of your internal process usually follows.

In addition to shock, numbness, hysteria, and denial, other reactions and experiences can be present in Phase 1, including seclusion, confusion, and chaos. Withdrawal can happen even when you're in the presence of others. The support from chosen family and friends is important during this phase. It's a time to guard against hopelessness. When you lose hope, you can sometimes no longer imagine what your next move will be, or even how to make it. Remember that you will shift in your own time.

Whatever you may experience in Phase 1 subsides when you move into other phases. Remember, this is a respite phase. Before you move into another phase, you might revisit this phase as a way to give your psyche a break; a time for emotional transition and metamorphosis.

Phase 2

Role Confusion

"A role can be defined as the actual and tangible forms which the Self takes."

~ Jacob Levy Moreno[44]

You develop and nourish many roles throughout your life—child, friend, student, spouse, parent, employee, employer, and many others. Think of the roles as an accumulation of masks that are part of the Self and the identity you've developed. They shift over time. Some roles stay with you, while others get dropped throughout the life cycle. The difference is that the Self, which is also a mask, is who you *are,* and the roles are what you present to the world. The roles are what you *do.*

Throughout your day, you can be a mother or a father, a cook, a designer, a peacemaker, a son or a daughter, and a teacher. And even when you're not actively engaged in any specific role, it influences the core of your personality. In the process of mourning, the roles that are intrinsic to you can dramatically shift whether you are experiencing a Big G or a Little G.

In Phase 2, you can experience a conflict between roles that are no longer needed after your loss and new roles that need to be cultivated and nurtured. This process of redefining your roles is both exciting and terrifying. It creates a crisis of the Self as you struggle to feel secure in what you identify as being *you.* Although you may not be aware of it, you're re-evaluating the Self and the roles you played prior to being in the dance.

Let's take a moment to understand how roles play a large part in how your Self develops, how you relate to others, and how your roles evolve over the span of your life.

"Identification" is a process through which you model the behavior of others to determine who you are and how you choose to behave. The early identifications are perhaps the most potent. They occur when children model the behaviors of their parents or caretakers. As the children develop, they can decide which modeled behaviors to retain and which to abandon. The identifications help shape and form the roles the child will play later in life. The Self is a distinct identity that is perceived by others through these roles.

Role development begins in the nonverbal phase of infancy, and continues as the infant becomes more socialized, matures into adolescence, reaches adulthood, and enters into old age. Sometimes those roles become almost calcified and don't shift even in the face of life changes. I've had clients who couldn't let go of their old roles and old ways: Their fixed roles kept them stuck and fused to their grief. They believed that participating in life, finding laughter, and experiencing joy were acts of unfaithfulness. They identified so strongly with the roles they played with their lost loved one or so committed to the role of victim, that they couldn't move beyond the self-inflicted wound that kept them fastened to their active grief.

"I'm so tired of making my mom think that the way she sees the world is ok, when the reality is, in being a mother to my mother, I realize how sick our relationship is . . ."

~ Paula

To fully engage in Phase 2, it's important to examine the roles you played before you entered into the dance of grief. Begin this conversation with your Self by taking out your journal. Allow for free associations as you read the following.

* What happens when you are no longer a breadwinner, or caretaker, or problem-solver, or mother to a child who has died (or any role with which you identify)?

  If you strongly identified with these roles and they disappear, a crisis of the Self can emerge. It can be confusing when what you have known and relied on is no longer stable or reliable. Some of the familiar roles have shifted into roles that are unknown to you, causing you to feel that nothing in the world seems real. You find some of the unfamiliar roles or masks showing up in how you react to your environment, perform at work, and relate to others. The roles are affected by your trauma and loss; they change, they feel different, and some take leave.
* If you are mourning the loss of a loved one, do you wear your wedding ring although many years have passed since your spouse died? If you lost a child, do you keep his or her room intact, frozen at the time of the loss? Do you talk about the loved one as if they are still alive? Does this keep the role of you being a wife, husband, or parent alive while also creating a time warp that allows your mourning to remain active?
* If you were caretaker to a parent and that parent died, you will always know you were a daughter or a son, yet are no longer in an active role of daughter or son, or in an active role of caretaker. This doesn't mean you will never be a caretaker again.

  If you liked caretaking, you may find other outlets for that role, volunteering your time to a hospital, for example, or you may choose to discard the role completely, which could produce an identity predicament. In that situation, you might be asking,

"Who am I without that role?" By holding onto a role that no longer has validity, you remain in a world of disillusionment and fantasy.

Hoarding can be an example of how the residue of a lost role can affect you. If you hoard objects that remind you of a time prior to an abusive situation or when your loved one was alive, you're not only hoarding to alleviate the anxiety you feel; you're also keeping alive the role that you had in relation to that time or to that person. Attempting to thrive in a role that no longer exists can feel like emotional torture, with little relief in sight. By holding onto that role, it's difficult to get the necessary perspective or balance that contributes to healing.

A healthy way to cherish memories is to hold on to a few items, keep them in a special box, or an album of photographs that you open or view whenever you want to remember your loved one, when you want to remember your role as a caretaker, or want to remember the role(s) you inhabited prior to your grief, loss, or trauma. You can create special rituals to mark surviving divorce, or acknowledge holidays, such as the loved one's birthdate or the anniversary of an important transition. Your memory then becomes the keeper of the roles that were sacred to you. Your old roles may be ready to be released so new roles can establish themselves.

When faced with extreme trauma, the brain creates many roles for you as an escape from something that is too physically or emotionally traumatic, such as repetitive abuse patterns, rape, or bullying. For example, some adults and children who are sexually, physically, or verbally abused will, while being abused, go into what is called a *dissociative* state. This means their personal conscious awareness is interrupted and a safe, protective emotional numbing takes over as a way of "removing" the person from the traumatic situation.

Peggy is a thirty-five-year old woman who came into therapy to process what had happened to her when she was a young girl. Her recounting of her experience accurately depicts a dissociative state:

> *I was nine years old when three neighbor girls asked me to join them at one of their houses. I thought we were going to play after school. Instead, once I was in the basement, they held me down and hurt me. I grieve the loss of myself, and though I am angry with them, I am angrier with myself that I didn't fight back.*
>
> *What's funny is that I just don't remember much after they held me down. It hurt, and then I went away. I know I was late for dinner, and I was sick for days. I never told anyone, until I realized that my life was not what I wanted it to be, and I sought help. I still don't remember much, and I am working to feel less detached and more connected to others. It only happened once, but it set me up for the rest of my life. I am a caretaker now, and I work with kids. They are so innocent, and I want them to stay that way. I fight for people and animals that are hurt or seem to be vulnerable. It is hard for me to get close to people, because I only let them in so far. I'm better than I've been, but I have a long way to go.*

In this scenario, you can see that for Peggy, emotional numbing functioned as a response that allowed her brain to shield and protect her mind and psyche as she suffered the abuse. The subsequent roles that contributed to her core self were developed and directly related to that time after the abuse.

When you're unsure about your identity, you can also become unsure about how to interact with other people, which, in turn, causes them to be uncertain about how to interact with *you*. Their view of you changes because you've changed.

Some people get stuck in the role of victim. What causes people to identify with the role of victim is multi-faceted. They may consciously or unconsciously gain attention by being in the role. Letting go of that role may be difficult and overwhelming, especially if there is a sense of helplessness that accompanies those feelings. Like a child having a tantrum, the victim who stays in that role experiences anger at not having been able to control the outcome. This perspective can create ambivalence about healing and results in keeping them bonded to being the victim. It's how they identify themselves. If you've based your interactions with others on being a victim, please think and respond in your journal about the following:

- What happens to the role of victim as you begin to heal?
- Can you release the role of victim and allow it to change into an inner voice of a *survivor*?
- How is the role of survivor different from the role of victim?
- Who do you want to surround yourself with? Other victims, or other survivors?
- What purpose does each role serve for you?

If you no longer need certain roles, you can experience a sense of loss when you give them up, and you might mourn what they represented even if it was necessary to let them go. You may also find yourself attached to certain aspects of those roles. For example, you may idealize certain features of an abusive relationship; because they are what you experienced as a child, you believe that attention, even if it's negative, shows you love. You might identify with a special object belonging to a departed loved one, or become attached to an item of clothing that you or your loved one wore before the traumatic event, or strongly connect to a piece of music that reminds you of a happier time.

When you lose a spouse or partner, it's especially difficult to shift from the role of *we* to the new role of *I*. It's one of the greatest challenges anyone who has lost a loved one will face. When you move from *we* and shift to *I*, you are recognizing and admitting to the loss.

Another challenging transformation is moving away from being *the victim* to becoming *the victor*. The victim who stays in this role as their sole identifier gets stuck in a self-made confinement that keeps them in one role. The mask of the victim is present to keep them safe. When limited to one pervasive role, even if for a sense of protection, the attachment to the role keeps the pain alive. Moving from victim to victor involves a process of letting go of the old role.

Here are some questions to ask yourself about roles and identification. This is an opportunity to respond to the questions in your journal/notebook.

- Do you define yourself based on who or what you lost?
- If you have been abused by someone of the opposite sex, do you take on the role of man-hater or woman-hater to stay safe?
- Do you take on attributes of the lost loved one? Do you find yourself walking or talking like your abuser or lost loved one? Are you attracted to foods, aromas, or activities that you weren't before the loss or trauma, yet now you find a hunger for them?
- Do you find comfort in wearing clothing or colors that your abuser liked? Or do you avoid any color that reminds you of your loss or trauma?
- What are the roles you played and developed before experiencing your loss?
- What roles have you needed to incorporate in your active mourning state?
- What roles did you drop?
- What roles are no longer necessary?
- What roles do you need now?

You have a repertoire of roles that will expand and contract as part of the healing process. As you go along on the journey, your grief will become more integrated as the roles become defined.

"Every day, just like me, grief puts on a new face."

~ Charlie Doherty

Phase 3

The Three D's: Distraction, Depression, and Detachment

"There is no detachment where there is no pain."

~ Simone Weil[45]

The three D's—*distraction, depression,* and *detachment*—do their own dance by weaving in and out, and playing off one another. The more distracted and detached you are, the more depressive your thinking can be. The more depressed you are, the more distracted and detached you can become. This threesome can devour you.

Distraction

A persistent inability to focus is part of Phase 3. It's understandable if you're disorganized and distracted because you have a lot on your plate in the wake of your loss, but beware: Disorganization and mental chaos often precede depression. Consider the questions below. Write down the time of day when you feel most aware of these symptoms. Note whether they occur when you're alone or with others, and note when the feelings abate (if they do):

* Have you been severely absent-minded or distracted? Does this result in a lack of follow-through on responsibilities?
* Do you find common errands or tasks overwhelming? If so, which tasks?

- ✳ Have you lost house keys or bank cards, forgotten appointments, or not shown up to work?
- ✳ Have you forgotten to put on a belt or worn mismatching shoes? (After Paul died, I once left the house wearing completely mismatched shoes.) Have you stopped essential self-care: No dental hygiene, irregular bathing, or stopped or increased your food intake?
- ✳ Do certain aromas catapult you into a sense of disorganization, detachment, or extreme perfectionism?
- ✳ Are you having major trouble concentrating? Do you find it difficult to engage in conversations and remain focused? Are you ruminating about how badly you feel?

If you answered yes to more than three questions, then you might be more than a little distracted. What follows are some coping tools that can help you break the Catch-22 of your distraction cycle. If you don't feel the distraction, how do you know it's there? However, if you consider any one of these elements, like losing your keys, this would not necessarily indicate a state of distraction. It's the quantity and frequency of symptoms that informs the degree to which you're distracted. The steps you can take to break the cycle of distraction are actually activities you tend to avoid when you're in that cycle. You want to break out of your distraction and be more present, but because distraction has become familiar, it can be difficult to break out of.

Depression is often a partner of distraction, and can often be responded to in the same way. One study[46] divided men and women with major depression into three groups. One group did aerobic exercise, one group took an anti-depressant, and the third group combined medication and exercise. All three groups showed a 60 to 70 percent rate of improvement. But after six months, the group with exercise alone showed fewer depressive relapses.

Exercise is one of the best ways to break your distractibility and depression. Push yourself to take a walk, starting with ten minutes a day and working up to thirty-five minutes. This can fire up your brain and release endorphins—which you want to do, because endorphins are on your side!

Imagine helping another. If you had a friend who felt the way you presently feel, what would you tell them? If you imagine how you would help someone else in a similar situation, you might be surprised to discover that you have the knowledge to help yourself.

Get plenty of sunlight. If you live in a place with little winter sunlight using a light therapy box can be effective in fighting depression.

Keep a log that tracks your negative thinking. Doing so (in your journal or on your smart phone) will help change the cognitive conflicts that come with depression. When is negative thinking most prevalent? Who or what contributes to the conflicting thoughts? Is it your interpretation of what you're hearing, rather than what you're actually hearing, that sends you into the depression abyss? Challenge your thoughts by changing the negative cognitions into positive cognitions. Challenge your choices by looking for alternative responses and actions.

Reach out to someone. In a state of detachment, you'll often feel an aloofness that leaves you feeling both protected and dejected. It may appear to others as if you don't care. On the contrary, you might care almost too much. The detachment keeps you in a safe zone.

Depression

A sudden death, a trauma such as divorce or abuse, or a sense of helplessness as a loved one approaches death can all trigger depression. Having too many unanswered questions, knowing too much, or remembering a long-forgotten trauma can also activate the depression.

Depression can feel like a deep sense of hopelessness and dejection combined with a sense of unrelenting misery. This can lead to damaged relationships with friends and family, or difficulties with concentration and productivity in the work environment.

Frustration, anger, and anxiety often accompany depression. Depression is different from a deep sadness or even melancholia. Look over the following characteristics of depression. See which of these resonate most with you, and document your responses in your journal/notebook:

* Overwhelming, persistent pessimism.
* Feelings of hopelessness, helplessness, worthlessness.
* Poor memory.
* Slow thought processing.
* Loss of interest in activities, such as sex, socializing, and eating.
* Insomnia or oversleeping.
* Thoughts of suicide or death. (If you have thoughts of suicide, call a hotline and reach out to a therapist or psychiatrist who can help you.)

"I can't stay as organized like I once was, can't keep up with my housework like I used to. Laughter, smiles, and fun don't come easy anymore. Actually, the whole year after her passing, I don't even remember."

~ Chara M.

Although most people who suffer a loss experience sadness, it doesn't always result in depression. If depression has hooked you, remember that you *will* get out of it. It's difficult to assess the depths of one's own depression. If the symptoms listed above persist for six months or more with no sign of improvement, consider counseling. Reaching out to a professional can help you break through the obstacles.

Detachment

Detachment can feel as if you're shut down, disinterested, dispassionate and indifferent, it is not a void. It's different from the experience of being numb. In detachment and in numbness there is a lack of attachment. The difference is choice. When you're numb you don't choose the missing attachments, while in a detached state, choice is a big part of it. Unlike being in a state of numbness, when unattached you know you could care and even might care, yet you don't.

Detachment is unlike depression and distraction, because it can work for you as it helps you disengage from people who may be over-bearing at this time and it can help you separate the Self from any chaos that may exist around you. Boundaries have an easier time getting created, especially as you engage in getting to know the new and emerging you. The boundaries you set feed into a better sense of what you need in this process and the people who are chosen by you to join the process.

Developing detachment is an art, and will help disarm some of the depression and distraction that are present. It's a choice, and while depression and disorganization are not chosen, they just are.

Think about the following questions:

1. What emotional, physical and spiritual boundaries do you need to establish? Think about people, places and things that need you to create more boundaries.
2. What promise can you make to yourself when it comes to healing and taking on your losses and trauma? Are you willing to challenge it; joining the pain, in order to contain it? (Remember when your pain does not have a container, one that you have created, more chaos occurs, and depression is part of it.)
3. What feelings/thoughts/memories do you need to take responsibility for and how can you give them less power. If you are more

detached, clarity will follow. Once you are clear, it is easier to engage in what you recognize as getting in the way of healing.

Use this opportunity to invite in the chance to be detached and discover greater clarity, a stronger psyche and the spirit to move into greater safety and discovery.

While the three D's can be confusing and disorienting, and make you feel as if you're losing a part of yourself, they might present an opportunity for you to go more deeply into yourself. Exploring regions of the Self that have been previously unknown will help you to dance with grace—and grit.

"I didn't want to wake up. I was having a much better time asleep. And that's really sad. It was almost like a reverse nightmare, like when you wake up from a nightmare you're so relieved. I woke up into a nightmare."

~ Ned Vizzini, *It's Kind of a Funny Story*[47]

Phase 4

Fear and Anxiety

"Anxiety is like quicksand: the harder we struggle to escape, the deeper we sink."

~ Paul David, *AnxietyNoMore*[48]

Fear and anxiety can overwhelm. They can physically and mentally exhaust you, especially when they accompany trauma or loss. When you try to run from them, chances are what you want to avoid will become more insistent. The task in this phase is to confront fear and anxiety. When you commit to engaging with that which is uncomfortable, you build a Self that's reliable, even when it's in pain, allowing you to stay your course. Staying in the fight and showing up even when your soul aches will help you move past fear and anxiety.

Fear and anxiety feed off each other; they're partners. Fear is often embedded in your feelings of anxiety. Fear and anxiety are intertwined, and because of this, you may find it difficult to tell them apart. Their dance sometimes feels like a nightmare. The challenge lies in adjusting your perception of the nightmare so you're no longer haunted.

The physical and mental responses to fear and anxiety can feel exactly the same. However, fear is often a reaction to something real—for example, when a burglar breaks into your home—while anxiety is the imagined, more projective response to being afraid of having your home burgled. If you're being burgled, that's a real threat to your safety. If you think you might be burgled one day, but have no evidence of immediate danger, this is anxiety/projection. It's imagination, based on your perception that a potential threat exists in the future but may never happen.

Real experiences you've had (for example, if your home has been broken into in the past) inform later responses of anxiety. To alter this response you need to break the hold of anxiety by staying in the present moment, rather than thinking about what can happen in the future—even if that future is in the next few minutes.

Most people want to hide their anxiety and fear. The desire to hide them can make them more potent and powerful, and can cause you to move into panic. If you enter into panic mode, your fear and anxiety will magnify and become harder to manage.

Just thinking about ways to control the feelings and white-knuckling won't release you. Rather, they increase the inner tensions.

The best approach is to acknowledge the fear. Acknowledge the anxiety. Separate the two. Call them by their names. Panic will often subside when you step into fear and anxiety rather than pushing them away. Respond to the triggers with resolve to face them, not simply react to them, and this will decrease their power over you. Your commitment to liberation will ultimately free you. Pay attention to what your body, mind, and soul are experiencing while in the hold of fear or anxiety. You can take actions to counter their hold on you.

Here are some examples of how anxiety or fear "speak" to you, and what can be done to slow things down. Take time to write your responses in your journal/notebook:

- Do you wake up with your heart pounding? Take your pulse and remember the number. Now hold your breath, and slowly release it. Do this three times. Take your pulse again. Did the number change?
- Is it difficult to take a deep breath? Hold your breath, then let it out slowly. Does that help? If not, hum an old song that comforts

you, one that you don't associate with trauma or loss. How are you breathing now?

* Are you imagining something that will happen in the future? What is that image? Do you like it? If you do, continue to hold on to that positive picture of the future. If the picture is negative, counter it by bringing yourself back into the present. You can do this by putting yourself in the present moment by using your senses. Lightly pinch your inner arm; spray perfume; text someone and say, "I am here."
* Do you find that no matter how busy you keep yourself, you cannot avoid the feelings? Acknowledge them. Counter the thoughts in your brain with a different kind of activity. Go for a brisk walk, jump up and down, sweep the kitchen floor, or engage in any sort of physical movement. Your intention is to interrupt the anxious energy, not ignore it.
* Is it hard for you to shut down the constant chorus of voices in your head? Write down what the chorus is saying to you. Do you believe what is being said? Why do you believe the hurtful voices?

As you answer the aforementioned questions, create a list of positive thoughts that counter that constant chorus. Let's revisit our list of Positive Cognitions from Chapter 1, see next page.

Making Peace with Anxiety and Fear

Anxiety and fear are demanding and exhausting. They take up a lot of psychic space. They affect you physiologically, psychologically, emotionally, and spiritually. Each of the five senses can be tapped into when anxiety and fear are present. Sometimes, it feels like you're having an out-of-body experience; that you've been split into an internal you and an external you. You become desperate to control what's happening so you can get back to what feels like *you*.

You can learn to manage the feelings by understanding how they're triggered, then responding with the self-help tools that you'll find on

I deserve love; I can have love	I can (learn to) take care of myself
I am a good (loving) person	It's over; I am safe now
I am fine as I am	I can safely feel (show) my emotions
I am worthy; I am worthwhile	I am now in control
I am honorable	I now have choices
I am lovable	I am strong
I am deserving (fine/OK)	I can get what I want
I deserve good things	I can succeed
I am (can be) healthy	I can be myself (make mistakes)
I am fine (attractive/lovable)	I can have (deserve) . . .
I can be trusted	I am significant (important)
I can (learn to) trust myself	I deserve to live
I can trust my judgment	I deserve to be happy
I am safe	I did the best I could
I am capable	I learned (can learn) from it

the following pages. Although anxiety and fear often seem to be coming from something or someone outside of you, remember that *you* create the responses to them. You cause your body and mind to react anxiously. Learning to respond differently to external forces will begin the process of dancing differently. Assessing your anxiety and fear isn't easy, but the more you do it, the easier it will get.

Triggers differ for everyone, and your reaction to them makes them more or less powerful. Conversations, aromas, sounds, sights, and even laughter can trigger anxiety attacks. You need to know what triggers you. Recognizing the first symptoms will enable you to stop the experience before it traps you.

Imagine that you're having a conversation with someone who says something to trigger your anxiety. Reactions are different for everyone, but some symptoms are common. At first your mouth feels dry. Then your heart starts to beat a bit faster, or you feel as if you can't take in a full breath. These physical responses are your "tells." They make you aware of something your body is reacting to. If you notice these tells, you have a good chance of changing your reaction the minute you notice them. Often, your breath can be your greatest ally in creating calm. If you have a phone, you can reach out to a safe friend or family member, reminding your brain that it has support.

If you try to ignore the feelings, they might balloon into panic. Pay attention to the indicators that signal when panic, anxiety, or fear are aroused within you.

One way to get to know your anxiety is to identify the times when you're *not* anxious. Take a mental picture of your body and mind when they're calm. Be aware of things you don't normally notice while in a state of calm, such as relaxed breathing or other signs of inner peace. Is there a place you go to that invites you to be peaceful? *This is your safe place.*

You can create many safe places in your mind, and thinking of these places can bring calm when anxiety is trying to envelop you. Write down all the safe places you've created. Take photos of places or people who help you feel safe when you can't access that feeling within yourself, and store them in your phone or on your computer. Refer to your list or pictures as reminders that you experience moments of inner tranquility. You can challenge the "all-or-nothing" thinking when you access memories of safety and times or places when you have felt less anxious. Those memories of calm and safety are your documentary proof that you're not consistently in an anxious state.

Another way to get to know your anxiety is to *rank* its potency so you can do the exercises that best quiet the response. Write down the numbers 1 thru 10. What does a 2 feel like to you? What does a 10 feel like to you? Document your responses and do this with each number. When you know your own personal anxiety scale and have noted that it's rising, accessing the appropriate exercises (on the following pages) can curtail the anxiety before it gets to a painful 10. The ranking also lets your brain know you're tuned into your body and its reactions and you're managing the reactivity. This calms the brain, which then tells your body, "No danger."

When your anxiety number is lower, the exercises are more effective. That's why I suggest using a scale between 1 and 10 (with 10 being the most anxious) to help you identify your level of anxiety and reduce it before it gets too high. To begin, follow these steps:

* Take a deep breath, hold it, and then let it go slowly.
* Do a body and mind scan. Take note of where your body is holding the anxiety. What thoughts, feelings, or experiences come up in the identified part of your body? Is it a thought about the future, or is it something happening right now?
* Ask yourself if you're experiencing fear or anxiety. Fear reactions are usually responses that are based on what's real. Anxiety can be a response to what is real, but it can also be a response to your perceptions and imaginings. When a family member is very ill, you may fear they will die. You might be anxious about the death, and anxious about scenarios that are yet to occur, like believing you'll lose your mind upon your loved one's death.
* What does anxiety feel like and what does fear feel like? How are they similar and how are they different? Is there something you currently need to fear, or are you creating a picture of the future or remembering something from the past?

In the following ranking system, I've broken the rankings down into three groups:

* Between 1 and 4 (emerging anxiety)
* Between 5 and 7 (moderate anxiety)
* Between 8 and 10 (extreme anxiety)

Within each group, I've listed some tools that can help relieve the anxiety.

You may experience a combination of these symptoms, or perhaps only one of them. You may experience symptoms I haven't mentioned. Be aware of any symptoms you experience and use these tools to bring you back to safety.

Emerging Anxiety and Fear—Ranking Between 1 and 4

You're more aware of your surroundings. Sounds and smells are slightly magnified. You don't want to get more anxious, and you're afraid someone will see that you're uncomfortable. You want to leave the situation. You feel queasy, imbalanced. Your mouth is dry. You become more conscious of your heart beating, body aches, or soreness. You feel tired, edgy, and irritable.

Tools:

1. This breath exercise is a bit different than the previous one. With one finger on your right nostril, close it off and inhale through the left nostril. Then, put one finger on your left nostril, let go of the right one, and let the breath go out of the right nostril. Do this breathwork very slowly, for a count of five in, and ten out. Repeat the in-and-out cycle ten times. This exercise lets your body know that you're breathing and helps regulate the breathing.
2. Write down what you're experiencing that may be triggering your fear or anxiety. Challenge the thoughts with what you know to be real. Your thoughts may be "future thinking," not based on what's happening in the moment. Look at a peaceful picture on your phone. Put on music that you like. Look around you and name any objects you see or can touch. Access the positive

cognitions that counter the future thoughts you're having. Talk yourself down.

3. Drink water. Take a few tiny sips at a time. This tells your brain that you can swallow, which can alleviate your dry mouth and allow your throat to feel less constricted.
4. Go for a walk; wash your hands; spray a scent that you like or that refreshes you. This is how you change direction away from the fear or anxiety.
5. Listen to the relaxation CD or download that accompanies this book. Log on to the website for the book and you'll get a link and code to access the meditation.

Moderate Anxiety and Fear—Ranking Between 5 and 7

In this level of anxiety/fear, you're hyper-aware of yourself and your surroundings. Your heart is beating faster, and you feel as if you can't swallow. You want to flee. Your palms are sweaty, sounds and smells are magnified, and you either want to seek help, or feel ashamed and want to be alone. Your surroundings are closing in on you. You feel doomed. Your self-talk is humiliating and critical. In your head, you repeat old stories that contribute to a negative self-concept. If you're in a more prolonged anxious state, your sleep can be erratic; you may find yourself bursting into tears with no apparent trigger; sensations such as sounds and aromas can become more acute; you may even feel increasingly distrustful of people and situations.

Tools:

1. Slowly take a deep breath and hold it for as long as you comfortably can. Let it go, taking twice as long on the exhale as you did on the inhale.
2. Look at your surroundings. Count furniture or patterns. If you're in your car, pull over and count the stitches on your steering

wheel or count the cars that are passing you. Perhaps only count the red ones, then the white ones.

3. Remember your safe place. If you can't remember it, pull out the paper where you have written the description. If it's on your phone, look at it and read it aloud. If it is an image, look at it closely. You can carry the idea of the safe place within you and know you have access to it whenever you need to tap into it. Imagine it as a small, colorful ball ready for you to grab.
4. Put on music, move your body, clap, sing, or if you're with other people, tap your feet, left then right and left again, and say silently to yourself as you tap, "I am calm." Continue the tapping as you say this. Nobody else needs to know you're doing it.
5. Leave the room if you can. Drink water. Keep drinking, as it will signal to your body and mind that your throat is not closed.
6. Put a rubber band around your wrist. When you feel the anxiety creeping in, snap the rubber band and say to yourself or even out loud, "STOP IT." Imagine putting the thoughts into a black ball and sending the ball into the sky. As you release the ball, your anxiety releases, moving out of you as it travels away into the atmosphere. As the ball moves farther away from you, a colorful ball begins to emerge from the sky, replacing the black ball, and enveloping your soul with positive intentions. As the anxiety moves away, a certain calm replaces it.

Extreme Anxiety and Fear—Ranking Between 8 and 10

You experience extremes of internal and external symptoms when you are at this level of anxiety/fear. Your heart rate is high; you feel like you might pass out; you're convinced you can't breathe. Your throat feels full; you may be shaking, trembling, and thinking irrational thoughts such as *I am dying*, or *I am in the worst danger*. You might go to the hospital, fearing a heart attack. You focus on all that has gone wrong in your life or has been done to you. You have trouble falling asleep or staying asleep. You are full of self-loathing.

Tools:

1. Try all the tools listed above. Although the goal is to catch yourself before you get to the extreme numbers, sometimes you won't be aware of being at the lower levels of anxiety. You can draw on any of the tools outlined here to help you when you are in an extreme state.
2. Call a friend, therapist, or family member you trust.
3. If anxiety reaches this level frequently, see your primary care physician, a psychiatrist, or a therapist for more help in alleviating the discomfort. It's hard to tame the brain when you're at this level of anxiety. Medication can help take the edge off the discomfort. In the short term, medication can calm the circuitry that is warning your brain of danger when there is none. When you're in the "flight-or-fight" mode, it can feel like you're losing your mind.
4. Self-hypnosis can help; the download that comes with this book can help you learn these techniques. Here is a link to one of the self-hypnosis exercises I use with clients.
5. GET ANGRY! Often this level of anxiety is based on unreleased or unexpressed anger. Find a private place to expel some of your anger. Hit a pillow or stomp your feet. If you can't find a safe place, then write in your journal, "I am so angry about . . ." Let it flow. When you acknowledge your anger, the anxiety usually clears. *(PLEASE NOTE: THIS DOES NOT GIVE YOU PERMISSION TO BE AGGRESSIVE TOWARD YOURSELF [SELF-HARM] OR TOWARD ANOTHER PERSON. THIS EXPRESSION OF ANGER IS CONTROLLED AND EITHER DONE ALONE OR WITH A THERAPIST OR GUIDE).*

6. Be kind to yourself. At this level, your inner Judge and Critic are more likely to show up and bring you down. Counter them by replacing their negative chat with positive thoughts. Along with the positive thoughts, create an image that supports the positivity.

The tools listed here can offer you tremendous relief. Just note that what works at one time may not work at another time. Keep the list of tools with you and try a different tool if one doesn't help. They are yours to help you take the lead and bring the dance with fear and anger under better control.

Marilyn came to therapy with overwhelming memories related to childhood sexual abuse. Her uncle not only abused her, he told her that something bad would happen to her parents if she ever told anybody, and that she'd be taken away and put into a foster home. She never said a word.

As an adult, she had trouble getting close to people, and recognized that the trauma was holding her hostage. Her numbers on the anxiety ranking scale have been a 10 at times, and in this state, nothing seemed real to her. She was hyper-sensitive to light and sound; her heartbeat was often so fast that she feared she was having a heart attack. After several trips to the emergency room, where she was told that her heart was fine and that she should see a psychiatrist for her anxiety, she finally took that advice. Once she started a regimen of therapy and medication, her anxiety levels stopped reaching 10, and she could process the pain of her abuse. Hopelessness and agitation quieted to a point where they were no longer a potent part of her day. Her brain had to re-learn how to react to situations without the force of anxiety crushing her soul.

Anxiety is often a manifestation of unexpressed anger. Anger is often unexpressed fear. (The two words have the same etymological origin, in the ancient Indo-European word *ang*.) The phases of anger and anxiety can sometimes intermingle in their own kind of dance—or you might have to dance with each, separately.

The dance with your anxiety can pave the way for you to come to terms with anger. The dance with your anger can also pave the way to understanding your anxiety. What Marilyn's story illustrates is when you avoid or try to ignore your anxiety, it gets bigger. By allowing yourself to drop into it, your brain learns that you're not afraid to face the feelings. Your grief will shift when your anxiety understands that it can no longer possess you.

PHASE 5

ANGER, RAGE, AND DESPAIR

". . . To rage, to curse all that is happy or contented, or trusting . . ."

~ Melba Colgrove, Harold H. Bloomfield, and Peter McWilliams from *How to Survive the Loss of a Love*[49]

As a powerful survival instinct, anger is integral to defending your inner core. We use anger to fight for boundaries and to communicate abject fears. These are the necessary and healthy aspects of anger. When feeling threatened or scared, you have probably used anger to defend yourself or to be heard.

In the mourning process, anger is one of the emotions that moves in and out like the tide. Sometimes it envelops you like a flood, and if you respect its power, you can learn more about how and why it operates. Instead of avoiding it or letting it mold you, you want to tap into the ability to converse with its core: Identify what fuels it and gain insight into what quiets it.

Respect anger's capacity to help you heal, while also understanding how anger can contribute to losing your sense of self. The experience of being lost in anger can feel like emotional whiplash. It can surprise you and rise within the body without caution or warning. The rawness of your anger filters into your life with a sense of chaos and emotional states of disarray. It can be frightening to be consumed by this seemingly destructive emotion. Naturally, you desire to disengage from its clutches. Do you ever wonder what would happen if you weren't afraid of anger? If you actually allowed full engagement with it, what do you imagine would happen within your psyche?

In Phase 5, two distinct impulses surge within you. The first impulse is to *externalize* the anger by lashing out aggressively to show others how you feel (and almost forcing them to feel it with you). The second is to *internalize* the anger by attempting to keep it hidden. The fear of letting the anger out may occur because you believe that once out, it cannot be concealed or controlled. You would be exposing a part of you that is volatile, explosive, and perhaps unmanageable.

Either internalized or externalized anger will result in the same sense of drowning and emotional deregulation, which can leave you feeling unstable. Whether you act out your anger through aggressive acts, or try to hide your anger, neither option resolves your emotional response. If the soul is not allowed to tangle with anger as part of the mourning process and anger is not given the reverence it deserves, this unresolved, internalized anger will erupt into rage, and despair will surely follow. When this happens, the abundant internal chaos takes up space and doesn't want to leave.

Anthony is a forty-two-year-old man who shared his thoughts on the anger he experienced as he was coping with his adoption:

> *I have never reacted with the degree of anger I have in my bones right now. My throat is tight, I am in a blind rage, and if I were an animal I would want to bite off someone's head. Some of it is not rational, I know this, yet some of it makes perfect sense to me. Once I'm in the cycle, it's a place of no return. My jaw is clenched, my nerves are activated, and I am just plain mad, mad, mad at everything! Frankly, I'm exhausted from being so angry. This is not who I used to be. I wish my birth mom had not given me up for adoption and then tried to contact me.*

Though the scenario of adoption may not be part of your experience, does the degree of rage resonate with you? Is it possible that Anthony is more afraid than angry, yet anger is the emotion he is connecting with and expressing?

One way to disconnect from this type of raging is to delve into the initial experience of your anger; especially if no one has taught you that anger is allowed. When you experience anger, often the first instinct is to hide it or shield yourself from it. However, this particular dance requires going into the depths of the soul so you can become aware of other emotions that serve as feeders to the anger in your grief. Fear of the unknown can lead to despair and may be a feeder to rage. Rage can be easier to express than fear.

Anger is on the opposite end of the spectrum from anxiety. When you are overcome by anxiety, if you think about and engage with your anger you may find that the anxiety disappears. Understanding anger as a tool for anxiety relief is critical to exploring any resistance you may have to expressing your anger.

Your initiation into this part of the dance is discovering that what has angered you is directly related to the sense of helplessness you may be feeling. In any loss, the lack of power to change what you've lost, how you were traumatized, or how you could have reacted differently is directly related to a sense of despair. It can be helpful to write in your journal/notebook as you begin to examine what may be feeding your anger by exploring what fears or anxiety have left you immobilized and feeling ineffective. No one likes to experience powerlessness. Once the anger is recognized and established, anxiety will often dissipate, and the anger finally comes out of hiding.

Understanding Anger

Self-Discovery Exercise

* What fuels your anger? Think about triggers: How you are spoken to, especially when someone makes assumptions about how you are handling your loss or trauma, when it seems you are not heard, when you feel helpless—these are a few examples of what could act as fuel for the anger.
* How do you express anger when it is present? Do you hold it in? Are you explosive, passive, outwardly agitated?
* What situations or people cause you to shut down?
* How do you care for your Self in those moments? Does self-care work? If it doesn't work to soothe you, try doing the opposite of what you've done in the past. Play with your options.
* Imagine shifting your frustration and anger by creating what you want. What do you want to say that has not been said? If your anger is a driver that pushes you to go beyond limits set by your loss and trauma, how can you use it in a positive, life-changing way?

Let's look at the difference between internalized and externalized anger and how they each lead to rage, and ultimately, despair.

Internalized Anger

Anger that is unexpressed or squelched is called *internalized* anger. Just because you don't have angry outbursts doesn't mean anger isn't bubbling up within you. Displaying anger is discouraged in certain cultures and within certain families. When anger doesn't have a chance to be expressed, it plays havoc within the psyche and leaves you externally silent, but internally out of control and blocked. Suppressing anger causes anxiety and fear.

Some of the common behaviors linked to internalized anger include an increased sense of negativity because of a bleak outlook (it's hard to get to "yes"), increased reactivity (even when the situations are insignificant or minor), and an inability to stop the force of the anger, which can manifest itself through perfectionistic attitudes, addiction, or harsh work ethics. Like lava from a volcano, it has to find an outlet.

With internalized anger, you may find those closest to you are complicit in maintaining the silence that fills a room without a sound and keeps your anger internalized.

Externalized Anger

While you may have intended to release the surge of anger and let the folks closest to you know what's going on in your soul, the result often prompts them to distance themselves from you. Anger can be scary for you and for those who witness it. A display of your anger can create the perception that you're an aggressor. Trying to honor what you feel and letting others in on it as a way of unmasking yourself, and then realizing you have pushed people away, is a slippery slope. If you become clear on your triggers, and establish different behavioral reactions, you might invite people in rather than pushing them away.

There are a variety of ways to express anger without being aggressive. Asserting yourself is very different from making an aggressive, physical move.

- Get clear about what is triggering your anger.
- Express the anger in non-passive and non-aggressive ways. Rehearse what you want to say before you say it. By doing this,

you've bought yourself some time to think about what needs to be said and how to say it. Time is a friend that enables self-reflection about the anger you are feeling, before you express that anger.

* Identify the specific emotions you feel. Use "I" statements, rather than an accusation of what someone has done, like, "You did . . ." Putting yourself and what you are feeling out there without accusation will get you closer to being heard. And isn't that what you ultimately want? To be heard?
* Pay attention to how people respond to you. Often when in dialogue with another, we tend to have our own internal conversation going, preparing our next response without really hearing what has been said by the person with whom we are communicating. Keep yourself open to listening.

If you don't have a specific protocol to follow when you're feeling angry, the outbursts create a combustible environment for anyone on the receiving end of a tirade. Often difficult to control, anger builds up when you're not being true to the Self. Before you know it, anger has turned into rage, and whatever emotions were previously harnessed are now out of control. You might take on the role of aggressor, because you want to feel empowered, yet ultimately you experience helplessness, vulnerability, and despair, because some people will retreat when in the company of an aggressor. When you don't feel heard, showing your temper in aggressive ways reduces your prospects for transformation. You land in the cycle of a dance that won't end unless it's interrupted.

When you release the anger, and learn that by doing so you actually restrict automatic and aggressive responses, the psyche opens up and experiences a less combustible way to be in the world. In consciousness, you can stay in the present, maintain relationships, and avoid the helplessness, the vulnerability, and the despair.

Constructive Anger Ends Despair

Understanding the depths of your anger is essential. You are a choreographer of sorts, and your role is to find the tools needed to build the bridge between internalized and externalized anger and establish a flow between the two. The flow creates a balanced exchange that leads aesthetic distance and calibration. (see Chapter 5).

Rather than accepting that anger is coming out of nowhere, acknowledge its potent presence without fear and meet it with, *"Oh, here you are. What can I be looking at within myself right now? What am I afraid of losing in this moment? What triggered me?"*

These questions make you aware of anger and enable you to engage with anger's temperament before you fall into its clutches. In those moments, you can access your hurt soul and soothe it. Catch anger before it catches you. You can do nothing to change the cause of your grief or trauma, but you *can* change your reaction to it. Despair will diminish when your anguish shifts from being paralyzed by muteness to voicing what is appropriate to share. To express your anger in a way that allows you to be heard, without distancing from others, requires you to modulate your voice and your intentions with self-control as you clearly articulate what you're experiencing.

David describes how he responded when he became a caregiver to his partner Andrew, who later died from AIDS as the result of a blood transfusion. David was overweight, but because Andrew didn't seem to care, David didn't care either. David was angry at the medical establishment for making Andrew sick, and was miserable at the thought of Andrew dying. He liked his role of caretaker because it made him feel needed, and after Andrew died, without the caretaker role to give him value, David sank into depression.

With the support of friends and therapy, he recognized that his loss became an opening to deeper self-awareness, and he developed a self-care plan. He has since lost 100 pounds, quit his job, and created a journey for self-discovery. He also learned that he was more of an ambivert than an introvert, and that his fixed personality style got in the way of seeing options in the world. David says, "Learning about me was my husband's legacy to me. I pay his life forward by living with gratitude and self-care."

What will help *you* build the bridge that moves you out of anger and into grace? Courage? Desire? Pain? Understanding? Self-confidence? In one way or another, all these tools are necessary for building the bridge. It's understandable to be angry at the person who abused you, or a doctor who misdiagnosed you, or a person who chastised you for your being transgender, or a boss who laid you off, or the person who left you in death. To continue living with an active, consistent state of rageful anger can cause an unknowing impact on your spirit. Rather than taking that journey and staying in it, tackle this experience by understanding your anger and finding practical ways to attend to it and honor its powerful teachings.

Take out your journal and ask yourself:

- Who are you angry with? The person who has died? The person who caused you harm? The doctors who misdiagnosed you? The drunk driver who injured/killed a friend or family member?
- What did they do?
- How did they leave you or hurt you?
- How did they treat you?
- What do you want to say to them?
- Will they be able to hear you?
- What would you write to them as a way to let them know your anger?

* Is it really his or her fault, or do you simply want to displace the anger and put it onto someone else?

You may also experience moods that feed a sense of inadequacy as you engage with anger.

* What voices speak to you when the inadequacy arises, and when do they surface?
* Are you thinking about the abuser, the person you lost, or the situation you could not control or change?

Become comfortable with the temperament of your anger. Anger is an active response to a sense of being threatened, exposed, or defenseless. Listen to it. Document your anger in your journal.

Note when you are angry, the circumstances that contribute to the emotion, your response, and the best action to take and incorporate if you were to have a do-over. Was it an internalized or externalized response? Learn to identify when anger is internalized or externalized. When your anxiety and fear are activated, and your anger is nowhere in sight, it's a telling sign that your anger is internalized. Anger's presence and role include guarding against perceiving and/or knowing your sense of self is being threatened. You can counter feeling threatened by understanding how constructive your anger can be.

To make your anger constructive, rather than destructive, think about breaking it down. Like anxiety, anger starts with an idea—a perception or a sense of something undefined in your unconscious. That idea is fed by both internal and external conflicts. The conflicts can be represented through an array of experiences such as fear, embarrassment, shame, or anxiety. When these experiences occur, they are expressed by an anger response that can be either constructive or destructive.

There is a wonderful parable about a father whose adolescent son was very angry.

The adolescent boy had uncontrollable outbursts that could get loud and scary. His father decided to give him a bag of nails, instructing his son to hammer a nail into the fence every time he had an outburst. The first day, the boy hammered thirty-seven nails into the fence. Over many weeks, the number of nails he hammered into the fence became fewer and fewer. He realized he would rather contain his angry outbursts than have to go to the fence with the nails. One day, he did not need to go to the fence. This went on for many weeks. His father told him how proud he was of him and suggested that for each day he held his temper, he should take out one nail. The son obliged the father's request. Once all of the nails were out of the fence, the father and son stood in front of the fence, and the father said, "You have done well, my son, but look at the holes in the fence. The fence will never be the same. When you say things in anger, they leave a scar just like this one. You can put a knife in a man and draw it out. It won't matter how many times you say, 'I'm sorry,' the wound is still there." **Nails in the Fence ~ author unknown**

Destructive anger can exist internally and externally, and in either case ultimately feels more isolating and self-annihilating. This level of response often happens over misconceptions of behaviors by others and within situations that seem familiar to you. When misconstruction of the anger occurs, it leads you into having a distorted reaction. The distortion often feels so real and results in feeling triggered. When you misinterpret the triggers that created the anger and react in a way that seems to come out of nowhere, as if from an unconscious state, you will often feel uneasy and off-balance because you know something is not right, yet you cannot access an alternative perspective. When in this place of distortion, it often causes others to react in ways that sadly result in you feeling internal unrest and fear. If you've felt you're not understood, then you're ripe for reactivity in the face of a situation that can trigger anger.

Aggression, when mixed in with low self-esteem, creates the right formula for anger to become destructive, affecting you internally and externally, and ultimately becoming unmanageable. It can manifest in many ways. Internally you might become sick with illnesses that could affect your belly, your gums, and even your hair. Externally, you might come off as a brute—mean and uncaring—which might result in people staying away from you.

Constructive anger shifts you from being out of control to assessing and communicating valid points that support your sense of self. Imagine doing an anger assessment: Delving into the pictures, thoughts, and behaviors that dictate the anger and discovering the ways in which anger possesses you. The goal is to find the victor in this process and not stay embedded in the role of victim. Repressed anger holds you as a kind of hostage, and you're a partner in that entrapment. Choosing to engage your anger, rather than avoiding it, leads to greater understanding of the Self in loss and trauma. It gives you a powerful stance that lets your psyche know you're unafraid to take on anger and its potential hold on you.

This is another way to engage the brain to change. Own what you learn. Don't put it on someone else. You're coaching yourself to identify when you feel angry so you can own it and do something about it.

To learn about your anger, you can ask yourself the following questions and write your responses in your journal:

* What is the purpose of the anger? To keep folks away? To feel more self-assured? To motivate survival?
* What is your anger defending? Could it be a fear you want to keep at bay?

To dig more deeply into the triggers for your anger, finish these sentences:

I feel angry . . .

When I think about . . .

When I smell . . .

When I hear . . .

When I remember . . .

When I perceive there is a threat of . . .

My anger scares me because . . .

My apathy appears when my anger becomes . . .

Now respond to the questions with, "This is what I can do about it." For example:

"***When I smell*** *that cologne, I am brought back to the kitchen where my mom hit me.*"

"***This is what I can do about it*** *. . . just because I am smelling this cologne does not mean danger is near. I am safe right now. No one is going to hit me right now. I'm going to smell something I really like, so I can be reminded of a place within me that is whole, and knows that I am in control now.*"

If you don't have the words to express the experience of anger, find other ways to see it and engage with it. I often give clients crayons and markers and paper to draw an expression of their anger. You don't need to be an artist to articulate anger through creative means. The drawings can be figurative and literal, or just random colors drawn on the paper.

One of my clients, Jerry, had a forty five year old daughter who was diagnosed with early onset Alzheimers. He sought help to cope with his inability to feel anything about the diagnosis. Watching his daughter lose memories of the past and the ability to care for herself, Jerry's helplessness left him emotionally over-distanced. He was unable to describe his reaction and did not understand how cold he felt within his soul, and was surprised at his lack of anger. I asked him to draw his anger, he drew a tree, with dead limbs. The limbs were symbolic representations of the parts of his daughter who was mentally withering away. He took a black marker, and slashed through the limbs, until the paper was shredded. He let out a loud howl, full of fear: It was the first time he released the anger that existed within his soul.

Often that which cannot be verbalized starts with the simplicity of drawing. Your drawings create a narrative for you. Watch how they change over time. You might find that once you begin to draw, your verbal expression will improve.

Writing can also facilitate expressing anger. You can write about what you're angry at, or with whom you're angry, or when you became aware that anger was part of your being. Often clients will write a letter (not necessarily to be sent) to their perpetrator or related to the situation they are angry with, or even at the part of themselves they're angry with. You can write about how you imagine expressing the anger or the best way to let it out. The two options may not be mutually exclusive. Once written down, the paper on which the feelings were written can be torn up, burned in a ceremonial way, buried, or kept for future reference. Keeping it isn't meant to reignite the angst or dwell in the pain. You keep what has been written as a reminder of growth and awareness; where you have been and where you are now.

Other ways to release anger include:

* Take a walk, be aware of your breath, and quiet the arousal of angry impulses by talking to your anger as if it is outside of you. This creates distance, changes the way you hold the anger, and enables you to gain clarity.
* Listen to music. Choose music that shifts your mood or reflects it.
* Hit a pillow—allow the emotions to flow through you and out of you. Limit the number of times you hit the pillow; for example, allow ten hits to the pillow. Stop the action. Then do a body scan and a mind scan to assess the anger. Take note of what you are experiencing most. Begin rhythmic breathing in this way: Breathe in for a count of ten and release the breath slowly for a count of ten.
* Communicate the anger to someone you believe will listen.
* Sit quietly and be with it. Experience it fully. Allow curiosity to be present so you can discover aspects of what fuels your anger.
* Get creative. Calming through creative measures allows the mind to process behind the scenes. In activities that are creative, you are engaging both mental and physical parts of you. Working with clay, coloring a picture, scrapbooking, and cooking are examples of activities that allow the unconscious mind to process the feelings. After the activity, revisit what aroused your anger and note any changes for you or if you have new information about yourself in relation to the anger response. You might be surprised by the answer.

PHASE 6

REGRET, GUILT, AND SHAME

"The difference between guilt and shame is very clear—in theory. We feel guilty for what we do. We feel shame for what we are."

~ Lewis B. Smedes [50]

This quote from Christian theologian Smedes accurately defines the difference between guilt and shame. Guilt is a reaction that occurs when you realize you've worked against another and have hurt him or her physically, psychologically, or psychically. A person struggling with guilt will try to fix or change the outcome. Shame is at work when you feel humiliation. A person in shame feels it physically, like the intensity of a blush, and needs to keep it hidden. It exists in a part of you that you don't want others to see. It resides in a very young place within the soul. Regret is a reaction to what was lost, like the loss of innocence. Repentance is a kind of sorrow for the path or choice not taken or something that has been left unspoken.

Deciding to face the discomfort of regret, shame, and guilt is not an easy task. It's much easier to find distractions that help you navigate away from the rawness of these emotional Tricksters. So often it can feel as if you have nothing to support why you feel regret, shame, or guilt. That's why they are Tricksters. They fool you into believing the experiences you're having within your soul over the losses in your life are unacceptable.

Misconceptions about how to counter their ferocity merely add to efforts to deny or avoid them. Regret is often confused with guilt, shame is often misrepresented as regret and anger, and shame mates with guilt so they can mingle and feed off one another. Shame is a powerful response, and it can be present when guilt is lurking about. However—and this is the tricky part—guilt does not rely on shame in order for you to experience it. Guilt and shame can exist on their own. They can also pair up to create greater internal havoc when they play off one another. Messages you tell yourself unfold as distinctions of unworthiness and dishonor; these are the hallmarks of the shame response. Often unyielding and forceful, shame coerces you to stay stuck in a story from the past where you were not the Hero. Replaying past events that caused you to feel shame pulls you into a vigorous whirl of darkness.

These Tricksters like to show up when you least expect them, usually because you've become an expert at keeping them at bay. Regret, guilt, and shame interact with one another in a kind of cross-pollinating interchange. Their impact comes at great velocity from many different directions, leaving you unable to process the barrage. Defending yourself doesn't seem to help. It can feel as if your psyche is being ripped apart. Shame, guilt, or regret can hold you in an unrelenting grip as they play a nasty game with your soul and disrupt your healing. They like to keep you caught in their nets.

The goal is to sink into the nets rather than trying to escape them. Knowledge and acute awareness of their presence enables you to face them head on before they have a chance to fully ensnare you. Stay alert to the nuances that emerge when you meet yourself in the grip of these Tricksters. Being alert means you track the internal cues that leave you in their clutches. When they show up, stop for a moment and track what preceded the feelings. Shock them by countering the thoughts with positive cognitions and don't release from the repetition of the cognitions until the feelings have subsided. Don't give them time to bloom.

Knowing the nuances gives you effective and commanding tools to change the confinement that guilt, shame, and regret often lure you into. They can be so enticing, because they keep you captive in your grief. You can learn to counteract their desire to align themselves with you by seeing them for what they are and engaging in a counterattack when you can identify which of them is present. Once you face them, you ultimately face yourself.

One example of rising above shame comes from pop star Christina Aguilera, who faced years of witnessing domestic violence when her father hit her mother in front of the children. She told *Us Weekly*,[51] ". . . I've always been pretty vocal and open about my own experiences in witnessing domestic violence in the home and neighboring homes around me, so it was something that was pretty constant in my younger upbringing . . . It makes people uncomfortable and there's a lot of shame around it. But that's why for me, it's so important for me to speak my truth and help others to find theirs and to find their own hope in a hopeless situation."

Turmoil and unnecessary trauma arise when regret, guilt, and shame break through, but with self-awareness, you can summon the ability to fight them. They show up in response to something that you're unwilling to address. You can manage their invasion by challenging your assumptions.

Imagine, for a moment, that you're dancing and inadvertently step on your partner's foot. This may elicit a feeling of guilt, and an inner critical voice attacks you for the misstep, which makes you feel as if your very existence is attacked. You determine, within the context of a black-and-white type of thinking, that you have two potential responses: You can choose to take dance lessons to become a better dancer so you don't have to continue to step on your partner's foot, or you can choose to fall into a shame or regret response, making sure to never dance again.

If you take dancing lessons, you have used guilt to motivate you to better yourself because you perceive that your misstep can hurt your partner. If you decide never to dance again, that's the shame response in action. When what can seem like an innocent interaction, like dancing with a partner, goes wrong, it can spark flashes that take you back to traumatic times filled with shame and regret. Memories of not being picked for team sports in school because you lacked coordination can trigger an "I'm not good enough" grief response, which could be why your psyche reacts with shame, for something as simple as having stepped on your partner's foot.

You might regret even having agreed to dance at all. In a calibrated state, you would be able to internally access more than two responses to the dilemma. Perhaps you could have said no to dancing, or you could have laughed about it, or apologized in advance to your partner for your terrible dancing and their stepped-on toes. Finding alternative reactions to the real and symbolic "missteps" in this dance in life is what balance and calibration offer. Shame and guilt are diminished when you're in the flow of calibration.

Obsessing about how your actions could have been different will not change what happened. You can't turn back the clock. Guilt can serve as a lesson that inspires healthy behavior choices, such as making amends, which can be transformative. Conversely, an unhealthy guilt response is psychologically harming if you hold on to it for a lifetime of self-inflicted punishment. When you choose to let it go, releasing the idea of perfectionism, the journey within the cycle of your grief gets easier. You are releasing thoughts that hold you back and impair healthy healing.

When you're in the depths of mourning, you may meet any number of emotional con artists who can trigger regression and play havoc with your internal calibration. They create disorder and mayhem as they challenge your sense of self. The urgent scenarios they dredge up from the past and present are confusing and often unrelenting. They colorfully and painfully illustrate and portray the disparaged state of the Self. They repeatedly invoke the image of the behavior that triggers guilt, regret, and especially shame.

When you change your relationship to guilt, regret, and shame, once again, you are modifying how the brain holds on to the associated behaviors. Here are some helpful actions you can journal about. Documenting is a terrific way to connect change with the brain:

* Explore what makes you react with guilt: What you did, what you didn't do, or what you wish you had done.
* Shut out shame by focusing on what you value in yourself. Stay in the here and now. The facts of the past cannot be changed. So, start with small, incremental steps. Simply by engaging with this book, it is clear that you place value on the desire to heal.
* If you let go of the image associated with shame, how would your life be different?
* How does guilt undermine what you know to be true about yourself? Sort out appropriate from inappropriate guilt reactions. Does your guilt arise from something you have actually done to someone? This is appropriate guilt. Identifying this type of guilt gives you a chance to seek amends. Or is it triggered by the way another person makes you feel? That is inappropriate guilt. This is a good time to ask: What is this guilt doing for you?
* Have you deliberately hurt someone because of your own pain? This is common for people who have suffered intense losses. They want others to feel what they feel. Determine if this scenario resonates with you. If it does, examine the interactions you've had with others. Have you caused pain to alleviate your own pain? When you want to lash out, take a time out, re-evaluate the reaction, and either remove yourself from the situation or get quiet.

When you separate, define, and understand the source material that gives the Tricksters their power, you're on the road to healing, and the voices of the Tricksters won't be as pervasive and annihilating. You hold regret, guilt, and shame, and only you can shift how they incite you.

First, face the facts of what you know about what fuels the Tricksters. Take responsibility for the part you played. Separate the guilt from the regret and acknowledge any shame. Have compassion for the part of you that interacts with the Tricksters. Know what is yours and what does not belong to you. If you believe that some of your actions didn't have integrity, can you do anything to act with integrity and gain back what you lost? Can you make amends with yourself and others who may have been hurt along the way? This is an opportunity for self-love. As you embrace the lessons of the Tricksters, you'll be able to fly even if you have only one leg to stand on. The Sandhill crane with one leg can be a totem reminder to allow yourself to be awakened into healing.

PHASE 7

SADNESS

"No matter how much suffering you went through,
you never wanted to let go of those memories."

~ Haruki Murakami

The emotional turbulence you've experienced in the other phases is not present here. The isolation, anger, depression, and anxiety are no longer as demanding. You recognize past hurt, have identified the segments of your grief and trauma that create obstacles, and you no longer feel overwhelmed. Sadness is quieter than anger, fear, despair, or guilt and often leads to greater vulnerability. Your veil is lowered, and your defense mechanisms are not as necessary as they once were. Sadness is adaptive and vital to your being. The dance with sadness is easier, slower, and more consistently calm than the other phases. It's fluid. It's tender. It's the poetry of loss and mourning in motion. The gift of sadness sets the stage for integration and healing. At this juncture, you have the capacity to be consoled.

Sadness offers your soul a very keen sense of relief. Tapping into it can occur as you move within the other phases. It offers a respite from the depths of depression, detachment, or disorganization. During the phase of sadness, you find the beginnings of internal peace. You're not as psychologically and emotionally conflicted as you may have been. Sadness is not an insistent or pervasive experience. Barbara Kingsolver said it best in her book, *The Bean Trees*: "Sadness is more or less like a head-cold—with patience it passes. Depression is like cancer."[52]

This sacred sorrow greets you without illusion or denial. It's part of you, and unlike the other phases, sadness is a personal lament. It isn't overbearing, and you can exist with sadness without trying to eliminate it from your life. It just *is*. It's part of you, yet it doesn't regulate or deregulate your moods. It's part of how you flow. When you're sad, you're reacting to your situation, but your sense of Self and core sense of safety are intact and in balance.

In an *Us Magazine* interview Robin Williams' daughter Zelda said in relation to her father's suicide, "Avoiding fear, sadness, or anger is not the same thing as being happy. I live my sadness every day, but I don't resent it anymore . . . I know how dark and endless that tunnel can feel, but if happiness seems impossible to find, please hold on to the possibility of hope, faint though it may be, because I promise you, there's enough nights under the same yellow moon for all of us to share, no matter how or when you find your way there."[53]

Like the other phases, your relationship to sadness changes over time. Be deliberate in the intention to integrate sadness into everyday living as you strengthen your footing. Although this phase is filled with challenges, you'll feel less foggy and more precise with your thoughts, reactions, and feelings. You can touch this phase and dance with the other phases. As the grip of grief lessens, you might find that you engage with sadness more frequently. Allowing this relationship between you and sadness is illuminating and freeing. This can be a time of enlightenment.

Ambivalence, an active feature of sadness, sets in although you may crave to be decisive about who you are, what you think, and how you will continue to live within the parameters of this journey. Surrender and let it be. Honor the ambivalence and the sadness when they surface. Not only will you recognize when sadness leaves, you will also know that at times it initiates the dance, while at others it follows your lead.

The essence of sadness is a form of reward because it's a sign that you have achieved more emotional balance. You've started to integrate the feelings that resulted from your loss or trauma. The realization of what you've battled, how you adjusted to what is behind you, and realization about what lies ahead can create both literal and metaphorical tears. Growing awareness, letting go, and forward motion leads to healing of what had been a shattered heart. As the wounded heart heals, you come to realize that it's okay to be sad. It's part of you. It's a gentle reminder of what you lost and what you've mourned.

Your psyche may become reactive at this phase of your journey. You might experience a new sense of isolation. Since you're now in a less fraught state, people who've been great supporters may now feel you're ready for them to be less engaged and less involved. As they retreat, they create an opportunity for loneliness to creep in. Ironically, a support system that has faded is challenging and gives you a chance to meet hidden strengths. This may cause you to revisit some of the prior phases. Just remember, it's likely and normal that throughout your life you'll continue to dip in and out of the phases.

Triggers may bring you back to anger or anxiety, yet once you've experienced the phase of sadness, you may not be as triggered by the other phases. Instead of fighting what's before you, drop into the deep conversation that your psyche wants to have. Walk willingly into each of the phases that speak to you. They're no longer strong enough to swallow you. Isn't it nice to know that you're dancing in a better place?

Shifting Sadness

Self-Discovery Exercise

Sadness shifts when you're engaged in working to strengthen three distinct elements that make up who you are . . . *brain*, *body*, and *emotion*.

These aspects of who you are need to be in sync with a sense of calm while at the same time capturing the ability to regulate and honor sadness.

The Brain

The following exercise calls upon your imagination. Deepak Chopra said it best: "The best use of imagination is creativity; the worst use is anxiety."[54] Habits get formed through repetitive actions. The neural connections in your brain have a chance to change when you work to shift the rhetoric in the brain. By devising consistent rituals, you create routine, practice, and find a sense of safety. You can use this exercise consistently to create a ritual for the brain to calibrate.

1. Calm yourself by taking in a deep breath, and then let it go slowly as you count to ten.
2. Do this three times.
3. Identify and focus on what is causing your brain to be tense. You know it is tense when retrieving and retaining information is difficult. Clearing your mind and creating calm interrupts the tension.
4. Let the thoughts move away from you by sending them away for the moment. Imagine the water, the sky or stars, or even a sacred box that can hold these thoughts until it's time for their retrieval.
5. Imagine a place of tranquility. What does that place look like? What does it smell like? Are people around, or are you alone? Is music playing or is it quiet? Creating such a place gives your brain a chance to balance itself. There is no stress here. It is calm. Peaceful. Safe.
6. Check in with yourself ten minutes after doing the four exercises. What differences do you notice about the tension you were holding before? Do you want to invite the prior thoughts to return, or do you see another option for changing your thought process?

The Body

Tell your body that it's time to give it a break. Here are some options:

1. Go for a sensory walk. Bring awareness to how your feet feel on the ground. How do they feel in your shoes? Bring awareness to each part of your body while walking. Smell the air. Feel saliva in your mouth. Blink your eyes. Then take in another breath. Tell the breath that it's a balancing breath.
2. Imagine the body is in a state of true balance. As if you're on a see-saw embodying true balance between the up and the down. Let that ground you.
3. Put your hands together as if praying. Take in a breath and let it out slowly. Disengage from that position, and place each hand on the top of your thighs. Feel the connection between the palm and the thigh. As you continue to breathe slowly, stay in that pose for a few minutes. Move from that position and massage your feet, your hands, or your jawline. Slow, meditative movements that massage and release tension will bring you into the present and foster balance.
4. If you have time, exercise mindfully. You can do this via free exercise videos on a computer, stretching (please engage in activities that are suited to your fitness level and ability; don't take on any exercise that may harm you), or take a yoga class.
5. For many folks, getting a massage, facial, or manicure (not for women only) can get them refocused on their bodies, allowing them to find a sense of flow, rhythm, and harmony.
6. Body exercises that reflect balance are easy. If you are not in balance, they are difficult to do. Try standing on one foot with your eyes focusing on a designated spot. Now try to close your eyes. Standing on one foot is harder with eyes closed, but with practice, as you teach your body balance, it will communicate that to the brain.

Emotions

Mindfulness exercises that express balance, contribute to a balanced emotional state. Sometimes before you move into action, you first need to imagine the process in action. It's a good time to honor this work by spending time with your journal as you explore a scenario.

1. Imagine a scenario of having compassion for another person. What does that look like? Is it giving food to someone needy? Donating time to an organization? What do you think about tapping into your compassion? Is it forced or easy for you?
2. Scan the emotions within your body. Identify the overriding emotion. Is it sadness, anger, or guilt? Then talk to it. Ask it what it needs. Ask yourself what desires you have around this feeling. Now give permission for new desires to be awakened within you.
3. Identify an overwhelming negative story that is part of your sadness. For every negative story, invite your emotions to welcome in a new image that is created by you, replace the old emotional scene with the new one, and welcome the alternative. Change it, replace it, and be in it.

The power to reframe the negative into the positive is an active way to care for yourself. Let the sadness know you acknowledge it. Transformation occurs through recognition.

Every emotion needs to be acknowledged. The harder you try to disengage from an emotion, the bigger it becomes. Healing doesn't mean forgetting; it means forging through the disenchantment that imbalance renders. Internal balance means you've become an advocate for yourself. You take on the role of champion as you strive to create the calibration that's so necessary for healing.

"But my sadness grew even deeper as I realized that my entire life, right down to how I interact with the world, had changed."

~ Bob Sullivan[55]

Phase 7, where you meet your sadness, has the most balance between under-distance and over-distance. The way you handle emotions that have surfaced in the dance is no longer on either end of the under-distanced and over-distanced spectrum because you can comfort you. Being in touch with the motivation to harness a sense of optimal balance, knowing it's within reach, enriches your engagement in the dance with sadness.

There is purity in this phase that allows you to *manage* your memories and your emotions rather than simply being overwhelmed by them or tolerating them. The sadness will probably never disappear entirely. That isn't the goal. The goal is simple and complex: You will remember the grief and the trauma; you will not forget it, yet the depths of healed despair are met with internal peace.

Phase 8

Forgiveness: Letting Go With Insight, Purpose, and Understanding

"Unless you let go, unless you forgive yourself, unless you forgive the situation, unless you realize that the situation is over, you cannot move forward."

~ Steve Maraboli[56]

Forgiveness is the intentional and voluntary process by which a survivor undergoes a change in feelings and attitude regarding an offense. In the process the survivor might release negative emotions held toward the perpetrator. When this occurs, a potential shift has a chance to materialize. The shift takes many forms and is an individual choice. One example of a choice in action, is wishing the offender get help.

Forgiveness does not require forgetting.

Significant and misunderstood, forgiveness is often difficult to integrate and incorporate into the dance of grief. It's a valuable concept that is part of survival, especially when facing grief and trauma. Without a pardon of the Self, and of others, the consequences for your mourning psyche become pervasive and omnipresent.

Your trauma and grief can seem like a festering wound that won't heal. It's a tenacious reminder of what caused the wound in the first place. A scar is evidence of what *was*, but an open wound keeps the past alive in powerful ways. The potential side effect of keeping the past alive by holding on to negative memories is an unnaturally prolonged relationship with active grief.

Hate and anguish thrive and feed on memories of abuse, grief, or trauma. Whether the memories are of your actions or of another's, when you don't forgive, self-abuse can occur and an extended relationship with pain and mourning is established. To let go, it's vitally important to release the set of beliefs you may think keep you secure, but they actually prevent you from moving forward. To explore what might be making it harder for you to forgive, write about the following in your journal:

1. List a set of beliefs that keep you from forgiving.
2. How do they keep you secure? Do the set of beliefs really keep you secure? If so, how?
3. What pain do they keep alive within you?
4. What pain would you like to get rid of? What pain do you need?
5. How do you define forgiveness? Create a definition that allows for the negative emotions to be released. The thoughts you have been harboring need to be liberated so you can set yourself free.

What has happened in your life will never be taken away from you, nor can the past be changed. Although you might wish for your memories to be filled with different images, they are a constant in the climate of your soul. You might find that happy images of your lost loved one cause conflict with your mourning, especially if the relationship was a healthy one, yet their death, or leaving, or illness caused you grief. The storyboards that exist in your mind, whether of a positive or negative nature, affect your body and play havoc with your ability to be in a state of balance and calibration. They are remnants of transgressions, either by others or self-caused, that might establish a desire for revenge and retribution—which are on the opposite end of the forgiveness spectrum.

It's difficult, if not impossible, to heal and change the course of your dance with grief when obstinately parked in the "no-go zone" of forgiveness.

To start moving, get out your journal and ask yourself: *How can I forgive* ___________________? Fill in the blank.

Imagine a time in your life when you may have had a different outlook, and you didn't have to prove who was right or who was wrong. The pain of any trauma associated with the cycle of grief will repeat itself in other relationships. When you won't or can't consider the notion of forgiveness, the desire for vengeance takes root. The balance that you want to nourish has nowhere to establish itself when you keep thoughts of your torment alive.

A mindset that allows you to forgive may seem like a foreign concept. Bear in mind that forgiveness is not for the other person's benefit. It's for *you*. It's a journey to personal liberation that ultimately frees you; it's not about or for anyone else. This process doesn't require you to directly confront the person, write to the person, or ever engage with them. In fact, it may not be safe or possible for you to do so. Focus on the internal action rather than an external one. If you forgive the doctor who made a wrong diagnosis, if you forgive the person who hurt you, or if you forgive your birth mother for giving you up, your action may have little or no effect on them. Remember, forgiveness is not for them. Imagine, just for a moment, the effect forgiveness could have on you and for you.

What if you create a definition for forgiveness that doesn't include forgetting? To let go of hostility does not mean forgetting. When you hold on to hostility or anger, your mental well-being and sense of calm cannot be summoned. Finding balance in the Self takes place when you can modulate the emotions associated with memories, people, and places. The goal is not to forget; it is to reduce the degree of stress that you live with every day, to gain new insights, and to find calm. While the idea of revenge is alluring, the negative voices that spur you toward retribution only create a powerful vortex that keeps you stuck.

Break out of revenge's grip and welcome a tangible outcome that entails engaging in resistance to the bond of bitterness. The trajectory of your mourning will shift, and your helplessness and wrath will be reduced. You can be in the pain of loss without being a victim to it. Instead of being a victim, you find the victor in you. Yes, guilt or remorse can take over, but if you confront them as part of your goal, you can challenge the ambivalence and the internal quandary surrounding forgiveness.

"I spend three hours a day thinking about this, and if I didn't think about it, I would be less stressed. I could enjoy more activities with friends instead of being emotionally charged, and I could feel less angry and suspicious."

~ Terry G.

Identify a thought, such as the thought that has been tormenting my client Lorraine for years: *I need to hold a grudge so I will never forget what the doctor did to my mother. His misdiagnosis caused her to die prematurely.*

If you have a grudge like this, challenge it. Create a different scenario and invite the new image to replace the old mental image. Imagine adopting a mindset that is a call to action. When Lorraine learned to challenge her thoughts, create a different picture, and change the internal dialogue, her attitude changed. She now says, "My mom is gone, and there's nothing I can do to bring her back. She gave me so many gifts, especially how to appreciate life. I am going to commit to myself to seeing the world as she'd want me to see it. Just having that thought, I already feel my body relaxing, my mind is no longer occupied by negative thinking. I have granted a kind of pardon, and I can see that it is more for me than it is for the doctor."

As someone coping with loss, you may see yourself as having contributed to the situation. You may not have done something wrong, but still have a sense of having *participated* in the loss or the traumatic event. That sense of being part of the outcome of the loss or trauma is a residual effect of having been a victim or survivor of what you consider to be a Big G. These feelings often arise out of a sense of vulnerability and defenselessness—feelings that are worth examining. The action is identifying the internal response you have toward yourself and how you master shifting that response. You can start to re-form your relationship with yourself by looking at and owning your part in the event, whatever it was.[57]

Many psychologists have written on the topic of forgiveness. Dr. Robert Enright, one of the foremost experts on the subject, has identified four phases of forgiveness. What Dr. Enright illuminates, for anyone dealing with the force of meeting forgiveness head on, is to understand what it means to forgive. He postulates that forgiveness is often misunderstood. The false assumptions about what it is stop the action of moving into a release. Holding on to bitterness or thoughts of retaliation creates obstacles to healing and interrupts the reconciliation process. Write in your journal about your thoughts on his perspective.

Enright's Four Phases of Forgiving: Uncovering, Decision, Work, and Deepening[58]

1. **Uncovering Phase**: Explore the pain experienced by the incident.
2. **Decision Phase**: Discuss the nature of forgiveness; commit to the journey of forgiveness.
3. **Work Phase**: When your focus shifts to the transgressor and you look to gain insight and understanding.

4. **Deepening Phase**: Victim moves toward resolution.

The question is: *What is resolution?* What does forgiveness mean?

Intrusive thoughts and images about past events can lead to further conflict. "The more people brood about a transgression, the higher are their levels for revenge."[59]

You can begin your relationship with forgiveness by looking at something I created called the FORGIVE perspective:

F—Find a definition for forgiveness: Forgiveness has nothing to do with forgetting!

O—Order and modulate your most intense responses to the loss or trauma

R—Regroup how you think about the loss

G—Give yourself a break, breathe, and create a new storyboard. *I choose to see myself as a survivor and that storyboard looks and feels vastly different than that of a victim. This is how it looks and feels to me . . .*

I—Invigorate the soul and find ways to feel safe

V—Vectors are paths that you choose, and there are many to create and embody on this journey

E—Energize healing by avoiding the lure of a vengeful mindset; elect to forgive, but not to forget

A common, but distorted mindset about forgiveness is one that contributes to a kind of magical thinking. Magical thinking is the belief that your thoughts, wishes, or desires can influence external outcomes. I often hear clients say that all they need to do is forgive their offender (an external influence), and the pain of their work will be done. Of course, it's rarely that easy. Yet, wishing for that outcome is a prominent desire for many folks confronting the Self and forgiveness.

The process of moving into a conversation about forgiveness involves a commitment to exploring an outcome that had not been previously considered. You may have believed the only way to live with the memories was to make a pledge and devote yourself to bitterness and retribution. When the intensity of sorrow and trauma soften, you move away from the obsessive thoughts that occupy the brain. Grudge-holding, revenge-seeking, and vindictiveness can feel powerful, yet they keep you stuck. Tangling with these thoughts and challenging your preoccupations alters the constant anxiety of being on guard.

Psychiatrist Gerald Jampolsky, author of *Forgiveness: The Greatest Healer of All*,[60] aptly stated: "When I am able to resist the temptation to judge others, I can see them as teachers of forgiveness in my life, reminding me that I can only have peace of mind when I forgive rather than judge."

The waves of mourning and healing are on a continuum, and when you least expect it, your angst (and your desire for blame or retribution) might be reawakened. When you honor the emotional narrative, the uninvited moment that catapults you into the past is far more regulated and balanced. Releasing the pain of loss and thoughts of revenge allows the festering wounds to close and turn into a scar. When you dare to enter the world of pardon, and you don't get stuck in the behaviors of condemnation, the body, mind, and soul can soar freely. Once again, your dance is made easier by you and for you.

PHASE 9

RE-PATTERNING, CALIBRATION, AND INTEGRATION

"I'm not suggesting you deny or suppress your emotions, but just discover for yourself what it takes for you to handle your emotions and stay balanced."

~ Wendy Hearn[61]

Integration is an imperative process that unfolds as proof that the mourning cycle has become quieter, slower, more comfortable, and less formidable. As you hold on to yourself as you move through it all, you'll find there is no definitive end or closure. Your brain is reorganizing itself as you move in and out of the phases. It's as if you've been introduced to a new route, and it has now become part of your life's path. You remember the previous road, now you've been exposed to alternate internal channels that are new and hopeful. The adventure has truly begun.

Re-patterning takes place when you've ridden the waves, been over-distanced and under-distanced, tasted balance, and collaborated with the psyche as it flows into calibration. When you re-pattern, integration occurs as you self-regulate the behavior patterns and physical manifestations of the mourning cycle. Patterns of behavior that developed from understanding the Big G are now processed, and will most likely contribute to developing a strong core throughout the rest of your life.

Robert Landy, one of my dearest teachers, wrote, "At aesthetic distance, the individual achieves a balanced relationship to the past . . ."[62]

In this phase grief's grip is unclasped, making the dance more calibrated. It's no longer ominously lurking in the background or clinging to you. As it fades, you find comfort in the new roles you've embraced. You assert yourself differently when facing the struggles presented to you as a survivor. The words or images that have held you hostage begin to fade, and you realize you had the internal strength to survive the Big G all along.

You know your sadness may never disappear completely. It's the emotion that's okay to hold on to and revisit. And you will. Yet your relationship with the sadness will change as you change. The emotions held by your psyche and the dance of grief become more manageable and tolerable. Phase 9 is a time for you to imagine and cultivate the life you choose to live. As you re-pattern, calibrate, and integrate your thoughts and emotions, the new patterns of thinking have gotten into your brain, and that is what allows you to shift. You are reaping the rewards of an identity that holds less bitterness, a clear sense of interior safety, and an empowered being. Being present is the gift you give to yourself.

PHASE 10

RESOLUTION

"You're so hard on yourself. Take a moment. Sit back. Marvel at your life: At the grief that softened you, at the heartache that widened you, at the suffering that strengthened you. Despite everything, you still grow. Be proud of this."

~ Author Unknown

Phase 10 is a matter of distinguishing between an active mourning cycle and a quiet mourning that gently ebbs and flows. Steadfast and purposeful, a calm resolve filters throughout your conscious and unconscious states. This is your healthy psyche in its glory.

Clarity abounds when you understand the wounds of the Big G no longer fester. They have closed to form a scar you bravely bear. The scar holds no internal threat, but is a reminder of where you've been and where you are at this moment.

Resolution is like the end of a play or movie. You've been through the ups and downs of the story and you're ready for the movie to conclude. You're excited that the next movie you watch will have a different plot and different actors. There may be some uncertainty at the start of the new movie; you may not know if you'll enjoy the second movie more or less than the first one, but you're sure the last movie will be memorable.

Resolution is a new dance with new roles and a new plot. You are the writer, choreographer, producer, and director. You can explore any of a vast number of dreams, and learn from them. Resolution includes transparency to others, about who you were at the time of your loss and who you are now. As your friends and family respond to the new you, sensing whom you can have faith in, and believe in, is an essential component of resolution.

This phase isn't really about closure. The past does not easily zip itself up and disappear. The strong emotions associated with your grief may be greatly diminished, yet the source that holds the memories is part of who you are. It doesn't mean you remain in a pathetic stance of victimhood. Instead, you understand that a part of you will notice triggers such as a scent, a piece of music, or even the way someone tilts their head. *Noticing them does not mean you will react to them!*

Your response to these reminders can transform over time. They can illicit and inspire connection and happy memories. This is a time for you to rescue the best reminiscences. The vestiges of sorrow grow softer over time. Remember, triggers don't reflect a lack of resolution. You know you've reached resolution when your reactions are more calibrated, when they aren't extreme. It's only when those reminders or triggers cannot be quieted that you need to do some further exploration.

I often find that movie analogies are quick ways to get a message across, and they can be evergreen. *The Wizard of Oz* is one of my favorite movies. It touches on aspects of grief and loss discussed in this book. In the film, if Dorothy hadn't first conquered the obstacles she encountered on her way to the Emerald City, and then been tasked by the Wizard to take on the Wicked Witch, the power of the ruby slippers wouldn't have been known to her or served her. It's because she survived each task that she could use the shoes.

You've done a lot more than simply click your heels three times in order to get home. The home of your grief is where you dance in a way that will remain part of who you are, and is a welcome part of you. You are now ready to meet the grace in your grief.

Phase 11

Grace

Grief is a teacher
Grace is peace
Grace is calm
Grace is flying
Grace is "I am"
Grace is coming out intact
Grace is abundance
Grace is beauty
Grace is breath
Grace is divine
Grace is duty
Grace is coming out alive
Grace is surviving
Grace is positive
Grace is knowing
Grace is understanding
Grace is role-shifting
Grace is a journey
Grace is infinite
Grace is . . .

Grace lends a certain dignity to the phases and gives the dance a special beauty. It transforms past pain into present pleasures, with fluidity, calm, and serenity. It encourages self-fulfillment. It lets you choose what will and won't define you. When you're in grace, you come to understand that grief doesn't have to define who you are; it becomes an experience that you've had, because it engages only parts of the whole Self.

I use the term "grace" to exemplify a type of internal spirit that encourages you to step into your transformed life through a relationship with your newfound tenacity and courage. The beauty of the dance emerges and is enhanced by you being grounded and balanced. Your healing psyche has gone through its own death and rebirth, and you've acquired emotional assets that can be counted on forever. This last phase honors your new understanding of the Self. Touching grace impacts the depths of your soul to such a degree that the journey of moving through your trauma and loss takes on spiritual and divine connotations. You conquer the darkness and move into a light of your own creation.

It often astonishes me that the outcomes in my life are both out of my control and in my control. When I began writing this book, I had only five phases. The more I worked on it, the more the phases developed. They actually wrote themselves. The last phase, grace, has the number 11 attached to it. This was not planned, and yet it is no accident. The number 11 is called "The Illuminator," "The Messenger," or "The Teacher," according to various world spiritual traditions. The process of coping with loss and trauma is a powerful teacher, and it imparts the importance of learning about yourself while you are in active mourning.

The phases of grief require time. If you don't give them time and space, they will assert themselves and demand your attention. They can enlighten you, and sometimes frighten you, as you explore the depths of who you are. You've entered the journey of self-discovery as you dance with your grief.

The goal is grace, and you attain grace through the integration process. Accepting, dignifying, refining, and illuminating, all allow you to meet the Self in your dance with it. Grace allows you to be you. *It allows you to honor the mosaic of your soul.*

Grace in Action: The Gifts of Grief

The dance of grief can be an inspirational guiding light that brings illumination while it raises spiritual awareness. Once engaged with grief, an unforeseen gift usually follows. How can any loss be a gift? Here are examples of people who survived sexual abuse or life-threatening illness, or experienced the death of a loved one, and used their personal trauma and bereavement to affect change in themselves and others.

- When her daughter was killed by a drunk driver in 1980, Candace Lightner created *Mothers Against Drunk Driving* (MADD),[63] the nation's largest non-profit that looks to protect families against drunk driving, drugged driving, and underage drinking. Had her daughter not left this world in the way she did, this organization would not have been created.
- Oprah Winfrey[64] was raped at the age of nine and survived repeated sexual abuses through her early teens. She experienced trauma and loss within her family life, and lost a baby when it was born prematurely. Her grief didn't control her, but it informed her work as a dynamic influencer and proponent of women's health and well-being. The gifts she has given to the public will not erase the pain she endured, yet she took the energy and perhaps even anger as motivators for change.
- Carolyn McCarthy became a Long Island, New York congresswoman a few years after a gunman killed her husband and severely injured her son. She became known as the "fiercest gun control advocate in Congress."[65] She touched many lives and was known as the "gun lady" in congress.
- Marilyn Spivak[66] founded the National Head Injury Foundation (now the Brain Injury Association) in 1980, five years after her fifteen-year-old daughter sustained a disabling brain injury.

* In 2006 activist Tarana Burke[67] started a Me Too movement. As a sexual abuse survivor, she started a national dialogue. That dialogue was reignited in 2017, when actress Alyssa Milano sent a tweet, #MeToo, which caused the impetus for a collective conversation to come out of hiding. Sexual harassment and abuse in the work force and in other places. The widespread, yet secret epidemic was finally exposed. Women around the world became part of a collective voice that continues to be heard. This movement affects any man or woman whose fear kept them from self-protection.

"With loss, I sometimes find a new quality in myself when having to step up to the plate."

~ Jody R.

Grief may inspire you to quit smoking, start a business, go back to school, volunteer for hospice, or overcome a phobia. A passion can bloom in the healing heart of the survivor. The desire to be an advocate, a teacher, or an agent of change becomes a new goal. When the world feels lonely, desperate, and frightening to you, small victories can mean a great deal. If you haven't been sleeping well, one night of really good sleep can be a gift. If you haven't found anything to laugh at for a while, and suddenly you find something funny, that can *shift* the momentum of grief. It is in such moments that a transition may begin.

As you read at the beginning of the book, the world becomes more real to you because *you* are more real to you. This process of meeting the Self is potent at any juncture and brings meaning to all the work you've done up to this point. Every time you make a shift, a new nuance or behavior can be welcomed by a growing consciousness that you are not the same person you were when you started this dance.

The Grief Recovery Tool Kit

CHAPTER 9

The Grief Recovery Tool Kit

"Healing doesn't mean the damage never existed.
It means the damage no longer controls your life."

~ Akshay Dubey, Author

Therapists often refer to having tools they use with clients in their practices. What they usually mean by this is they have collected a variety of techniques and strategies to help people cope as they seek to understand their core senses of Self. Therapists look for concrete methods to tap into the hidden soul, and create personalized interventions suited to your needs.

In the following tool kit, you'll find an array of exercises, calming processes, and effective techniques that will help you deal with the emotional complexities within the psyche. These include recommendations that focus on relief, insight, and awareness. You can personalize several of these practices, based on your interpretation of the tasks ahead of you and the depth to which you want to explore your grief.

Rituals

Personal rituals are sacred ceremonies that are integral for marking turning points in our lives, such as birth, baptism, baby naming, coming of age, marriage, and death. Ritual can be important to the individual, the family, and the community.

You may not realize how deeply rituals are ingrained in your daily life. When you drink coffee from your favorite cup every morning before going to work, or you eat dinner at the same time, sit in the same place at a restaurant you've been to myriad times, sleep on the same side of the bed, eat the same foods, or shop at the same store, there is ceremony and ritual in each of these behaviors.

In the book *About Mourning: Support and Guidance for the Bereaved,* Savine Gross Weizman and Phyllis Kamm aptly describe the importance of ritual during this process: "Rituals and traditions are helpful . . . They provide a model for behavior, a structure to carry you through the initial period of mourning."[68]

Creating rituals reinforces the belief that you're in control when loss and trauma are alive within you. The ritual produces a sense of containment. You can create any type of ritual; its interpretation and execution belong only to you.

One ritual I frequently suggest to clients is a "cry box." This is an imaginary container that will hold tears, pain, and memories, and is especially useful when you cannot immediately express what is going on inside you. When emotions bubble up and you would rather not expose your pain, the cry box is there as a vessel to hold your secrets.

The cry box can be a metaphorical box, or you can create a physical box. It doesn't even have to be a box. Think of it as a vessel belonging only to you. Sit quietly and imagine what your cry box might look like. Is it large or small? How is it decorated? You can make it as ornate, beautiful, or simple as you like. Think about it as a personal container that stores your feelings. You can cry into it, yell into it, or pray into it. Whatever you need. There will be times when it's inappropriate for you to cry, for example during a business meeting or at your child's school play. At those times, you mentally imagine putting feelings, images, and thoughts into the cry box, and you commit to revisiting them later. Keeping them in this sacred container is a way to honor them at a time when they cannot be freely expressed. Remember, it doesn't push the feelings away or repress them forever; it puts them on hold until you craft a private space to meet them head on and deal with them appropriately.

Family Stories

Family stories are also a form of ritual. The family gathering together at holidays, weddings, births, or deaths creates opportunities for the family stories to come alive. Think about your family and the stories you tell. Are there particular stories that come up at every family gathering? In your journal, write about the following:

1. When you think about the family story, how does it integrate with your grief and trauma?
2. What does your family story teach you?
3. What part of the story is real to you and what part no longer bears any resemblance to what you know to be true?
4. Were family stories told to reinforce certain behaviors?
5. Were they told to keep fond memories alive, or edited to keep certain memories at bay?

Photographs also elicit stories and memories. It may be difficult to remember details of a past trauma as you mourn. An image may enable you to fill in elements or concepts that weren't previously available to you. The more you understand, the greater your sense of safety. Not everyone is able to look at photographs or tell family stories, and if it's uncomfortable for you, respect what your soul can tolerate. Believe in your instincts. Start slowly.

The rituals you've known in the past, even the little ones you might not readily recognize, can become disrupted after a traumatic loss, and this can add to your sense of disconnection from yourself. Re-framing old rituals or creating new ones will help you return to balance. The rituals that once soothed you may no longer do so, and what once worked to abate anxiety, anger, or depression may not achieve what it once did.

A common example is a person who was once involved in attending a church or synagogue, but can no longer tolerate that practice because of their anger at God for their loss or trauma. That doesn't mean the person won't return to their church at some point or has completely denounced spirituality. Many spiritual options encourage community and provide support without emphasizing a traditional understanding of God or a higher power. Another example of an old ritual that no longer works would be joining the family for a holiday celebration. If the thought of being with your family of origin brings up complicated memories or if the abuser is part of the celebration, you can create a new ritual.

When you find old rituals no longer work, it's time to craft new ones. Don't worry about the status quo. Be creative. Listen to your heart. If we use the last example of the family holiday gathering you no longer choose to attend, here are some choices you have in creating a new ritual.

* Acknowledge that the old ritual is not working for you. Seek to understand the reasoning that supports your choice. What makes you uncomfortable about the old ritual? What does it remind you of?
* Imagine scenes in your mind that could replace what you experienced when the ritual was rewarding and calming.
* Test each of the scenes in your mind. Imagine going to a friend's house. Who would that friend be, and why is it that person? If

that image doesn't work, consider going to a workshop or a vacation or even a spa during holiday time. Could self-discovery, or exercise, or learning something new take the place of a family holiday gathering? Could you have a friend join you? Would you rather go it alone?

* How about a bucket list ritual? If, for example, you don't want to be with family during the holidays, you have options. Try engaging in something you've always wanted to explore. For example, go to a museum, or challenge the status quo by driving to an unknown, random place. Or find others who, like you, would rather be around friends than family at holiday time. Changing this ritual is about making your own history, story, and celebration.

Physical Exercise

Physical exercise reduces both acute and chronic anxiety, as well as both acute and chronic depression. If you're usually sedentary, exercise can act as a stimulant and boost your immunity. If you exercise daily for twenty minutes or more, it will change your brain chemistry.[69,70] When you exercise, mood-enhancing endorphins are released throughout your body, acting as a sedative or an emotional booster, bringing euphoria or aiding sleep.[71]

Yoga is a wonderful method to reduce stress and regulate breathing, and it can be done at any skill level. It's extremely effective for people who have experienced trauma and loss. It helps with concentration and self-calibration, and serves as a nervous system reset. It's a process that only requires the Self. You don't need to take a class. If you would prefer to do it at home, there are many free online yoga classes that are easy to access. Bessel van der Kolk, MD writes about the curing properties of yoga in his book, *The Body Keeps the Score: Brain, Mind and Body in the Healing of Trauma.*[72]

Stretching as a daily practice gets the blood flowing to all parts of the body. This type of stimulation positively affects the brain and emotions. In as little as ten minutes per day, slow, rhythmic movements help create balance. You are in control of your body at all times as you stretch. Realignment can happen while you stretch, bringing your body into balance and achieving more fluid function.

Walking is another way to engage with the Self while in movement. This activity is known to help with health issues, provides comfort, and helps you digest thoughts, moods, and dis-ease. Some people prefer walking on a track, while others prefer taking a long walk in a park or around a neighborhood. Taking in the sights, the sounds, and smells in the surroundings gives you natural stimulation based on the external environment. Being one with nature can bring you into a sensory experience that momentarily overrides potent emotions. Whatever you choose, taking a walk for five or fifty minutes can make a difference in your emotional experience and in the way you dance with your grief.

Meditation

Meditation requires nothing but you and your breath. It's proven to reduce stress, calm nerves, and improve concentration. It can change the way your brain holds on to stress. Some people call meditation aerobics for the brain.[73] It's a wonderful way to get a break from your grief.

Here is a simple meditation you can try:

1. Take five minutes out of your day to *stop.*
2. Find a quiet place. Turn off your phone and any other electronics.
3. Loosen your belt, take off your shoes, and find a comfortable position sitting on the floor, in a chair, or lying on your bed.
4. Breathe slowly, imagining that your breath is moving from your feet to the top of your head.

5. Follow your breath. Be aware of its rhythm.
6. Try slowing down your breathing.
7. If your mind begins to wander, shift your focus back to your breath.
8. Try counting as you inhale and exhale. Breathe in for a count of five, and breathe out for a count of five. Then increase it to seven, then ten.
9. Each week, increase the amount of time you spend meditating by one minute.
10. If you don't have five minutes, just three long, slow inhales can create a sense of balance, clearing your mind and opening your lungs.

Journal Writing

Writing in a journal is an excellent way to record thoughts, experiences, and observations about your personal journey. Recording your thoughts or responses to questions has been at the core of some of the exercises you've experienced in this book. What you write is for you and only for you. You don't need to share these private thoughts with anyone. Privacy allows you to open up and express thoughts and experiences you might not speak of to another person. The journal represents a good friend that will never disappoint—it's receptive and doesn't criticize.

Keeping a journal may give you new insights into your attitudes and behaviors. Moving away from recording your thoughts and feelings on a computer, and using paper and pen/pencils/markers, creates a connection between the brain and the emotions. Simply thinking about the thoughts and feelings, without recording them, makes it easy to forget what you've learned, how your journey through this dance has evolved, and what the magnitude of your growth has been. Journals don't have to be written. They can be drawn, recorded, or creatively constructed.

Here are some tips for creating a journal.

* Find a quote that mirrors your state of mind or inspires you. Write it in your journal and jot down your reflections on the quote.
* Find a picture that reminds you of your growth, your pain, or your present emotional state. Paste it into the journal. What words best describe what you emotionally experience as you look at the picture? What do you experience in your body? What people come to mind when looking at the picture?
* Dialogue Journaling: This is a conversation in writing. Think of a past conversation you've had and rewrite the dialogue. Write what you would have liked to say, or what you wanted to hear in response. Write down the outcome you'd like to see.
* Responsive Journaling: Record your reactions to notable events that occur in the course of your day.
* Topic-Driven Journaling: Choose a topic for the day, such as a phrase or an emotion (anger, regret, guilt, or sadness). Write about that topic.

Other forms of journaling include writing poetry, scrapbooking, coloring in a coloring book (especially with the mandala or complex pattern), mask-making, knitting, crocheting, or any form of art that might provide a creative outlet that seeks balance, self-expression, and self-discovery.

Art and Hobbies

Creativity in all forms will make it easier for you to heal because it is, by its very nature, transformative. Whether you recognize it or not, you are creative simply by being alive. A path you choose to walk on, a choice of clothing, or how you manage your day are acts of creation. Trauma and grief, as they cycle throughout your psyche, need respites that encourage getting out of the head and into the heart.

The term *art* is broadly defined. Think of it as including drawing, painting, storytelling, creating poetry, working clay, playing music, dancing, and anything else you believe to be creative.

As an artist myself, I found that in my most wounded state, my art became my go-to source of solace. I could rely on it; no one could take it away or demand that I progress within a certain timeline. I became a ceramic artist, and clay was my best friend. It never disappointed me. It always showed up and was ready for anything. The results were immediate, whether I was making a piece on the potter's wheel, or I was engaged in hand-building. As the creator of the art, I could manipulate it, change its shape or contour, or destroy what I had done. Emotions had a place to express themselves in ways that were not self-destructive or avoidant. What I noticed was how many types of hobbies or art were available to the beginner as well as for folks who have studied the arts. Jewelry making, wood working, and scrapbooking are examples of crafts that don't require any special education or skills, nor do they require anybody to help you. When I was engaged in my art, time had no meaning. My brain had a chance to get away from the struggles like a kind of reset, and when I returned to "my life" I had a renewed sense of self-reliance. My grief was present; I moved *with* my grief, rather than fighting it.

Knowing that you don't need to rely on someone else to create is often a relief. If you're shy about taking a class, you can also find information in books and on the web. Becoming engaged in arts, crafts, or hobbies is similar to yoga or meditation in terms of relaxing the mind. When the mind calms, the body and psyche do too.

The collaboration between creating art and the physiology of the body is quite amazing. Scientists have studied the effect that art and music have on mind states. They've discovered there are electromagnetic fields that build around us when we're engaged in art, music, or hobbies. These fields can put us into a kind of altered state that causes the deep sense of relaxation I shared about my own experience. Engaging with art and hobbies actually affects the brain's neurotransmitters, your hormonal state, and your nervous system. Your body handles stress, emotions, and pain when the brain is transformed through this process.

Find the time to discover what activities might help you through your cycle of grief and trauma. If you can't imagine taking the time, start by listening to music that feels soothing or comforting. Not everyone likes the same music or even feels a response to certain music. However, one of the best resources I've used for music is by composer Stephen Halpern. His music has allowed many of my clients to align with their inner resources. You can find out more about his music at www.stephenhalpern.com.

Create. There is no right or wrong in this context. Give the psyche a break from the consciousness work of the dance and allow the unconscious to take over.

Self-Soothing Techniques

Whatever techniques you choose to use in quieting the chaos or shifting from either the over-distanced or under-distanced states, they require time and repetition. Having the techniques at your disposal requires a willingness to meet with them multiple times during the day to gain the benefits. In a minute, with practice, you can bring anxiety down to a manageable level; in two minutes, you can shift your breathing; and in three minutes, you can shift hopelessness to a sense of comfort. The primary goal is to calm your very active nervous system, which is aroused when it senses danger or threat. If your brain realizes it can be soothed when it's in turmoil, a shift will occur.

Service

The gift of giving is a platform for healing. We often overlook the possibilities of donating time, energy, and presence to shelters, houses of worship, schools, and other organizations that help others help themselves. Many of these organizations look for volunteer support. It may feel as if you don't have the energy or emotional balance to offer help to others, but that feeling of listlessness yearns to be released. You can achieve healing, integration, and self-discovery when you're willing to step out of your zone of comfort. This is a new type of dance in grief: A dance of giving while grieving.

Calming Through the Physical Senses

Sight: Look around you. Select one element in your field of vision to focus on, and break it into smaller parts. For example, if you're looking at trees, look at the width and height of the tree, the branches, the colors of the leaves, and the individual leaves. If you're in a city, watch one person as they pass and focus on their shoes until you can't see the person any longer. Go to a flower shop, select a beautiful flower, and look at how the folds of the petals connect and fit together with one another.

Smell: Identify a scent that is soothing. Allow your brain, psyche, and body to respond to that scent. Where did you go? Flowers, perfumes, and soaps are easily accessible items that can be used for this task. Take a cotton ball, dip it in your favorite scent, put it into a baggie, and when you need sensory self-soothing, smell the cotton ball.

Sound: Listen to a song or instruments that engage and calm you. I personally like Native American flute music. All I need to do is hear the first part of the music, and I experience an interruption of my present mind state and a reduction of my internal chatter.

Taste: Identify your favorite flavors or foods. Smell them. Put them in your mouth, and before you swallow, allow your tongue to be aware of the texture, temperature, and flavor. That focus will soothe you, even if only for a moment. Close your eyes when you taste the food, be aware of what you notice when they're shut versus when they're open.

Touch: Keep a piece of fabric around that feels good to you. Silk, cotton, or fleece can be comforting. If you have an animal, cuddle with it, or even touch your own hair to feel its softness or coarseness. Wash your hands in warm water. Wrap yourself in a favorite blanket.

Each of the sensory awareness exercises cause your brain to stop what it's been focusing on. The break lets your brain know you're in charge and can interrupt the cycle for the benefit of brain, heart, and soul.

Be in This Moment

Amazingly, when you concentrate on one moment and focus attention on one part of yourself, soothing can occur. Try this: Put your palms together and push. Create tension between the two hands. Focus on that pressure. While doing this exercise you're in the moment. Nothing else infiltrates your thinking.

You always walk around with your body. Select different body parts for your undivided attention to help sustain focus. This is grounding and calibrating.

Peter Levine introduced what he calls Self Holding Exercises for Sufferers of PTSD—Part 1 and Part 2,[74] which can be seen on a video he produced for The Psychotherapy Networker blog in October 2014. He advises, "Pat yourself all over, to point out to yourself where your edges are. Sense into the feeling of having edges, the place where you end and the rest of the world begins."

With this exercise, confirm the space you occupy in the world and the space you deserve to fill. Claim your space. It starts with the Self.

Breathwork

We all breathe. If we didn't, we wouldn't be alive, but we're often unaware of this life-perpetuating function. Although breathing happens automatically without our thinking about it, breath can be applied as a healing and calming resource, whether you're coping with the depths of the grief cycle or simply getting in touch with your own breath flow. Do you know most people breathe shallowly and well below capacity? The breath, especially when you're experiencing physical or emotional tensions, often disrupts the rhythm the body craves when in those states. For example, your physical rhythm and flow are interrupted when you hyperventilate because you're frightened or hold your breath when you're tense. Being in touch with breath is a means toward being in touch with the Self.

Breathwork itself is a form of therapy that has been used for many decades to enhance states of wellbeing and to aid in breaking through states of depression and anxiety. Practitioners throughout the world are trained in breathwork to initiate clients into a journey of Self. This is known as Holotropic Breathwork, which was developed by Dr. Stanislav Grof and his wife, Christina Grof. Its orientation is spiritual, and its goal is to help people heal by bringing them into non-ordinary states of consciousness. This type of breathwork should not be done on your own. Practitioners are listed on their website, GTT Holotropic Breathwork and Grof Transpersonal Training, at www.holotropic.com.

A simple breathing technique that doesn't need the guidance of a professional and that you can practice any time is: Take in a long, deep breath and feel it as if it's being drawn into your body from the base of your feet all the way up to the top of your head. When you're full, release the breath, slowly, from the top of your head down to your feet. That's all there is to it.

Be curious about your breath. Don't take it for granted. Notice how your body feels when you allow it to take in a long breath. Does it handle the intake of the breath well? Does it want to hurry the inhalation? Or does your breath catch as you're trying to draw it in? This information mirrors some of what your mind, body, and psyche may be experiencing.

Adding the breathing exercises as daily rituals to your toolbox can have long-lasting effects. You might find your energy is higher, your ability to sustain self-exploration is improved, and you create an alchemy that turns the negative into the positive, helping you move from an over-distanced or under-distanced place to a more calibrated place.

CHAPTER 10

Moving Forward

There is always a glimmer in those who have been through the dark.

~ Atticus—ancient philosopher c.175

Never forget that you are a work in progress. Some days will feel like you're in a self-discovery mode and the grip of grief has lessened, while other days may feel as if the grip of grief has got you, making it seem as if you've regressed. As you slowly create a new image of your Self and your life, composed of new puzzle pieces you've forged through adversity and fit into your re-developing psyche, you'll let go of some of the old pieces that no longer fit. Engaging in the dance has helped you to establish new borders. Now you can imagine what they might look like because by doing the work, you've initiated movement and change. As you come to understand your own limitations, a certain level of self-respect will emerge that honors your soul's need to combine the remnants of the old puzzle with the new puzzle pieces to create an image of the new you.

Your loss and trauma do not define you. *You* determine how much you allow grief and mourning to take over and how much you choose to integrate them. As you encounter and interact all the parts of you, they support the essential essence that is *you*. You have met the fighter in you.

You've met the different archetypes within you. You've met the masks that weave in and out, the interplay among all the wonderful parts of you. Complacency is no longer part of your internal dialogue. You've pushed through the dis-ease. You've met your motivation and it pushes you to escape from the underbelly of despair, denial, and detachment as you understand that you can embrace awareness, presence, and internal peace.

Moving through the pain is essential because it enables you to create a daily plan for healing. Practice, practice, practice! Every day, take yourself on in ways that may be uncomfortable yet can ultimately reap rewards that enable you to create a balanced state of being. When you have used a healing technique from your toolbox, and it has worked for you, take note of it and don't shrug it off. You've just discovered a valuable tool. This is *essential*, because your brain is listening! Change happens over time. Change does not happen overnight.

It's important not to judge yourself. You will heal in your own time, and that timeframe is yours to determine. Don't underestimate the power of time. In the play, *The Little Foxes* by Lillian Hellman, the mother says to her daughter, "Time heals most wounds."[75] Take this quote, and change it to, "In my own time, my wounds will heal."

The more you adapt what you've learned about how to help yourself out of the hungry and dark vortex, the greater the prospect for succeeding and healing. As you reawaken and come out of the fog, new insights, new friendships, and new beginnings may become part of your world. If you've learned to use some of the tools from the Grief Tool Kit, sought out a support group, seen a counselor or therapist, or worked with a doctor to find a helpful medication, you are setting yourself on the path to grace.

Anxiety, depression, and anger can lure you back into their clutches, yet their presence is part of the process of healing. Discomfort often accompanies growth. Although it may feel like regression when you re-experience an emotion that you have already examined, take it as an opportunity to delve into its reappearance as the person you have become.

Keep the Grief Tool Kit close at hand. It can help to enlighten the power of each potent and valuable emotion.

How you care for yourself as you continue to heal depends on your desire to develop new skills that stimulate self-revelation while ultimately creating more internal balance. That calibrated state contributes to developing a certain kind of flow: It's the flow of the dance. Once you've experienced the flow, you'll also notice when you disconnect from it.

Self-care and self-discovery require continuity. The desire to maintain balance requires a commitment to careful planning. A plan doesn't mean you lack spontaneity, because how you achieve the goal is up to you. It means starting with a vision of what you want to experience as an end result and working backward from there. Activate your awareness and curiosity. The elements of curiosity include being inquisitive and interested in achieving the outcome. The outcome is best realized with commitment.

Use your grief to learn about who you are to *yourself* and to share your knowledge of the grieving process with others. Meanwhile, create the life you want. Be the person you believe you can be. Feel your heartbeat and your breath, and know you'll find your own kind of grace. In that grace is YOU!

Endings are beginnings. If you've taken one small piece from this book and it has helped you, that is your cherished beginning. The relationship you have with your loss will change over time. You'll become stronger, develop a greater sense of self, and learn that you are more than your grief.

In this profound journey, you will learn to dance with each new challenge as it presents itself. You will take on your soul in very big ways, and in little ways, and you will live the life created by you. As my dad always said, "Don't look at where you are as an ending; it is nothing more than a new beginning."

Remember the Sandhill crane at the beginning of the book? She had survived in the wild with only one leg. Trauma and loss does affect the Self, and like the Sandhill crane, you had to find a certain strength to survive in the wild nature of grief. Within these pages, you tested your resilience as you learned to fly with a metaphorical missing leg, meeting your strength and your potency. The part of you that knows the wound of loss quiets, finds its space, and regenerates into a new and exciting knowledge of the Self. As a result, the dance of self-discovery allows for full use of the many parts of you so you can fly with the intimate grief that is by your side—yet is not who you are. Navigating through the darkness allowed you to find your own personal light. The image of the Sandhill crane is a reminder of what is possible. Fly with what you have learned, be curious for what will come next and know that you've met, within you, a personal strength that comes with knowing the Self through trauma and loss.

Your spirit has been given the opportunity of self-discovery. Learn the twin gifts of grieving and grace. One dance step at a time, one dance step at a time.

Acknowledgments

Though writing is a lone process, there is a noisy adjacent room full of people who have inspired, touched, and impacted every written word, thought, and intention. Included in that room are teachers; some I have met and some I have not, yet they served to inspire my curiosity, emotional depth, and internal tenacity. Oh, to have them all together in my mind is often piercing, mystical, fun, and soothing. Thank you to Carl Jung, Murray Bowen, Alice Miller, Wayne Kritsberg, David Schnarch, John Holland, Sallie Foley, Neil Cannon, Robert Landy, Bessel van der Kolk, and especially to Thomas Moore, who deepened my understanding of integrating all the parts of the Self with grace.

In that room, there are potent women and men, friends who have taught me about resilience, love and trust, Suzane, you witnessed the pain of loss after my mom died, possessed a certain strength and understanding of the tender moments while lending support without judgment. Arlene Love, you knew how to give unconditional love, and your untimely leave-taking from this planet has left an ache in my heart. Carol Gatto, thank you for your brilliant feedback and creating relief by finding humor in the little moments. Robin Marshall, oh that laugh, oh that determination, so many ohs! Patricia Johnson, past and present you have been a dear friend, sharing intuition, and learning. Terry Eagle, you are a healer of the body, the heart and the soul, truly from another planet, sista! Lizanne Corbit, a watcher, a seeker and a knowing soul with links to that which has no name. The soul knows in recognition, and we knew. You are all that, my potent goddess. Susan Lipkins, conversations like none other, and the great, yes you can! Andrea Martone, you are an unfaltering gatherer and seeker of all the Wild Women and the men and women who support them.

My clients are in that room and taught me about the soul and the spirit. They allowed me to enter their worlds, and showed me how tough and robust they were in light of their grief, their losses and their traumas. They taught me to recognize the brain in transition. They taught me how pliant and durable they were, and engaged in healing as they got to know the Self.

The past has been kept alive and re-patterned with two talented and exceptional women. They remind me how the past can be renegotiated in the mind, the body, and the soul. Elena Greenburg, thank you for the powerful conversations. As an artist and a therapist, you have found a way to honor both. Paula Hoffman, you are steadfast and honest, a bright star that lightens the darkness with insight and a constancy that is forever. Through tears, and agitation and laughter, you were the midwife in this process. Certain things will never be forgotten.

A deep admiration goes to Jennifer Ho, always there, always grounded as she assisted, offered friendship and perceptions that were nothing less than brilliant.

I have two families. The family of origin and the family of choice. Both of these families are exquisite, intricate and complex. To Ira and Elizabeth Nathan, my parents, who taught me to fight for truth, and live for loyalty. Andrew and Leanne, my brother and sister-in-law they got it right, are devoted parents who know how to love. Thank you for being the allies in this in so many ways. Ally, Kevin and Dana thank you for being a constant through this journey. Dannah and Ronit, proud to know and love these two powerful women, who have shown amazing perseverance in their professions and in their lives, filled with internal abundance and beauty. Jonathan and Jake, against the odds, made it look easier than it was. Fannie and Lou Rosen, my grandparents who were present in my heart and part of the healing that was needed in order to write this book.

Thank you Joseph Dobrian, Terri Daniels, and Sheila Curry Oakes: You each brought a different point of illumination while editing and re-editing this book. You respectively created a texture that allowed each piece of the puzzle to find its proper place. Thank you to Catherine Traffis, for being a dedicated copy editor and Peter Letzelter-Smith, for your perfectionism. It's not done 'til it's done and who knew there would be so many pieces involved in finding the finish line. Dave Cutler, thank you for the artistry in your image: when I saw it, I knew immediately that it was right for this book. It creates a conversation within these pages that speaks to the inherent risk of taking a leap of faith, especially when facing the many aspects of grief. 1106 Design, a woman-owned business, made sure to complete the tasks needed to get it done. Ronda, the project manger, took the manuscript and worked as a guide and a shepherd, and did so with extreme patience.

My partner, my friend, and my most ardent supporter is my husband, Chris Koehler. You listened, you read, you listened again, you read again, and through it all, you remained calm and precise and showed me that love can be realized and remain tender and profound; in life, in death, in grief, and in desire.

Support and Support Groups

Suicide

IMALIVE:

www.imalive.org

National Suicide Prevention Life Line:

www.crisiscallcenter.org—800.273.8255

Suicide Helpline:

Suicide Resources: www.psychcentral.com

Children

Acts of Simple Kindness:

actsofsimplekindness.org—800.422.4453

National Alliance for Grieving Children:

www.childrengrieve.org

Infertility

The National Infertility Association:

http://resolve.org/

Parents Grieving Loss of Children

Compassionate Friends:
www.compassionatefriends.org—877.699.0100

Trauma and Abuse

Child Abuse:
Childhelp National Child Abuse Hotline www.childhelp.org
800.422.4453

Domestic Violence and Abuse:
SAFE http://www.thehotline.org—800.799.7233

Rape, Abuse & Incest National Network:
https://rainn.org—800.656.4673

Safe Horizon for Child Abuse:—800.621.4673

Adoption

Child Welfare Information Gateway:
https://www.childwelfare.gov/pubs/f-postadoption/—1-800-394.3366

National Counsel for Adoption:
703.299.6633

Veterans' Issues

Veteran Crisis Hotline:
http://veteranscrisisline.net/—800.273.8255

Gender Issues

World Professional Association for Transgender Health:
www.wpath.org

National Center for Transgender Equality:
www.transequality.org—202.642.4542

Empty-Nesters

Empty Nests Support Group:
https://www.dailystrength.org/group/empty-nests

Divorce

Divorce Care:
www.divorcecare.org

Loss of Spouse

GriefShare:
https://www.griefshare.org/

Soaring Spirits:
http://www.soaringspirits.org/

The Widdahood:
http://www.thewiddahood.com/

National Widower's Organization (for men):
http://www.nationalwidowers.org/

The Liz Logelin Foundation for Young Widowers:
http://thelizlogelinfoundation.org/

Websites

Holotropic Breathwork:
www.holotropic.com

For lectures and workshops:
Email: gtt@holotropic.com
Phone: 415-383-8779

Endnotes

Intentions

1. William Blake, "The Marriage of Heaven and Hell, " in *The Complete Poetry and Prose of William Blake* (New York: Doubleday, 1988), 39.
2. Anaïs Nin, *The Diary of Anaïs Nin: Vol. 2* (New York: Swallow Press, 1967), 97.
3. Tony Crisp, "Where Am I," Tony Crisp webpage, http://dreamhawk.com/poems/where-am-i/.

Chapter 1

4. Lucius Annaeus Seneca, *Troades*, 786.
5. Scarlett Lewis, *Nurturing Healing Love: A Mother's Journey of Hope and Forgiveness* (Carlsbad, CA: Hay House, 2013).

Chapter 2

6. Thomas Moore, *Care of the Soul: A Guide for Cultivating Depth and Sacredness in Everyday Life* (New York: Harper Perennial, 1994).

CHAPTER 3

7. Lori Deschene, "Overcoming the Fear of Loss: 5 Steps to Get Unstuck," *tiny buddha* website, n.d., https://tinybuddha.com/blog/overcoming-the-fear-of-loss-5-steps-to-get-unstuck/.
8. Martha Graham, "I Am a Dancer," in *This I Believe: 2*, ed. Edward R. Murrow, Hector Bolitho, Adlai E. Stevenson, and Carl Sandburg (New York: Simon and Schuster, 1954).
9. Erica, "Angry At Everyone After Husband's DUI," *AngerManagement Resource* website, n.d., http://www.angermanagementresource.com/angry-at-everyone-after-husbands-dui.html.
10. "Obituary of Marianne Theresa Johnson-Reddick," *Reno Gazette-Journal*, September 13, 2013, http://www.rgj.com/story/news/2014/06/25/full-text-of-marianne-theresa-johnson-reddicks-obituary/11321891/.
11. Esther M. Sternberg and Philip W. Gold. "The Mind-Body Interaction in Disease." *Scientific American* 287 (2003): 82–89.
12. Judith Orloff, *Emotional Freedom: Liberate Yourself from Negative Emotions and Transform Your Life* (New York: Harmony, 2010).
13. Kacey Mya. "Five Ways to Infuse Your Home With Soulful Energy," *Sivana east* website, n.d., http://blog.sivanaspirit.com/infuse-home-energy/.
14. Paul Laurence Dunbar, "We Wear the Mask" in *Lyrics of Lowly Life* (New York: *BiblioLife*, 2014, first published 1896).
15. Shel Silverstein, "Masks," in *Every Thing on It: Poems and Drawings* (New York: Harper, 2011).

CHAPTER 4

16. Bil Keane, *The Family Circus* cartoon, 1994.
17. Carl Jung, "Instinct and the Unconscious," *British Journal of Psychology* 10 (1919): 15–23.

CHAPTER 5

18. Carl Sandburg. *The School Musician Director and Teacher* 43 (1971, as quoted without source.
19. Lynne B. Hughes, "How Did GRIEF Get an Expiration Date?," *Hello Grief* blog, n.d., http://www.hellogrief.org/how-did-grief-get-an-expiration-date/.
20. CaraBeanHer, "I get sick every anniversary of my brother's death," *Yahoo! Answers* blog, n.d., https://answers.yahoo.com/question/index?qid=20130701201329AA1h7jG.
21. Winnie M. Li, "On the Anniversary of Your Rape," *Huffington Post*, June 14, 2014, http://www.huffingtonpost.com/winnie-m-li/on-the-anniversary-of-you_b_5139345.html.

CHAPTER 6

22. Johann Wolfgang von Goethe, *Conversations of German Refugees: Wilhelm Meister's Journeyman Years, or, The Renunciants* (Princeton, NJ: Princeton University Press, 1995).
23. Belle Beth Cooper, "Are You An Introvert Or An Extrovert? What It Means For Your Career," *Fast Company*, August 21, 2013, http://www.fastcompany.com/3016031/leadership-now/are-you-an-introvert-or-an-extrovert-and-what-it-means-for-your-career.
24. Steven Monahan, "New Study: You May Not Be an Extrovert or an Introvert," Steven Monahan website, February 6, 2014, https://stephencmonahan.wordpress.com/2014/02/06/new-study-you-may-not-be-an-extrovert-or-an-introvert/.
25. Carol Kearns, *Sugar Cookies and a Nightmare: How My Daughter's Death Taught Me the Meaning of Life* (San Francisco, CA: Melgar Press, 2009).
26. Thomas J. Scheff, "The Distancing of Emotion in Psychotherapy," *Psychotherapy: Theory, Research, and Practice* 18, no. 1 (1981): 46–53.
27. Ibid.

28. Tamiko, "And the Acting Award Goes To . . . YOU! Yes, You with the Chronic Pain!!," *my foggy brain* blog, May 6, 2014, https://myfoggybrain.com/2014/05/06/and-the-acting-award-goes-to-you-yes-you-with-the-chronic-pain/.
29. Sharon Fieker, *I Choose This Day: Mournings and Miracles of Adoption.*
30. John Green, *The Fault in Our Stars* (New York: Dutton, 2012).
31. Peter A. Levine, "Nature's Lessons in Healing Trauma: An Introduction to Somatic Experiencing® (SE™)," YouTube video, Somatic Experiencing Trauma Institute, October 15, 2014, https://www.youtube.com/watch?v=nmJDkzDMllc.
32. Judith Viorst, *Necessary Losses: The Loves, Illusions, Dependencies and Impossible Expectations That All of Us Have to Give Up in Order to Grow* (London: Simon and Schuster, 1986).
33. Xburtonchic, "I'm not the same person anymore . . . ," Bluelight discussion forum, n.d., http://www.bluelight.org/vb/archive/index.php/t-600903.html.
34. Lynette L. Craft and Frank M. Perna, "The Benefits of Exercise for the Clinically Depressed," *Primary Care Companion Journal of Clinical Psychiatry* 6, no. 3 (2004): 104–111; Helen Macpherson, Wei-P Teo, Luke A. Schneider, and Ashleigh E. Smith, "A Life-Long Approach to Physical Activity for Brain Health," *Frontiers in Aging Neuroscience* 9 (2017): 147; and C. H. Hillman, "I. An Introduction to the Relation of Physical Activity to Cognitive and Brain Health, and Scholastic Achievement," *Monographs of the Society for Research in Child Development* 79, no. 4 (2014): 1–6.

Chapter 7

35. David Morris Schnarch, *Constructing the Sexual Crucible* (New York: Norton, 1991).
36. Murray Bowen, *Family Therapy in Clinical Practice* (Lanham, MD: Rowman & Littlefield, 1994).

37. Ibid.
38. Murray Bowen, 1913–1990, founder of systemic family therapy. "Emotional cutoff" and differentiation are major foundations of his work.
39. Donald Winnicott, "Transitional Objects and Transitional Phenomena," *International Journal of Psychoanalysis* 34, no. 2 (1953): 89–97.
40. Bowen, *Family Therapy*, 243–548; see also Roberta M. Gilbert, *The Eight Concepts of Bowen Theory: A New Way of Thinking about the Individual and the Group* (Falls Church, VA: Leading Systems Press, 2006).
41. Michael Homan, "One of the Millions of Hurricane Katrina Stories," ieterna foundation website, n.d., http://www.ieterna.com/index.php?option=com_k2&view=item&id=286:one-of-the-millions-of-hurricane-katrina-stories&Itemid=345.

Chapter 8

42. Brandiw, "Numb . . . lost . . . I can't lose my baby:'(," *Momtastic baby and bump* blog, December 12, 2012, http://babyandbump.momtastic.com/gestational-complications/1564553-numb-lost-cant-lose-my-baby.html.
43. Michelle Cruz Rosado, "9/11 Twin Tower Survivor: Her Story of Shock and Healing Post Attack," *KirstyTV* blog, http://www.kirstytv.com/911-twin-tower-survivor-story-shock-healing-post-attack/.
44. Jacob Levy Moreno, *Psychodrama*, vol. 1, 4th ed. (Beacon, NY: Beacon House, 1977).
45. Simone Weil, *Gravity and Grace*, trans. by Arthur Wills (New York: Putnam, 1952).
46. "Understanding Depression," Harvard Medical School blog, June 9, 2009, http://www.health.harvard.edu/mind-and-mood/exercise-and-depression-report-excerpt.
47. Ned Vizzini, *It's Kind of a Funny Story* (New York: Hyperion, 2015).

48. Paul David, "Helpful Anxiety Quotes," *Anxiety No More* website, n.d., http://anxietynomore.co.uk/anxiety_quotes.html.
49. Melba Colgrove, Harold H. Bloomfield, and Peter McWilliams, *How to Survive the Loss of a Love: 58 Things to Do When There Is Nothing to Be Done* (New York: Lion Press, 1976), 55.
50. Lewis B. Smedes, *Shame and Grace: Healing the Shame We Don't Deserve* (London: Triangle, 1993).
51. Rachel McRady and Ingrid Meilan, "Christina Aguilera: My Experiences With Domestic Violence Inspired Me to Help Others," *Us Weekly*, November 13, 2015, http://www.usmagazine.com/celebrity-news/news/christina-aguilera-experiences-with-domestic-violence-inspired-me-20151311.
52. Barbara Kingsolver, *The Bean Trees* (New York: Harper & Row, 1988).
53. Joyce Chen, "Zelda Williams Talks Dad Robin's Death in Emotional Interview with Chelsea Handler," *Us Weekly*, August 18, 2016, http://www.usmagazine.com/celebrity-news/news/zelda-williams-talks-dad-robins-death-in-emotional-interview-w435223.
54. Ann Wycoff, "Deepak Chopra: Why He Loves La Jolla, Oprah, and SNL," *San Diego Magazine*, n.d., http://www.sandiegomagazine.com/San-Diego-Magazine/November-2012/Interview-with-Deepak-Chopra/.
55. Bob Sullivan, "When Lucky Died: A Grief Observed, on Social Media," *A Letter to My Dog* blog, November 12, 2013, http://www.alettertomydog.com/tag/bob-sullivan/.
56. Steve Maraboli, *Unapologetically You: Reflections on Life and the Human Experience* (Port Washington, NY: A Better Today, 2013).
57. M. A. Cornish and N. G. Wade, "Working Through Past Wrongdoing: Examination of a Self-Forgiveness Counseling Intervention," *Journal of Counseling Psychology* 62, no. 3 (2015): 521–28.

58. Robert Enright, *Forgiveness Is a Choice: A Step-by-Step Process for Resolving Anger and Restoring Hope* (Washington, DC: American Psychological Association, 2001).
59. Michael E. McCullough, "Forgiveness: Who Does It and How Do They Do It?" *Current Directions in Psychological Science* 10, no. 6 (2001): 194–97.
60. Gerald G. Jampolsky, *Forgiveness: The Greatest Healer of All* (Hillsboro, OR: Beyond Words, 1999).
61. Wendy Hearn.
62. Robert J. Landy, *Drama Therapy Concepts and Practices* (Springfield, IL: C. C. Thomas, 1986).
63. Candace Lightner created Mothers Against Drunk Driving (MADD), September 5, 1980, California.
64. Oprah Winfrey, www.oprah.com, American Media Icon and Philanthropist. A public opinion influencer known for the "Oprah Effect."
65. Carolyn McCarthy, "McCarthy Unveils Gun-Control Bill," *Politico*, January 13, 2011, http://www.politico.com/story/2011/01/mccarthy-unveils-gun-control-bill-047565.
66. Marilyn Spivak, Cofounder, past president of the National Head Injury foundation, she is a neurotrauma outreach coordinator at Spaulding Rehabilitation Hospital/Boston, 1980.
67. Tarana Burke, African American Civil Rights Activist Bronx NY. Founder of the Me Too Movement in 2006. Girls for Gender Equity.

Chapter 9

68. Savine Gross Weizman and Phyllis Kamm, *About Mourning: Support and Guidance for the Bereaved* (New York: Human Sciences Press, 1983).
69. Steven J. Petruzzello, M. Landers, Brad D. Hatfield, Karla A. Kubitz, and Walter Salazar. "A Meta-Analysis on the Anxiety-Reducing

Effects of Acute and Chronic Exercise," *Sports Medicine* 11, no. 3 (2007): 143–82.

70. Mark Muraven, Roy F. Baumeister, and Dianne M. Tice. "Longitudinal Improvement of Self-Regulation Through Practice: Building Self-Control Strength Through Repeated Exercise." *Journal of Social Psychology* 139, no. 4 (1999): 446–57.
71. "Exercise and Depression," *WebMD*, n.d., http://www.webmd.com/depression/guide/exercise-depression.
72. Bessel A. Van der Kolk, *The Body Keeps the Score: Mind, Brain, and Body in the Transformation of Trauma* (London: Penguin, 2015).
73. Dorene Internicola, "Aerobics for the Brain? Fitness Experts Praise Mindfulness Meditation," *Reuters*, June 3, 2014, www.gmanetwork.com/news/story/363835/lifestyle/healthandwellness/aerobics-for-the-brain-fitness-experts-praise-mindfulness-meditation.

Chapter 9

74. Peter Levine, Self Holding Exercises for Sufferers of PTSD-Part 1 and Part 2, September 29, 2013.
75. www.new-synapse.com Lillian Hellman, *Four Plays: The Childrens' Hour; Days to Come; The Little Foxes; Watch on the Rhine* (New York: Modern Library, 1949).

Bibliography

Atticus. Ancient Philosopher, circa 175.

Batman Forever. 1995, American superhero film. Directed by Joel Schumacher. Produced by Tim Burton. Writers: Akiva Goldsman, Janet Scott Batchler, Lee Batchler.

Blake, William. *The Complete Poetry and Prose of William Blake*. New York: Doubleday, 1988.

Bowen, Murray. *Family Therapy in Clinical Practice*. Lanham, MD: Rowman & Littlefield, 1994.

Brandiw. "Numb . . . lost . . . I can't lose my baby:'(." *Momtastic baby and bump* website. December 12, 2012. http://babyandbump.momtastic.com/gestational-complications/1564553-numb-lost-cant-lose-my-baby.html.

Brooks, Philip. American Episcopal Clergyman and Author 1835-1893.

C. Used with client permission, furnished upon request.

CaraBeanHer. "I get sick every anniversary of my brother's death," *Yahoo! Answers* website, n.d. https://answers.yahoo.com/question/index?qid=20130701201329AA1h7jG.

Chen, Joyce. "Zelda Williams Talks Dad Robin's Death in Emotional Interview with Chelsea Handler." *Us Weekly*, August 18, 2016.

http://www.usmagazine.com/celebrity-news/news/zelda-williams-talks-dad-robins-death-in-emotional-interview-w435223.

Cochran, Larry, and Emily Claspell. *The Meaning of Grief: A Dramaturgical Approach to Understanding Emotion*. New York: Greenwood Press, 1987.

Colgrove, Melba, Harold H. Bloomfield, and Peter McWilliams. *How to Survive the Loss of a Love: 58 Things to Do When There Is Nothing to Be Done*. New York: Lion Press, 1976.

Cooper, Belle Beth. "Are You An Introvert Or An Extrovert? What It Means For Your Career." *Fast Company* website, August 21, 2013. http://www.fastcompany.com/3016031/leadership-now/are-you-an-introvert-or-an-extrovert-and-what-it-means-for-your-career.

Craft, Lynette L., and Frank M. Perna. "The Benefits of Exercise for the Clinically Depressed." *Primary Care Companion Journal of Clinical Psychiatry* 6, no. 3 (2004): 104–111.

Crisp, Tony. "Where Am I." Tony Crisp webpage. http://dreamhawk.com/poems/where-am-i/.

Doherty, Charlie. @charlielougirlx, Twitter.

Dylan, Bob. Simple Twist of Fate. Blood on the Tracks. Released 1975. Written and sung by Bob Dylan.

Enright, Robert D. *Forgiveness Is a Choice: A Step-by-Step Process for Resolving Anger and Restoring Hope*. Washington, DC: American Psychological Association, 2001.

Erica. "Angry At Everyone After Husband's DUI." AngerManagement Resource website, n.d. http://www.angermanagementresource.com/angry-at-everyone-after-husbands-dui.html.

Fieker, Sharon. *I Choose This Day: Mournings and Miracles of Adoption*. Paperback, 2006. Christian Books and Bibles, Tate Publishing.

G., Terry. Used with client permission, furnished upon request.

Gilbert, Roberta M. *The Eight Concepts of Bowen Theory: A New Way of Thinking about the Individual and the Group*. Falls Church, VA: Leading Systems Press, 2006.

Goethe, Johann Wolfgang von. *Conversations of German Refugees: Wilhelm Meister's Journeyman Years, or, The Renunciants*. Princeton, NJ: Princeton University Press, 1995.

Graham, Martha. "I Am a Dancer." In *This I Believe: 2*. Edited by Edward R. Murrow, Hector Bolitho, Adlai E. Stevenson, and Carl Sandburg. New York: Simon and Schuster, 1954.

Green, John. *The Fault in Our Stars*. New York: Dutton, 2012.

Grollman, Earl A. *Living When a Loved One Has Died*. Boston, MA: Beacon Press, 1977.

H., Carol. Used with client permission, furnished upon request.

Hellman, Lillian. *Four Plays: The Children's Hour; Days to Come; The Little Foxes; Watch on the Rhine*. New York: Modern Library, 1949.

Hearn, Wendy. @WendyHearn, Twitter.

Hillman, C. H. "I. An Introduction to the Relation of Physical Activity to Cognitive and Brain Health, and Scholastic Achievement." *Monographs of the Society for Research in Child Development* 79, no. 4 (2014): 1–6.

Hughes, Lynne B. "How Did GRIEF Get an Expiration Date?" *Hello Grief* (blog), n.d. http://www.hellogrief.org/how-did-grief-get-an-expiration-date/.

Internicola, Dorene. "Aerobics for the Brain? Fitness Experts Praise Mindfulness Meditation." *Reuters*, June 3, 2014. www.gmanetwork.com/news/story/363835/lifestyle/healthandwellness/aerobics-for-the-brain-fitness-experts-praise-mindfulness-meditation.

J., Michael. Used with client permission, furnished upon request.

Jamie. "I'm a Woman in a Man's Body." *Now to Love* (blog), December 10, 2011. http://www.nowtolove.com.au/news/real-life/im-a-woman-in-a-mans-body-30605.

Jampolsky, Gerald G. *Forgiveness: The Greatest Healer of All*. Hillsboro, OR: Beyond Words, 1999.

Jung, Carl. "Instinct and the Unconscious." *British Journal of Psychology* 10 (1919): 15–23.

Kearns, Carol, and Jean Shinoda Bolen. *Sugar Cookies and a Nightmare: How My Daughter's Death Taught Me the Meaning of Life*. San Francisco, CA: Melgar Press, 2009.

Kingsolver, Barbara. *The Bean Trees*. New York: Harper & Row, 1988.

Lamott, Anne, used by permission from author Anne Lamott

Levine, Peter. "Nature's Lessons in Healing Trauma: An Introduction to Somatic Experiencing® (SE™)." YouTube video, Somatic Experiencing Trauma Institute, October 15, 2014. https://www.youtube.com/watch?v=nmJDkzDMllc.

Lewis, Scarlett. *Nurturing Healing Love: A Mother's Journey of Hope and Forgiveness*. Carlsbad, CA: Hay House, 2013.

Landy, Robert J. *Drama Therapy Concepts and Practices*. Springfield, IL: C. C. Thomas, 1986.

Levine, Peter. Peter Levine Self Holding Exercises for Sufferers of PTSD-Part 1 and Part 2, September 29, 2013. www.new-synapse.com

Li, Winnie M. "On the Anniversary of Your Rape." *The Huffington Post* website, June 14, 2014. http://www.huffingtonpost.com/winnie-m-li/on-the-anniversary-of-you_b_5139345.html.

Longfellow, Henry Wadsworth.

M., Chara. Used with client permission, furnished upon request.

Maraboli, Steve. *Unapologetically You: Reflections on Life and the Human Experience*. Port Washington, NY: A Better Today, 2013.

Macpherson, Helen, Wei-P Teo, Luke A. Schneider, and Ashleigh E. Smith. "A Life-Long Approach to Physical Activity for Brain Health." *Frontiers in Aging Neuroscience* 9 (2017): 147.

McCullough, Michael E. "Forgiveness: Who Does It and How Do They Do It?" *Current Directions in Psychological Science* 10, no. 6 (2001): 194–97.

McRady, Rachel, and Ingrid Meilan. "Christina Aguilera: My Experiences With Domestic Violence Inspired Me to Help Others." *Us Weekly*, November 13, 2015. http://www.usmagazine.com/celebrity-news/

news/christina-aguilera-experiences-with-domestic-violence-inspired-me-20151311.

Merzenich, Michael M. *Soft-Wired: How the New Science of Brain Plasticity Can Change Your Life*. San Francisco, CA: Parnassus, 2013.

Monahan, Steven. "New Study You May Not Be an Extrovert or an Introvert." Steven Monahan website, February 6, 2014. https://stephencmonahan.wordpress.com/2014/02/06/new-study-you-may-not-be-an-extrovert-or-an-introvert/.

Moore, Thomas. *Care of the Soul: A Guide for Cultivating Depth and Sacredness in Everyday Life*. New York: HarperPerennial, 1994.

Moreno, J. L. *Psychodrama*. Vol. 1. Beacon, NY: Beacon House, 1977.

Murakami, Haruki. www.harukimurakami.com. Born Kyoto, Japan 1949. Author of several books including *Kafka on the Shore*.

Muraven, Mark, Roy F. Baumeister, and Dianne M. Tice. "Longitudinal Improvement of Self-Regulation Through Practice: Building Self-Control Strength Through Repeated Exercise." *Journal of Social Psychology* 139, no. 4 (1999): 446–57.

Mya, Kacey. "Five Ways To Infuse Your Home With Soulful Energy," *Sivana east* website, n.d. http://blog.sivanaspirit.com/infuse-home-energy/.

Nin, Anaïs. *The Diary of Anaïs Nin: Vol. 2*. Edited by and Gunther Stuhlmann. New York: Swallow Press, 1967.

"Obituary of Marianne Theresa Johnson-Reddick." *Reno Gazette-Journal*, September 13, 2013. http://www.rgj.com/story/news/2014/06/25/full-text-of-marianne-theresa-johnson-reddicks-obituary/11321891/.

Paula. Used with client permission, furnished upon request.

Petruzzello, Steven J., Daniel M. Landers, Brad D. Hatfield, Karla A. Kubitz, and Walter Salazar. "A Meta-Analysis on the Anxiety-Reducing Effects of Acute and Chronic Exercise." *Sports Medicine* 11, no. 3 (2007): 143–82.

R. Jody. Used with client permission, furnished upon request.

Rosado, Michelle Cruz. "9/11 Twin Tower Survivor: Her Story of Shock and Healing Post Attack." *KirstyTV* (blog), n.d. http://www.kirstytv.com/911-twin-tower-survivor-story-shock-healing-post-attack/.

Sandburg, Carl. *The School Musician Director and Teacher* 43 (1971), as quoted without source.

Scheff, Thomas J. "The Distancing of Emotion in Psychotherapy." *Psychotherapy: Theory, Research, and Practice* 18, no. 1 (1981): 46–53.

Schnarch, David Morris. *Constructing the Sexual Crucible.* New York: Norton, 1991.

Shakespeare, William, *Much Ado About Nothing.*

Silverstein, Shel. *Every Thing On It: Poems and Drawings.* New York: Harper, 2011.

Smedes, Lewis. *Shame and Grace: Healing the Shame We Don't Deserve.* London: Triangle, 1993.

Sternberg, Esther M., and Philip W. Gold. "The Mind-Body Interaction in Disease." *Scientific American* 287 (2003): 82–89.

Stevens, Jean. "A Loving Wife and Sister." Ashland Christian Church website, July 6, 2010. http://www.connectcallcultivate.com/2010.07.01_arch.html.

Sullivan, Bob. "When Lucky Died: A Grief Observed, on Social Media." *A Letter to My Dog* (blog), November 12, 2013. http://www.alettertomydog.com/tag/bob-sullivan/.

Tamiko. "And the Acting Award Goes To . . . YOU! Yes, You with the Chronic Pain!!" *my foggy brain* (blog), May 6, 2014. https://myfoggybrain.com/2014/05/06/and-the-acting-award-goes-to-you-yes-you-with-the-chronic-pain/.

Toeplitz, Shira. "McCarthy Unveils Gun-Control Bill." *Politico*, January 13, 2011. http://www.politico.com/story/2011/01/mccarthy-unveils-gun-control-bill-047565.

Van der Kolk, Bessel A. *The Body Keeps the Score: Mind, Brain, and Body in the Transformation of Trauma.* London: Penguin, 2015.

Viorst, Judith. *Necessary Losses: The Loves, Illusions, Dependencies, and Impossible Expectations That All of Us Have to Give Up in Order to Grow*. London: Simon and Schuster, 1986.

Vizzini, Ned. *It's Kind of a Funny Story*. New York: Hyperion, 2015.

Weil, Simone. *Gravity and Grace*. Translated by Arthur Wills. New York: Putnam, 1952.

Weizman, Savine Gross, and Phyllis Kamm. *About Mourning: Support and Guidance for the Bereaved*. New York: Human Sciences Press, 1983.

Winnicott, Donald. "Transitional Objects and Transitional Phenomena." *International Journal of Psychoanalysis* 34, no. 2 (1953): 89–97.

Wycoff, Ann. "Deepak Chopra: Why He Loves La Jolla, Oprah, and SNL." *San Diego Magazine*, n.d. http://www.sandiegomagazine.com/San-Diego-Magazine/November-2012/Interview-with-Deepak-Chopra/.

X., used with client permission, furnished upon request.

Index

B

C

H

I

J

K

L

R

S

T

Milton Keynes UK
Ingram Content Group UK Ltd.
UKHW020913110924
1589UKWH00029B/290